YV88

YV88 is not necessarily what the Sierra Club envisions as the future of Yosemite Valley. It is the authors' vision of opportunities we may have to live more harmoniously with our environment and to use technology to make this possible. They have chosen Yosemite as the setting for their vision. It is for you to decide whether it could work as well in other places too.

YV88

An Eco-Fiction of Tomorrow

Christopher Swan   Chet Roaman

Sierra Club Books   San Francisco

The Sierra Club, founded in 1892 by John Muir, has devoted itself to the study and protection of the nation's scenic and ecological resources — mountains, wetlands, woodlands, wild shores, and rivers. All club publications are part of the nonprofit effort the club carries on as a public trust. There are some 50 chapters coast to coast, in Canada, Hawaii, and Alaska. Participation is invited in the club's program to enjoy and preserve wilderness everywhere.

Address: 530 Bush Street, San Francisco, California 94108

Library of Congress Cataloging in Publication Data

Swan, Christopher.
  YV 88.

I. Roaman, Chet, 1939-   joint author.
II. Title.
PZ4.S9699Yad [PS3569.W245]   813'.5'4 77-7596
ISBN 0-87156-195-6 pbk.

Cover design by Jon Goodchild

Book design, paste-up by Christopher Swan, Chet Roaman

Printing coordination by David Charlsen & Others

Printed in the United States of America

contents

Being the account of the first scheduled trip of the Yosemite Railway (YR) to Yosemite Valley. Riding on the first of three solar-powered electric trains from Merced on the morning of October 3, 1983.

contents

contents

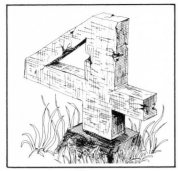

contents

San Francisco

Merced

Los Angeles

TRAINSCRIPT

Thomas turns, ordering a coat and leather satchel into a neat pile on the wooden seat. A slight sense of imbalance. He swings back to a willow branch wiping across his nose, leaves combing his hair. The train is moving.

The show has started. The audience, all of us, focus our attention on the moving theater: how the train feels, moves, operates; where to sit, what's to drink, where's the john, what's to see, who's here, what am I missing, will I like it? Now, looking out and down at the people of Merced lining the sidewalks, standing on small automobiles, I grab the wood-smooth rail, not out of need but unconsciously, assuming the train would vibrate and rock like every other I've ever been on.

It doesn't.

The train's a 250-meter-long squared aluminum tube set on a dark steel-enclosed frame interrupted only by the gaps between cars and the openings that contain wheelsets. She's low to the ground, three-quarters the height of the two big semi's that stand in the street waiting for the crowd to clear; her slightly expanded width accentuates her snake-in-the-grass appearance. Only in her case, the grass is the trees lining the streets.

With the exception of the baggage and open observation cars, her sides flash glass: large, clear windows at regular intervals set flush with polished, almost white aluminum. At floor height, where aluminum meets steel, a continuous blue stripe underlines elongated Roman letters spelling out "Yosemite Railway."

Looking down to the nose or back to the tail, she's a long rippling mirror reflecting surroundings on glass, color on aluminum. Only the open platform doors at the end of each car break the image: heads sticking out, hands waving to create an additional dimension to the surreal painting.

He looks down the side of the open car to the cab up front, along the reflection of Merced's industrial guts. The crowd shimmers on the front cars' horizontal windows. Children running, threading in and out of the adults. A baseball-capped acne-faced kid half-sitting on his bike, one leg draped over a wooden Department of Public Works barrier only centimeters from the moving train. The boy smiles as he looks at him, but reservedly: you can't get too carried away when you're up against a moving train.

Thomas gets caught up waving at everyone, not a steady look for anyone any longer.

The first time I've ever been ON a parade.

Only minutes before sitting, half-sleeping in that ancient, rocking, dusty, air-conditioned Southern Pacific relic through dawn-lit fields of shadowy crops, bisecting California's central cornucopia, the San Joaquin, to the base of the Sierra Nevada's mass of granite stretching half the length of the state. That massive geological tilt we call the "range of light."

The Yosemite Valley Railroad (YV), opened in 1907, covered 78.43 miles of track with grades between 1 and 2 percent, achieving a total rise of 1900 feet. Over 63 miles of the line were grades, and 32.9 in curves (505 exactly)

2

Dawn in San Francisco: riding to connect with this inaugural run of the Yosemite Railway. In the Merced yards promptly at 8:45 A.M., mingling with the famous and the barely recognizable as well as those whom I've come to know through writing about this project—Yosemite Park. Most arrived here by car or plane, apparent in the glazed look of people still warped by fast, conventional, "disposable" forms of transport.

The station covers a long rectangular block almost entirely protected by willows and trellises, he continues recording diligently into the machine on his upper arm. *Its shed structure is supported by laminated beams below an arching wood and solar-skin roof. A clerestory opens the top of the curve to the morning sunlight that streams into the dusty air to streak and spot the three glistening inaugural trains. We were on Number One on opening day.*

In front of the temporary reviewing stand, I heard some grumbling about the influentials who rated instead of "those who had fought for and built the damned thing in the first place."

"Smells so new in here. When was this train finished?"

"About a month ago."

Behind the station in the next block is a four-story enclosed parking structure, the Merced Inn, Yosemite Railway offices and the freight station. I couldn't see much of that complex or the restored 30s-style Doric-columned SP station nearby. It should suffice to say that the whole area looks like an island of new against a sea of used and tired, he stops recording.

Merced, epitome of a farming town—still showing its agricultural pragmatism with numbered and lettered streets—whose stores offer only necessities. There used to be one frivolous thing, though, about Merced: a steel-frame neon sign over what was Highway 99, "Merced, Gateway to Yosemite."

Looking at this strange town: it sure has updated its style, soil in the hands brushed into the illusions of Los Angeles' collective chambers of commerce. How odd a place for the Yosemite project: in four years a 342-kilometer railroad complete with 26 tunnels, over a hundred pieces of rolling stock and God knows how many bridges.

Riding the overpass across Southern Pacific's main line on which he'd entered twenty minutes before, he can see practically all of Merced's thirty-square-block area, a grid of maples, elms and oaks. The arching bridge carries the train from the railway's terminal at 15th and O Streets over boxcars rusting behind the Yosemite Lumber Company's office to a more northeasterly direction, R Street. From here most of the buildings along the railroad's tracks, and to the freeway two blocks west of the station, are boxy, practical structures built for mechanisms, not people. But right in the middle between M, N, O, 15th and 16th Streets is this complex of brand new structures, forms not related to industry or maintenance, but the womb of a journey east to the Sierra.

with a maximum curvature of 15 degrees. Sixty-eight bridges or trestles crossed water.

He sits down on the varnished pine seat curving out from the car's side. *Comfortable.* Passing between a dusty shopping center and a Taco Bell with broken windows and graffiti-scarred For Sale signs. The two tracks are laid in a grass- and flower-lined strip right down the middle of R Street.

What's moving? The train is so steadily reflected in the mirror-coated lenses of a few scary-looking cops, it's hard to tell whether the town is moving past us or we past Merced. Those glasses, a tint of 1984 in 1983.

People standing on cars in the Safeway parking lot waving till I feel their arms must be aching. It's like a real old-fashioned inaugural. Reminds me of seeing the last steam-powered trains with my father in the 50s; we'd ridden through some small mountain towns with whistles blowing and locomotive belching black smoke for the camera-laden crowd. A year ago when the YR was going through the usual construction hassles that occur, always, just before any big project is finished, there were real doubts about whether this ride would ever take place. But here it is, the train is passing by these pastel stucco houses, merely four months behind schedule.

—"Of course open it anyway. It'll be finished, won't it? In that way we can use the winter to smooth it out, get it to ride! It'll take the public awhile to get used to using the park all year long."—

Accelerating to 40 kph intensifies the sense of the powerful electric motors under the car. Whirring sound of urging. Enough to propel us into the Sierra Nevada? Why am I having these doubts? I can't get over how unnatural it feels to be on this solar-powered train traveling through this town so out of sync with it and Yosemite. This day is even odd: a train so unlike any other, the weather so obliging for October, and celebrities and other grotesques converged in a town that normally sees them only on wall screens.

About to cover 35 km of flat, open grassland north. Virtually a straight line of track across rangeland greened by occasional small farms. Then the Merced River's delta, across it and up east into the Sierra, 110 km. For most of that distance, the train'll parallel the river on tracks laid just above its course in a deep canyon formed by an ancient glacier's runoff. A gentle cleft at first, deepening with rocky walls trimmed with dry vegetation, then dense pines above scattered outcroppings of rock, the river path narrows to a gorge of water-stained white granite faces before finally opening into Yosemite Valley.

I don't know why, but I just reached up and grabbed a leafy branch passing by. Just about cut my hand open. Dumb.

Bringing his green-tainted hand to the railing, brushing and rubbing it, Thomas' attention is caught by the old man who moments before had sat down next to him.

"There's still a child in you," the older man decides with eyes laughing, eyes of a child.

Still in the center of R Street, but now it's a wide 60s-style boulevard lined with maturing city-gray trees and aluminum streetlights. Car and city noises bouncing off the hot asphalt. Past a school and the end of pavement, instantly into open grassland where, by its previous absence, silence is emphasized.

"How many people working this train?"

In comparison, the Yosemite Railway (YR), opened in 1983, spans 490 kilometers of light- and heavyweight track with grades up to 8 percent, achieving the 3000-plus-meter rise of Tioga Pass. All but 30 kilometers are

"Two drivers, two conductors, must be five working in the dining cars, which is more than there'll be on regular service."

Even though I've written two stories on the construction of this railroad, I'm amazed at the simple things I don't know, but well, my man, you have been doing other things, too.

"You know, Merced is really the oddest place to begin a railroad to Yosemite."

"Never thought about it myself, but now you mention it I guess it's because of the old railroad. You know that we're riding on the old right-of-way—opened in 1906—and will be for most of the way to El Portal?"

"Really? Why do you think they used this old way? The rails are long gone. . . ."

"I imagine it has something to do with it being the natural way into the park from the west. This one's more or less following the middle route. If they'd used a southern one and built a whole new right-of-way, it'd favor the people coming from the south. And a more northern route from Modesto would've favored people coming from there. A compromise, I guess, probably the same reasoning they went through surveying the original in 1895. It's probably the shortest way also, now I come to think of it."

"Makes sense."

"You bet it does. I've lived up near La Grange—that's north of here, 'bout thirty miles, sorry, that's about fifty kilometers; anyway I've lived here for most of my life. Grew up in Merced. It was always a slow, quiet town, but this project has livened things up a bit."

"What do you think about it?"

"The railroad?"

"Yeah."

"Well, it's good. I'm a bit biased you understand. I work for the project part of the time. Yeah, I like it. It's basically a good thing. I'm thinkin' though, it can be stolen away from the people. I've seen that happen too many times. After awhile you just assume people'll get too lazy to decide for themselves; they'll let some kind of authority get the edge on them."

The silence of agreement.

"Do you think there'll be space in the nose?"

The old man looks around. "Probably not, that's the best seat in the house, but maybe. People movin' around a lot. This train's chaotic; people aren't sittin' anywhere too long."

"I'll give it a try."

"Good luck."

Judging from the design of the seat, I would be able to place my small bag beneath it on a regularly scheduled train.

But this train is anything but that: more people than seats, constant milling about from one end to the other. I'll have to go back a few cars and check my bag before going forward to the nose. These opening day insanities; I've got to ride this train in normal

grades, and 380 kilometers are curves (if completed, they would equal 800 circles) with a maximum curvature of 38 degrees. There are 170 bridges or trestles; 70 percent of the track is on the old highway right-of-way

service. *The low distant range of purple hills is already visible to the east. I hope I'll get a seat before we reach the mountains.*

Through the other two crowded open observation cars, he walks with the rushing wind pushing him towards the back of the train and blowing long sparse light-brown hair across his bald spot and thinning forehead. Startling windmill shadow hurries across the crowd as the train passes a small farm.

Crossing Cardella Avenue: one of those perpendicular endless stretches of asphalt shimmering as the train streaks past at what seems like 80 kph. How can anybody live out there, it's so flat and glaring? What I can't understand is why people in flatlands don't build more towers. Seems like the best thing about living in the flatland would be looking across the sea of grass. But these folks aren't like me, which is why I'm not living here and they are.

Bellevue Road extending out from our crossing gates as far as I can see. Randomly spaced patches of growing things in between acres of dry, yellow grass: some overgrazed down to the hard reddish-brown soil, others separated by old fenceposts. Twisted meandering barbed wire forced into this eternal marathon dance by the years of cattle that've leaned into them. To my right as I turn my head, a frozen image: a green house trailer with white roof paint peeling off in curls like old playing cards in puddles. This, in front of a tottering whitewashed barn patched with occasional sheet aluminum and fiberglass rectangles. Next to a 77 Buick almost entirely gutted. Imagining flies buzzing around the torn upholstery. Windows shot out with .22s. The bullets are recent, the brass hasn't tarnished. I know these odd things.

So far I've seen two restored farmhouses all painted up and surrounded by thick multivegetabled gardens. I can see they're the latest thing: organic gardening in the land of corporate growers. Wonder if it'll catch on the way they say it's going to?

Wind is hot now. I can feel the moisture evaporating off my skin. Observation car looks like a 3-D movie theater in the 50s; and those few who aren't wearing dark glasses are squinting as if they were looking at snow.

Walking the length of this train entails passing through the vestibule, a space that separates yet connects, where you are neither outside nor inside: in transition. On conventional trains the vestibule and its accompanying diaphragm—the flexible passageway that allows the cars to bend independently around curves—were dirty spaces entered through awkward, heavy steel doors and filled with the smell of steam heat and rotting rubber. On this train you enter the vestibule through an oak-framed sliding glass door divided at waist height by a carved oak panel. Its leaf design culminates in a round red plastic spot triggering the door at a touch to slide open effortlessly. Bridging the vestibules is the diaphragm, a clear plastic tunnel-like device through which you can see the four couplers connecting car to car. They are bright aluminum castings that strongly resemble clasping hands, expressing function while also suggesting an intrinsic relationship between machines and life forms.

while 11 percent of the track is on the old railroad right-of-way, the remaining 19 being new right-of-way.

He enters the vestibule just as a woman dressed in a fox-fur coat, dark glasses, bright orange head scarf, deep purple neck scarf and heavy leather bag dangling from her left arm comes through the opposite door and stops to contemplate the bridge between moving platforms. She has a drink in each hand.

"Honey, do me a favor, will ya' take one of these? I'm not going to make this trip without a free hand."

He gingerly takes the cup from her outstretched hand. She passes him and the door behind him slides open, letting a blast of warm air rush into the space as she enters the open observation car he has just left. He stretches his arm back before the door closes. "Here, the worst is over, your drink."

"Keep it, sweets; he doesn't really need it anyway."

Unoccupied sign on bathroom door to the left. A sliding door that rolls back in the wall with slats like a rolltop desk. I really didn't want to use the john in that ancient steel can operated by the Southern Pacific. This one: wooden walls, look like light oak, polished stainless steel sink and toilet. I'll just sit down on the wood seat and make myself at home.

Simple instructions. A flushless toilet that operates even when the train isn't moving. Methane collection tank beneath the floor. Sink water coming from a tank in the ceiling. One red, yellow and blue blown-glass ball above, striping the walls at night with streaks of color. Soap, just a small bar, none of that dispenser crap; soap's the cleanest thing in the world. Real towels with YR in green on blue. Somebody's going to steal these towels; do they think they won't? Perhaps this one plastic wall around the side etched-glass window—you can see out but I presume not in—is intended for graffiti. "Squatters' Writes" already chalked in. As well as, "Flush twice, it's a long way to LA." Sliding door also triggers occupied/occupado sign.

". . . and now they're getting into ecological restoration, whatever that means. How can you make a place like it was? You can't go back. How can you make a wilderness again? It's a contradiction in terms."

"I wonder what it'd be like if there was no transportation at all to the park. Setting the whole region off as a wilderness gotten to only by trails. Did anyone consider that?"

". . . ."

"I bet there's a relationship between effort expended to get there and appreciation of it. If you had to walk, you'd really be into it by the time you got to the valley."

"Did driving here make us appreciate it less? I don't know. And people taking this train there, if they really look at the land they're passing through to get to the Park, will they appreciate it more having seen all this territory leading up to it?"

Involved in this train. People are beginning to wake up, loosen up; the atmosphere of the train's getting to them. Guess I'll have to come out of my morning stupor and train lag. God, here I am on a brand new 15-car train rolling along a newly completed track buried in grass all the way to Yosemite Valley. Along with politicians, celebrities, press, construction workers, California socialites, artists, kids, bureaucrats, planners, scientists

When the Yosemite Railroad took its first full-length trip on March 15, 1907, twelve passengers left Merced on the three-car train that offered an official "speiler" to describe the sights the passengers were seeing.

and maybe some people. A veritable linear party, a rolling brunch complete with national TV coverage just in case I want to see it all again on the 11 o'clock news.

"You know, the idea of the train. It's like going backward."

"Backwards? We're movin' ahead just fine."

"No, what I mean is going back to a previous, outmoded technology."

"Previous, outmoded? That's the fallacy! Whatever's usable, practical, beneficial, that's what we use. A simple and elegant answer to a problem doesn't have to be abandoned just because we have something newer. Because electricity is a real advance over kerosene lamps doesn't mean railroads have lost their function. We don't have to get caught refining and redefining. We can go on to something else."

Through the sixth car in the train, an enclosed coach, with at least a dozen "pardon me's," and "excuse me's."

"Excuse me, do you happen to know how far apart the inns are between Merced and Yosemite?" *The conductor looked startled. Hearing nothing but demands and complaints all morning, a pragmatic question can be a stopper.*

"They're a day's walk or about half a day apart on horseback—that's the way they were spaced."

Another three steps leads him to: "I resent the fact that I can't drive up to Yosemite anymore. It's simply not fair."

"What's fair?"

"That's not the point. It's goddamn irritating. There were good roads up here and they took them out. What's wrong with a few parking lots and a gas station? What we'll have now is trains and tracks all over the place. Dirty cabooses.

"I mean people used to come up here for a few days to relax. They could bring all their stuff—everything they needed—in a camper or a car and really lay out for a while. Now if they want to come, they have to bring their stuff on the train and that means just cutting everything back to a minimum. It's restricting and I don't like that. It just doesn't seem fair."

"If you remember, there was virtually an urban encampment in the valley. Hotels and other shelter structures, buildings, restaurants, stores, garages, barns, banks. The valley's only about 11 km by less than 2 wide and too much of that space was taken up by those buildings, things having nothing to do with the actual experience of being there, seeing there. After all, that was what we went there for, most of us at least."

Finally the baggage car, eight cars back.

Shelves full of bags, backpacks, purses, suitcases, packages, coats, and TV cables behind a low wood wall down one side of the car paralleling the corridor and broken only by two center counters next to the sliding outside doors, large enough to take in a canoe if carefully angled in. It was hanging from hooks in the roof, the canoe's painted canvas skin glistening orange under the clerestory-admitted shafts of sunlight.

Someone on this train intends to float back from Yosemite!

Even though I was his only customer, the harried young man looked overworked this morning, probably hoping regular service won't be like this. He finally exchanged my bag and heavy overcoat for a small composition coin—a tickadisk—stamped with the YR insignia.

Now back up front for a try at the nose. One door out the baggage car to enter into the shimmering plastic diaphragm. A moment to look out the side. What a beautiful day this is, the few clouds are crisp and sharp in the distance. White and light gray against the low horizon's light blue. I feel kind of dizzy, drunk, maybe from the vodka in that orange juice or the craziness in the station or the lack of sleep. God, it's such a strange feeling to notice your blood tingling as if it were suddenly charged with electrons. Maybe it is. Damn, shouldn't have stopped. Senator Fale is coming through the door, walking forthrightly despite the train's slight, lateral undulations as it passes thorugh a switch. Could he and his entourage be charging into the diaphragm especially to interrupt my moment of peace? Many California politicians think of this project as a frill; Fale was for it early, even if he did use it for his own ends. I may as well talk to him now and get it over with. Even this early in the morning his tired face looks made up, just like he looks on TV.

"How are you, Senator?"

"You work for that West Coast scientific magazine, don't you?"

"Yeah, we're continuing to feature this project. Would you care to . . . ?"

"In awhile, awhile."

He extends his hand, shakes Thomas's and uses that gesture to slide past him.

Maybe the couplers suggested it.

This vestibule is reminiscent of open platforms on 1880s passenger cars. It bridges the gap between inside and out: a private porch.

Running through long tangents of straight track alternating with gradual curves around low rolling hills. Three or four shallow cuts that are eroded with miniature grand canyons, cuts made over eighty years ago for the original railroad. A cluster of cottonwood and oaks sheltering some Herefords from bright morning sun. Short bridge over an irrigation ditch, past a small pond crowded by cows standing in thick black mud. Tableland: flats of land extending in meandering lines, trimmed with slightly higher grass off into the distance. A pickup leaves a trail of light brown dust against still distant Sierra foothills, blueish in the ground-bound haze.

He steps through the diaphragm, swings sideways from the aluminum grab bar into the next car's open platform. He can see the two-lane highway paralleling the track crammed with a long clot of cars. There's one crazy in an old, rattling half- but not well-restored Volkswagen Beetle that's attempting to pass the cars and the train. His exhaust is open and roaring, totally breaking the steady hum of steel wheels down there in the grass. He roars by one group, slips in, roars by another, slips in, then finally passes the first three cars. In a cloud of

In 1904 Congress granted the Yosemite Railroad its right-of-way through National Forest land in exchange for $100 annually.

```
CAR:.......... 5/15 Inaugural Special (Pompompassos)
TIME:.......... 0921
DATE:.......... 3 Oct 1983
SPEED:.......... 81 kph
DIRECTION:...... 12 degrees N/NW
GRADIENT:....... 0.01%
ALTITUDE:....... 57 m
From ORIGIN:.... 21.31 km (Merced)
To DESTINATION:. 123.27 km (Yosemite Valley)
Est Arr TIME:... 1224
NEXT STOP:...... Snelling 0929
TEMPERATURE:.... 20.5 degrees Celsius
WEATHER:........ Clear, occasional showers north Sierra
........ low: 12, high: 22
........ wind: 5-8 kph E/SE
NEWS:.......... Governor Green meeting YR inaugural
trains at Valley Station
.......... Wildfire 3 km south Lake Tenaya
.......... Second Mediterranean Eco-Restoration
Conference meets in Venice
```

blue smoke, he's gone. Through all of it, those other drivers, so busy trying to drive, watch the train, wave and take pictures, don't even notice him. The train's doing 85 kph; he's got to have been hitting over 100.

Looking down the side of eight cars to the last one. Five giant black ravens flapping up from a patch of blood-stained grass to the side of the highway and only three or four meters from my rolling theater box. Their wings cast fleeting shadows across the last car's shiny skin, a surface that like a chameleon's becomes the environment it passes through. A last glance back as we round a curve. The inevitable comparison between the waving dry grass we've just passed over, covering our path as if it were not there, and the dead highway: dark gray, black-patched, white-lined asphalt.

I remember these trains as plywood and cardboard mockups in an office that looked like a dilapidated farm in the hills near Merced Falls—where we'll be in another fifteen minutes. My visits to the Yosemite Railway project office: the reasoning behind every last bolt, stick of wood and pane of glass was expressed with the determination of people who knew what they were doing but were still surprised at their ability to do it. All the sophisticated minds became childlike about the becoming railway. They had discovered the potential of a near-forgotten, too often romanticized connection: people and trains.

A closed interior that is soft with upholstered structural framing between windows, seats of thick leather-covered foam that cradle the body, bright carpet illuminated through walls of clear untinted glass, sliding glass panels in the lower portion of each window allowing passengers to feel fresh air. Warm interiors made of soft materials that by nature respond to our delicate, damageable bodies. Acknowledging by form the inevitability of a mistake, an accident.

He's walking forward, into the sixth car, then the fifth.

They look so trusting. We are such fallible creatures, yet we place so much faith in these elaborate creations. Even though this is a relatively simple machine, it's still liable to potential error. I wonder if that lady who so breathlessly and starlike rushed through the car has any idea how quick and alert the drivers have to be at all times? Does she even know there are two drivers responsible for her safe passage?

A clerestory above down the center of each car's roof; a second roof rising 25 cm above the ceiling and punctuated with small windows admitting sunlight, or moonlight. Light from windows as large and frequent as the structure will allow. Multicolored route maps or fine prints of Yosemite scenes and an information screen at the end of each car. In the computer trade it's called a "databoard"; nothing more than a flat television wall screen about thirty centimeters high and fifty wide carrying a continual display, constantly changing, of relevant information.

It's hypnotic to stand here and watch the numbers from origin go up, to destination go down. The graphic printout can be replaced instantaneously with an image in one of the cars, or a view ahead or behind the train. Right now it's showing an image of the buffet setup, behind some dignitary munching away while talking into the camera. Another view flashes: Tom what's-his-name of CBS looking official with his camera and memo pad. He doesn't have anyone to interview. Surely in that entire coach there must be someone capable of answering his questions.

"This is the first curve in five kilometers."

I don't believe someone said that!

"Tom Ricker wanted in the baggage car." *The voice over the PA system was quiet and unobtrusive, not that blaring tin I'd assumed was unavoidable with any public address system.*

"Who built this train?" A concerned mother gasps to a young woman wearing a YR button.

"You'd have to look at the signature plate on the end platform to be sure. I think a company near Redding that used to build recreation vehicles built at least three of 'em."

"Are you kidding? I wouldn't trust a company that'd been building those plywood and aluminum cardboard boxes! My husband and I once had . . . ."

"Maybe so, but there were a lot of craftsmen in that plant whose skill wasn't being used on RVs. I read that that particular company went through some changes over the building of these coaches. It had been owned by a conglomerate that couldn't see any other product but RVs. They waited for the RV business to come back—everyone in the company knew damn well it never would. Finally the employees formed their own company, bought the controlling interest—the founder who had sold it to the conglomerate in the first place helped—endured some pretty lean months and finally landed a YR contract. They built these cars for half what a railcar company would've charged, and it seems to me they did a much better job."

"How did they do that!"

"You mean build them? The working drawings were designed so that anyone could follow them. All they are are step-by-step instructions on how to build the whole body. It's only welding, bolting, sawing and bending. Most of the nuts and bolts are common hardware store items, off-the-shelf stuff. Only the wheelsets, interior electronics and some unusual castings have to be specially made. It came as quite a blow to the large corporations, this getting back to real people capitalism."

That's a good point; now where can I use it?

He walks towards the next car, sliding past Tom and his impressive little handheld color TV camera pointed like a Colt .45. He looks over Tom's shoulder; there's nothing on the pad.

Jesus, what a mob, the lead car is jammed. I have to walk sideways more than before; but the pressing bodies hold me up. Nothing but politicians and half-remembered media faces pressing right up to the end door. Feel like I'm in campaign headquarters or at a fund-raiser in some whitewashed art gallery.

"Thomas Sutter, is it you?"

I can't see through the talking heads. There she is, Sally somebody, haven't seen her

After surveying, the grading of the line from Merced was supervised by James "Horse and Carts" O'Brien, a San Francisco grading contractor who had never built a railroad.

12

for awhile. Can't remember what she does, think fast. Connected with this railroad? She must be. Fake it.

"This is Serge." *And they continue their conversation, occasionally glancing to see if I'm interested. I'm interested in getting through this mob and finding a seat in the nose. At the moment it looks like I'm going to have to work for my view.*

"Don't you agree?"

"Umm."

Serge: "People aren't interested in careful planning; they just want to see it happen fast. Progress is the result of careful, professional planning."

Salli: "Don't you see. We weren't in a hurry so much as we had to keep the spirit growing. Planners tend to hold people back. Justifying their professionalism, that becomes their work, not solving problems. Planning becomes an excuse for action."

Serge: "Salli, you can't just throw a track down anywhere. That Midpines branch has water seepage problems; everyone but the planning team agreed to build over that soft spot; we advocated surveying a grade around it."

Salli: "But it's operating isn't it? The planning team wasn't in complete agreement, some members recognized the value of getting it done and not trying to plan for *every* eventuality—if we'd followed your suggestion it wouldn't have been done even now. As it turns out, we'll have operating revenue, and it'll be easier to fix things like that as we go along."

Serge: "That's like constructing a dam without really preparing for its impact over the long run. It would have been so much simpler to build the track right the first time."

Salli: "Easy to say in hindsight. When you talk about something's being 'right,' you're speaking ideally. Reality is never right. We seek perfection, not build it!

"I'm going to try and get a seat in the nose. Nice to have met you . . . eh. See you later, Salli."

"Excuse me"—"Pardon"—"Hi, who are you?"—"Yes, I'll just slip by, thanks."—"Oops, sorry, I'm sure it'll come off in the wash. Try Zap; it gets everything out organically."

"Funny thing about biodegradable: it also means life-diminishing."

"Huh?"

"Say, ah, you that guy who used to be on the radio, uh, . . . now what was it . . . ?"

"That's right."

"Haven't heard you for a while."

Oh, Christ, not this again. I want to get up front.

"What've you been doin' lately? I sure enjoyed your humor."

"Writing a lot, that's been taking up my time."

"You gonna write about this ride? Say, I've got a real bunch of stuff ya'can use. How 'bout an in'erview?"

Does he think he has an inner view?

"Excuse me, but I've got to talk to the driver."

Be human now.

"Maybe later."

Up to this constriction, this forward car's configuration has been much like the other coaches except that it contains movable wicker foam-cushioned lounge chairs instead of fixed seating. There are two drivers whose feet are visible through eye-level openings on either side of the passageway. I can look up and see one driver's hand holding a bright green handset that resembles a telephone mouthpiece. A triumph of miniaturization: a handful of electronics capable of transmitting the driver's response to the terrain and the train's response to the driver's action. A row of tiny bright buttons are within the concave inner surface around a screened circle that looks like a microphone. Its elliptical shape is topped by a bright red knob on which his thumb rests: the throttle.

Literally, he's got the whole train under his thumb.

The nose: a space, 3½ meters long by 3 wide and high, surrounded by glass. There has been no attempt to temper the bright glaring reality totally transfusing this grotto-like space. The feeling for an instant is like being within a WW II bomber, a B-29's glass pit.

I don't really know whether it's pleasant or not.

To either side of the brown carpeted path that recedes to the front of the train are low foam seats that encourage sitting back with knees up or perching cross-legged on the thick landscape. People who are sitting there are snugly pressed, not packed. I count, besides myself, 15 hypnotics whose stare of wonder at the rapidly approaching track isn't disturbed by my slithering down into the green-covered softness and nestling my spine into the seatback.

"That old highway sure looks pitted; they just aren't maintaining them like they used to."

Images of ancient Roman roads; patches of neatly laid stone isolated on lonely English hills. Every culture assumes its imposing public works will last forever, that nothing will diminish the achievement. Yet we forget how many millions it took to build and maintain the highways. Those amounts aren't appropriated for these uses anymore, and it is becoming increasingly apparent that California can't maintain its network of car roads.

Ahead: rails lost in grass only 5 or 6 meters in front of us, though for brief seconds silver lines gleam a hundred ahead. With the exception of small columns barely visible below the rails, the track structure is buried. Totally camouflaged. There are no wooden ties, no gravel ballast, only two indistinct sinewy threads hovering above living earth, carrying this vehicle and then disappearing from sight.

More like a miniature bridge than a railroad track. Smaller animals can even get through underneath the rail. Only the infrequently passing train interrupts their freedom. And since the grass grows all around and through the track, there

In 1905, three years to the day (December 18) of the incorporation of the line, in order to comply with charter regulations, the first "regularly scheduled" runs began from Merced to a point three miles east. There was no

```
CAR:..........  5/15 Inaugural Special (Pompompassos)
TIME:.........  0925
DATE:..........  3 Oct 1983
NEWS:.........  Wildfire 3 km south Lake Tenaya declared
                freeburn.  Expected direction: Sunrise
                High Sierra Camp.  Probable affected area:
                Long Meadow.
          .......  President sends congratulatory message to
                inaugural ride stating, "...if I were
                William Howard Taft or Teddy Roosevelt
                I'd be there!"
          .......  The IntraCity Community Loan Bank announced
                today that loans financing solarskin con-
                version of living and office buildings in
                Los Angeles, Santa Barbara and San Francisco
                have already exceeded 25 million dollars in
                the first three months.
```

aren't any dead zones, continuous disruption of plant and animal patterns. Nor is the surface geology of topsoil disturbed. Water is absorbed into the ground just as it was before the track was laid.

Bell above the headlight: ringing. The track has turned through the trees to the east. Speedometer dropping, 30, 29, 27, 24. Odometer lights up 28.72 km from Merced. The crowd at the Snelling station appears with the third peel of the bell. A red, white and blue ribbon across the track.

Snelling's ten-block area reiterates the sleepy, southern delta atmosphere. To his left, north, visible through the intricate contrasting greens of the tree-shaded lanes, the beginning of the grassland—North Dakota in the summer. Bells ringing, the train crawls between two platforms closer to the stretched band.

Within a few feet of the train, people wait in conversational knots: uncomfortable men wearing their Sunday best in a town where that still means something. Enveloping warm, moist air surrounds light cotton clothing, dark glasses and a smattering of curl-rimmed, sweat-stained Stetsons. Men with fieldwork tans standing among ladies whose shapes attest to the quality of their cooking. Teenage boys, arms lazily hanging at their hips, legs indistinguishably outstretched, assume assured attitudes that don't quite conceal their lack of ease.

"Are we going through that ribbon?" A lady behind him addressing no one in particular. "Doesn't look like we have any choice."

The poster to the right on the shadowed wall of the rock-and-wood station displays Half Dome and the words, "Our First Day, October 3, 1983" below. That image again pointing up the incongruity of this place, over a hundred kilometers west of and a thousand meters below Yosemite Valley.

I'll never know what it's like to work a farm in Snelling, in the eastern corner of California's San Joaquin Valley. Or what I would think of a national park so important it requires its own railroad. Yet it was these people and all the others in all the other small towns and hamlets in this five-county area whose agreement and work and courage made it possible. Not the politicians and not the hype artists and not the media. Their parents and their parents' parents helped build the old railroad nearly a century ago. Honoring that, they built Snelling's new station near the site of the old.

The snowplow pilot touches the crêpe, breaking through blue, then white, then red. The crowd outside goes off in a rush of celebration like a lit fuse. Those inside applaud, more in anticipation of leaving Snelling: the mountains are clearly beckoning.

Two tracks instead of one. I've heard someone planted golden poppies along this entire section. For a moment, imagining it in the spring.

In Merced, on the highway north of town and now along the paralleling highway east of Snelling, all those people just wanting to watch the train. Why do we become

station where the train stopped, and the chief engineer would fix a fare for those who took the ride.

fascinated by certain machines? Why do we think about them, write about them, sing their songs, talk to them, give them names, love them almost to the point of physicality? And of all the machines we've romanticized, I think we cherish trains the most.

Now in the ninth decade of this century, we're witnessing the revival of this fantasy. The railroad is recapturing the imagination of a generation that has grown up racing other strangers on concrete highways. Is this just another fad or a significant change in collective outlook?

All around our path now are windrows of rock, more dredge tailings I assume, but they're so extensive that seems hard to believe.

"What left those behind?"

Here I am asking questions directed at no one and everyone. I guess that's what happens on trains. You just start muttering to all your fellow travelers.

"Gold-dredge tailings. Left behind after the dredges worked this area around the turn of the century. We use 'em for building." It was a guy he'd seen before.

"You live here?"

"Not far from. Down back around Merced."

"Work for the railroad?"

"Yeah. In the yard at Merced Falls."

The land is ravaged here. Tailings dragged around. Birch, poplar, cottonwood and oak, some twisted from the repeated assaults of the bulldozers pushing the rock. Down in a hollow between two ancient house trailers is a rusting one partially hidden by dirt and leaves and cobwebs. A strange landscape. I feel almost guilty looking into the scattered backyards of shack-like houses and seeing occasional human scenes in this land of waste. But then I remember I'm a journalist.

"What's your name?"

"Arthur Jimenez."

"Mine's Thomas Sutter. How do you rate a ride on this train?"

"Oh, I won the draw. Along with half the other workers. Didn't have room for the families though. I guess that's all right."

Dark brown eyes reflecting the passing trees and the river now barely visible beyond me. He seems to be waiting for my curiosity to surface in words.

"People don't care about this land, do they?"

"No, this is garbage land, used and wasted. When a place has been discarded and left without pride, it gets ugly. Then only people with great strength and vision and energy can reclaim it. I hope they come here."

Dredge tailings diminish in size and frequency, Merced River visible in the south. To the right a two-lane blacktop still crammed with cars seen between the low piles of weed-grown rocks.

"Why are we slowing down?"

"I think they're going to add another car to the train."

"How long will that take?"

"Less than a minute. They have to slow to about twenty though."

"While we're moving?"

The government refused to give up more right-of-way beyond El Portal, so the Railroad built a wagon road to the the valley that cost $73,260.24. This became the Arch Rock entrance to the national park and the YV was never

"Yeah. We've already uncoupled into two halves. See the car over there on the left ahead? The coach on the parallel track?"

"It's moving?"

"Right. Now watch this. It's all gonna happen behind us. It sure took practice. See if you can feel it."

We're moving between the platforms of the board-and-batten Merced Falls Station and Inn whose clocktower showing 9:42 and 2142 coincides with the reading in the car. The crowd in the station's paying more attention to what's happening behind us than to the actual arrival of the train. Ego deflating after the previous adulation shown us.

"Did you feel it?"

"Feel what?"

"Great, you didn't. New car just coupled up. You have to have done it many times before you can sense the slight bump when they meet. How 'bout that?"

"The vibration, you mean?"

"That was the rear half of our train coupling to the new car. Now we're together again. Sixteen cars instead of fifteen."

"How come they . . . ?"

"Showin' off partly. We have to be able to add cars quickly while in motion past the yards; that's what this particular track is for. We can routinely add cars to scheduled trains now while they're in motion."

"Flexibility."

Accustomed as I am to writing about industrial plants that look like giant insects jumbled in battle, this whole scene is a revelation. The place where much of Yosemite Railway's equipment is assembled, maintained and repaired looks like a neat Kentucky thoroughbred farm, not a railroad yard. Lively contrasts exist between traditional architectural forms that might've been used a hundred years ago and highly sophisticated steel-and-glass tetrahedrons flashing sunlight off faceted surfaces. Between rows of hard-edged steel rails, the loose, mottled shade from regular rows of fig and olive trees fall across stored trains. The earth in this yard is alive and productive, not dry and wasted as it too often is around industrial areas.

Over another low overpass and into a few gradual curves. Under an oak bending shadow over the train. Then, between cuts, a view to the south: the highway, like an extended black line on the yellow-brown hills, disappears south to Hornitos, close by the dammed Merced River: Lake McSwain it's called here.

Black rocks looking volcanic in color and form. Shards of once-melted, then compressed deposit, standing up like tombstones, laying over loosely as if thrown there and wedged in forever. Yesterday for this rock is a million years.

compensated for its investment.

The kid behind me frantically snaps his tiny Nikon. I can hear the motor advancing the film while simultaneously feeling the train's motors bite into the grade. It's so sudden a climb. Two minutes ago flatland, the yards, the highway junction. Now we hold at 72 kph. Beginning to climb the Sierra Nevada.

Not knowing the people noises, bluejays leap to flight from their perches on the rail ahead. The birds have taken to the rail; it's a perfect lookout for seeds, insects and grubs in the grass below. A bright flash of sunlight from a peak maybe 45 degrees up and north maybe twenty kilometers.

I'm not certain but I have a hunch it was the reflection off the globe of a solar generating station, maybe the one powering us now.

Slowing before a sharp curve. Suddenly the motors lose their whirring sound, becoming muted as the wheels' noise overwhelms the engine's sound. Crawling around the bend and there, maybe 25 m in front, are three Herefords. Only one eyes the interruption on top of the rails overgrown with thick, tasty weeds. The train crawls, the cows start walking away but paralleling the track closest to the steep hillside. Couldn't pass without hitting one of these dumb, expensive bovines. The train starts to get angry: bell and whistle vibrate until there's enough noise to make them amble down a narrow arroyo that the train bridges.

Once we started working up the grade, I realized why we slowed before we could see the animals: the drivers have a sonar-like device that sends a signal through the rails, generating a band of low-frequency sound to either side of the track. A sensor in the train then detects any variation; this, in combination with an infrared scanning device for night travel, gives the drivers a view of what their eyes cannot see.

Clipping along through cuts, over bridges, route like a wavering line passing through perpendicular ridges in the steep, folded, oak-covered hills. Most of the railfans have given up. Only a few cars on the highway, now an access road to the dam the voices behind tell me we're approaching. I hear someone else talking about these mountains; he must be from the East: out here these are hills, what're coming up are mountains.

It's rangeland but feeling more and more like wilderness. We're alone out here. A rolling party in the middle of the dry Sierra Nevada foothills. I wonder how many of these people could survive walking across this land. I wonder if I could.

A tunnel, an old one, it's so much bigger than the train. Designed for the old railroad and still showing soot over the keystone date at the top of the arch. 1924. Little steam engines once chugged up this grade. Hard to believe an engineer and fireman could sit in a black steel locomotive only feet from a hot firebox filled with roaring oil.

Inside the tunnel is very cool, almost cold. I'm thankful, even though the hot sun made my forehead burn, that the Yosemite Railway doesn't air-condition its cars. The air is only cooled, not filtered, refrigerated and dehydrated. You can feel the change in climate, air quality. I've been able to taste the difference between the dusty lowland and the cleaner foothill air.

While the YV was being built it had three competitors: the Southern Pacific's Merced Canyon Railroad, which got as far as having surveyors; the Fresno electric line; and the Sierra Railroad's Yosemite Short Line.

18

"I see you did find a seat up here. It's amazing: those people back there are really crazy."

For a few moments the old man from the observation car adjusts his perception to the new and somewhat scary onrushing view. The train rolls around curving rock shelves that are the leading edges of steep ridges. Then, crossing the highway leading to the dam, the train immediately rides over a steel bridge spanning a long drop to a dry creekbed.

"See that tunnel there?"

Scanning the folded hills, Thomas is trying to see in a notch or behind a tree. Only after a cluster of oak flashes by within meters of the glass does Thomas make out a concrete opening. The main dam is about a hundred meters high spanning a narrow gap between two hills. Just to the north on the other side of the hill is a small depression walled with another, smaller portion of rockfill. The tunnel is below that smaller dam and appears to go through the hill and into the lake.

There are cuts in the ridgelines everywhere, including one huge cleft up above the main dam where they quarried the blueish-white crumbling rock that forms the dam. I imagine a surgeon performing an appendectomy with a meat cleaver and pitchfork. Tearing up the skin of the living Earth as if it were so much junk mail.

"We're not going through that tunnel, too?"

"Not unless you know a way this train can become a submarine!"

"That tunnel was built for the second route of the original Yosemite Railroad back in the 20s when they relocated track around the first dam. It's now covered by the water behind this dam, built in the late 60s."

"You mean we're on the third route?"

"That's it." The old man smiled. "First one was down along the river all the way to El Portal. When the dam was built, it was relocated around the lake at a higher elevation. Then, long after the old YV was abandoned in 45, the lake was raised by a large earthfill dam built in front of the old concrete structure. So to build this railroad, they had to survey yet a third route. That's what we're on now."

"So there's this old concrete dam drowned down there in the murky water! Did you ever ride the old YV?"

"Oh yeah, back in 41. Must've been 22 or so. Just before I went into the army; that's how I remember it."

"What was it like?"

"Wasn't like this."

They look ahead, the laughter breaking the conversation enough to bring back looking at the view: a long and dense green ridge to the left quite high above the train. Straight track, a few gradual curls across what seems like a long plateau just behind the first range of north-south foothills. Lake McClure occasionally sparkles in a view to the east through open patches breaking the low, mixed and tangled forest. The water's low, exposing maybe forty or fifty meters of coffee-and-cream-colored hillside like the stain in an old bathtub.

It suddenly occurred to me: there's been no river since Merced Falls, only two stagnant, washwater lakes.

"It was quite a railroad. Oil-burning steam locomotives, old wooden or steel coaches; why I can remember the open-ended observation car had seats, wicker I think, just like this car. Cause the grades were so steep, used small engines pullin' short trains. Not as steep as some we've just come up, but you know a locomotive pullin' a train can't climb a grade anywhere near as steep as an electric train with all wheels powered."

"Why was it abandoned?"

"Why? Money—like always. Equipment was ancient, less and less mineral and lumber freight, highway was completed all the way into the valley. People just as soon drive all the way. Back when it was abandoned, I heard a lot of loose talk, like maybe the buslines and auto companies helped along the railroad's demise."

"Wouldn't surprise me. Back in the 30s, Detroit put together a holding company to buy up old electric transit systems that were shaky. After they got them, the red ink really began to flow. So they were able to close down once-profitable, efficient nonpolluting competition. And of course they replaced it with buses and cars that the parent companies just happened to make. Wouldn't surprise me if they pulled the same stunt with a steam railroad, particularly a rural and out-of-the-way one like the YV that ran through an area with such a potential for car recreation."

"I don't know, maybe you got somethin' there. Don't make no difference now. People were fanatic about cars then; it was easy for big corporations to pull somethin' like that. Seems now like there's a renewed interest in trains for ground transportation. People have started recognizing that automobiles everywhere was just what was destroyin' what we used the car to go and see. Couldn't return railroads everywhere, but a few in special places like this, why that's just what's bein' cried out for.

"People saw the Sierra Railway north of here—it's makin' money hand-over-fist crryin' tourists behind ancient steam engines—they'd think we could build one like that to Yosemite. Well, they had the right idea but the wrong tool. Old oil-burnin' steam locomotives may be romantic, but they're not efficient. Besides, who needs more air pollution? Lots of folks thought this idea old-fashioned, trains and all.

"Finally someone named . . . damn, what was that guy's name? Anyway, somebody suggested an electric railroad powered by solar generators. Then they begain to reconsider and realized what a good, basic idea a train was. Sure it was old, but that didn't mean it was no good. So that's how the railroad idea took hold."

"It wasn't just the railroad . . . ."

The governor and other dignitaries had been invited for a golden spike celebration of the first trip, but a flood a few days earlier had washed out the roadbed and apparently the celebration too.

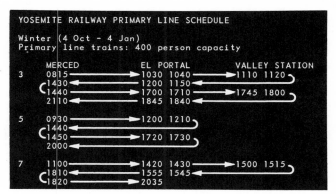

"Hell, no, that was just the seed. Any plan to restore the wilderness of Yosemite, and that was bein' talked about for a long time there, had to begin with transportation. Unless we could get in and out of the valley without the pollution of cars, tryin' to restore the ecology of the place was the cart before the horse. I remember seeing some of the early proposals in the press and the local papers—not all of them were warm to the idea. Many people seemed to think, and I suppose still do, that the very idea of a region without cars was un-American. It wasn't strange to hear people get up in public meetings and talk about the tie between patriotism and machines.

"The railroad became the core idea. Fairly simple research proved that one out and other ideas began to water: inns along the approaches to the Park, removal of buildin's in the valley, a railline over Tioga Pass, buildin' up El Portal, gardens, restoration projects, community technology and ownership. What started out as a solution to a problem became a kind of release for everyone's bottled-up fantasies. Everybody started in on gettin' the cars out of Yosemite. Not one person I talked to in those days really thought it possible, but everyone saw the possibilities in it. Funny, it was as if people didn't want to think their dreams could be realized."

"I followed those developments, but I just didn't see the overall way it changed basic assumptions. But now that you've refreshed my memory, I remember all the controversy, articles, letters, editorials and all the comment in the local media. I was intrigued by it and alternately irritated by the talk. Now, riding this train, living the reality of it, now I feel how powerful all that was."

"In all my years around California, I've never seen anythin' like it. Why, what's happened here is something *new*. Who would've guessed that similarities rather than differences would grow from the cynicism and fear and catastrophe of the 70s?

Bridge visible ahead, a sign: Barrett and a broad curve around the point of a black volcanic rock ridge. We're about to go over Lake McClure. Feeling that curious depletion of energy after you've solved a basic question with the simplest direct logic, yet know that that's not all there is to it.

Over a short concrete arch, speedometer dropping from 55 kph, whirring motors generating electricity as they brake over the main bridge's wooden decking. Rolling slowly out over the lake on a large bridge: a two-spanned, tunnel-like, over-four-hundred-meter-long structure.

From yellow-brown grass hills with ridgetops of thick oak and manzanita among sharp outcroppings of black volcanic rock splashed with orange and chartreuse lichen, hills no higher than three hundred meters, deeply folded and disguised with vegetation, the bridge connects to a new land: mammoth escarpment stretching north to south and rising steeply up from the lakeshore.

Across the bridge and we notch a geological step like a climber going from talus to steep granite slope.

Bell begins to sound. Wheels clicking through switches opening into two tracks. Passing a stationary worktrain: office, lodging, flatcar, woodworking cars. Men in paint-stained coveralls with power saws, hammers in hand.

Four horses tied up at the end of the bridge. Riders sitting on stacks of lumber eating fruit, their sunny spot framed by the alternating triangles of the bridge's structure.

"Ladies and gentlemen, Barrett: five-minute unscheduled stop."

No welcoming committee, no crowds of people. Only a banner of surveyor's tape hastily strung across the center track between two sawhorses. Train stops just short of it.

"Arthur, why didn't we stop in Snelling or Merced Falls?"

"What? Oh, well . . . eh." He pulls out an ancient, deeply scratched conductor's pocketwatch, looks at it with concern, mumbles something about the second train and replaces it in his worn cowhide vest.

"We didn't stop there because this is a special train. But most through trains won't stop either; they'll go straight through to El Portal or Yosemite. These are local stops."

"Locals? Didn't really consider them before."

"Oh, yeah. Locals, mixed trains, railbuses, railtrucks; everything on this railroad. We ain't runnin' just for Yosemite tourists. Lotta local traffic, too."

The old man leans over, a neat spot of sunlight illuminating his clear face, the collar of his red shirt and making his silvery hair glisten. I had questions about this bridge but said nothing.

Then: "Take this bridge; it's a perfect example of what we were talkin' about. Most people down in Merced and the other towns wanted continued access to the lake for boatin' and fishin'. While the railroad people wanted to pull out the road, partly for esthetic reasons, partly because they needed the revenue from the fishermen who'd ride the train. And there was this problem: people wanting to continue pullin' their boats up every weekend, even though gas keeps gettin' more expensive. Not everyone wanted to moor their boat on the lake, and besides, McClure's a reservoir, so the water level changes throughout the year: in the summer the water's low and the shore is steep and rocky; in the spring the water's much higher. So a dock would have to be built that could take the up-and-down seasonal movement as well as horizontal movement while maintaining a tie with the changin' shoreline; all together a tricky and expensive proposition. It all seemed like a stalemate, like the whole question of the national park—everyone proposing what they wanted, but no one agreein' about what everyone wanted, together.

"Then this friend of mine, a local accountant who by the way loves to fish, came up with a suggestion at a meetin' in Merced. Now there had to be a railroad bridge over the lake. The bridge would have piers out in the water, well away from the changin' shoreline. So why doesn't the railroad build a pier with

The advertisements for the first YV said "The Iron Horse now makes its way to the very gates of the National Park." San Francisco newspapers called the line "the Baby Road of the Mountains."

stairs inside and a collar-like marina dock that rises and falls vertically? This would do away with the problem of maintaining a connection with the shore. That did it. Minutes before everybody in that meetin' hall had been angry and frustrated. But they got over that quick as they began to jump in on the idea, worryin' it."

"Just great!"

" . . . There were difficulties, of course, how it would be paid for and so on. But once people decided what they wanted, the money didn't matter; again, it's living the experience, not counting the paper value that's important.

"So now the road to the lake has been removed and this has had the unplanned but interesting side effect of discouraging casual visitors, while encouraging people who really want to use the lake, mainly locals. You can imagine how that added to the sense of community; people feelin' they have a private place that the whole world doesn't know about, even if that whole world's gonna pass above it. Plus people have been usin' their boats more since they don't have the long drive to deal with or the cost of gasoline to get there. So when regular service reached here, anytime they liked they just got into a quiet, relaxin' train, got off right where we are now and just about stepped into the boat."

"Is that a traveling crane above us?"

"Yeah, it was built for the bridge construction. It was converted for loadin' and unloadin' the boats."

"It really all fits, though I wonder if it's all too well planned, too neatly worked out. Know what I mean?"

"It's what the people wanted, and it just turned out to be easy to do this way, just as easy as doing it sloppily."

"Easy? That bridge looks like a quantum leap in engineering."

"Well, in combination with the solarskin, there's a temperature-differential turbine located in the bridge's piers. Designed by a guy who used to work on nuclear reactors before that industry fell apart. He's a genius, I guess. Figured out how to integrate the functions of the two systems. When cold and warm layers within the lake move, that relates to the wind condition or somethin' like that. It's all monitored and the bridge reacts to the changes. You'll have to ask him, I just don't understand all of it."

"Amazing. I think I have an idea about what you're saying. You know, it's interesting to watch these different stations go by: Snelling, Merced Falls, this bridge. Imagine making it possible for twenty people or so to live and work right on it, a sort of bowdlerized London Bridge . . . and I'm not talking about Lake Havasu."

"I think it shows how people, individuals, have contributed to the project, mostly people with an abidin' sense of relationship with the planet. Outsiders, designers and builders who work on a job, they construct buildings to fit the place. But here people deeply involved with what they're doing, try and make their structures come to terms with the place. There's agreement, contributing rather than forcing. Then, instead of conflict there is harmony.

It became the "route of the celebrities" as California Governor James Gillett came in June 1907, as did South Carolina Senator Benjamin R. Tillman. William Randolph Hearst drove in a 40-horsepower Thomas Flyer to

"Next time you're in any large city, take a real look at the large structures, the buildings made of steel and glass. They're industrial, hard and polished like a machined part just off the assembly line. From a period of design that confused forms with functions. We were so overwhelmed with our powerful machines that everything we made began to look like them. Regardless of where the building was or what it was used for. Seems the basic idea of wholeness was missing. People weren't aware of the integrity of place."

"ALL ABOARD!"

Releasing air brakes clicking, workmen waving in time with the bell. Shrill whistle scaring the horses, their flanks quiver as if shaking it off.

Surveyor's tape doesn't break. Two men near the train start to laugh. The sawhorses are pulled along the sides of the train. Snap, flying yellow and orange streamers. Cheers and smiles from the onlookers. By the horses, then the stacks of bright yellow pineboards and through the final span of steel frame turning the view ahead into a mosaic pattern like a giant stained-glass window.

Through the last arch, new steel dark brown, its protective rust already formed. Steel supporting pea vines, pea vines intertwined with steel. Green claiming the harsh brown edges exemplifying a relationship of growing things with all the structures seen so far along this railroad.

Merced Falls station, Snelling, the yards and maintenance buildings have convinced me that there has been a lot of thinking about the relationship between climate and building forms: overhanging eaves that keep warm air close to the buildings in the winter and cool air near the windows during the hot months. The stone walls and deeply set windows evidence a building philosophy that maximizes the natural air-flow and essential temperature retention and loss characteristics of materials.

Around a broad curve into the lake's eastern shore. A parallel track dropping below, barely visible were it not for a slowly passing railbus clinging to the vertical mountainside like a steer picking its way through brush. Only the two silver rails indicate the path without revealing the slender concrete supports that vanish into the thick manzanita, in turn into the mountain itself.

"Ladies and gentlemen, our unscheduled stop in Barrett was caused by a leaking air brake connection. It has been repaired."

"Will they have mechanics on every trip?"

"The engineers and the conductors know these trains as well as the designers. A system's only as efficient as its maintenance. By the way, my name's Arthur, Arthur Jimenez and this is Thomas Sutter. I've met you, haven't I, before?"

"Royce Gamble."

We shake with the broad smiles of friends reintroducing ourselves. Orange-yellow light reflecting off autumn-turning trees; the change in light washes over the faces I'd

Merced, James B. Duke, the tobacco king, attached the Colonel, *his private car, to an afternoon YV train. Even the confirmed hiker John Muir made the trip by the rail, with a party of writers and naturalists.*

almost forgotten were right behind me. Up here in the nose, you're lost to the train behind and drawn into the color and form outside.

"By the way, meant to mention it before: odd about these lakes; this one and those north, virtually every river flowing west out of the Sierra . . . ."

I'm looking at him, not at the steep dropoff to the water below.

"These lakes were made for irrigation and hydroelectric power. In the 50s and 60s, in order to get the funding through, the agencies—like the Corps of Engineers—emphasized the idea of recreation—fishin', water skiin', campin', houseboats—more than the real reasons they needed these river lakes.

"Well, it never occurred to me—don't know why—that most people of voting age then would consider a lake's having recreation value, but they wouldn't think this about a wild river. Most people then were recent to the area—no more than one or two generations. In the areas they came from, eastern United States, Europe, lakes were perennially the recreation spot, geologically ancient lakes with accessible shorelines. They just didn't see that, here in the West, damming a wild river is a recreational loss.

"Their children—the generation that's responsible for the Yosemite project—grew up swimming and rafting down western whitewater. That's why access to the Merced via this railroad was so important to them."

"Interesting, never occurred to me either."

A sign almost lost in the thick red poison oak: "Hunter Valley 1.0 mi, Horseshoe Bend 2.5 mi" arrows carved in the old sign, dated by miles, point to trails little more than deer paths through dense chaparral: dry, shiny-leaved, gnarled evergreen bushes interspersed with scattered scrub oak and stubby digger pines. A tightly interwoven tangle of vegetation so thick it makes foot or horseback travel impossible.

Chaps, leather leg coverings, were named for chaparral whose jungle-like growth tears skin with rasping, stiff leaves and barbed branches. Train speed is slow here, just as it would be on foot. Deeply convoluted land makes us proceed on bridges, cliffs, through tunnels and always in curves.

Speedometer: 36 kph.

Speed here is dependent on the land. Out of Merced we raced across the grassland. Now the hills have slowed us. The railroad could have been built for more speed: straighter, more tunneling, less circuitous. It would've been less an experience, less the process of travel, more the product. Getting there fast. Where is there?

I've driven this country by car, enjoying the twisting mountain roads, vanishing corners, cavern passages through overhanging trees. Tantalized by the surrounding, almost enveloping mountains, I was too busy trying to keep the car within the white line and shoulder to experience the passage. Now I needn't worry, so I'm free to look and search out all those nooks and crannies that flash their beckoning temptation. So many places I'll have to backpack along this route—there is a paralleling trail—and explore the detail in leisure.

The train is really into the canyon now. The river down below flows over rocks and driftwood in a wide channel coated with fine brown silt; this reveals the gorge, usually under high lake water most of the year, rendering it abstract.

The $5 million financing of the railroad was achieved by two 30-year bond issues, the second of which, representing $2 million, came due January 1, 1963.

```
CAR:............ 1/16 Inaugural Special (Pompompassos)
TIME:........... 1010
DATE:........... 3 Oct 1983
SPEED:.......... 52 kph
DIRECTION:...... 15 degrees E/NE
GRADIENT:....... 2.3%
ALTITUDE:....... 274 m
From ORIGIN:.... 60.03 km (Merced)
To DESTINATION.. 84.55 km (Yosemite Valley)
Est Arr TIME:... 1227
NEXT STOP:...... El Portal 1156
TEMPERATURE:.... 19.9 degrees Celsius
WEATHER:........ Clear, occasional showers north Sierra
........ low: 12, high: 22
........ wind: 4-9 kph E/SE
NEWS:........... Congress passed additional 5%
                defense budget cut by narrow vote
........... Worldwide harvest prediction
            7% below original projection
```

Driving a car up the road to Yosemite: in ten trips with thousands of furtive glances, I might get to see a tenth of what I've seen so far on this trip. Now, this way is known to me by its land and life, not by the quality of drivers I haven't run into. By the Merced River, rather than the frequency of passing lanes or gas stations.

A tunnel. Dark and noisy. Another bridge. Chaparral extremely dense and high around the portal; like coming out of a black jungle into brightly lit vistas above the forest.

Royce looks back, then at Thomas. "You know that guy, the one with the mustache and Levi jacket?"

"I just couldn't figure it out before, but now I know. He's a guy named George Spencemuller. He's a civil engineer I used to know when the railroad was being surveyed. I'd come up to do something for the magazines I was freelancing for, *Technology Digest* or *Co-Evolution*, and we'd get to bullshitting about the project. I thought he was in Rio on the Pan American Railway."

"I met him a couple of times in El Portal. He's the one who put the whole route together; overviewed the survey."

"Yeah, an incredible engineer. Understands life systems and geology, which is why he worked on this project. Could've made more money elsewhere, but this railroad was more his style. He wanted to construct one that would really open up people's eyes to the land."

"I think he did. I've ridden a lot of the line during construction. There's some views along here, some surprises you won't believe."

An unusually long view up ahead. Chaparral covers the mountainside almost totally. Only occasional splotches of dry brown grass in the dark evergreen and then only around the track where the earth is still unsettled after the construction. Mullein plants have taken over the bare ground. Their wide fuzzy leaves are turning brown in the October sun, tiny yellow blossoms are almost gone. A few digger pines stand forlornly on points of distant finger ridges. Looking like last survivors of a once-extensive forest. A sign passes: Bagby 9.9 km. An older one: Horseshoe Bend Camp 1 mi.

In the comparative silence of this long, oddly straight run, the overheard conversation comes into focus:

" . . . highways began to be built everywhere as cars became more powerful. Steeper roads in more difficult terrain became common. Railroads avoided regions like this. Avoided building anything greater than a 5 percent grade at a time when highways were being built up 7 and 8 percent grades. Even though subways and streetcars could climb such grades, and did everywhere in the world, mainline U.S. railroads stayed within a frightened perception that calm terrain and gentle grades were their province. People assumed—even engineers—that the railroad couldn't climb steep grades in the same way it couldn't carry anything but long trains; not trucks, cars or buses."

"Jesus, sure took them a long time to consider anything but long freights over long distances. Took Amtrak to force them to see passenger service as a possibility again. I guess the railroads were sittin' in that victim attitude; assuming they are victims of economy, not makers of it."

"It's a question of values. Has nothing to do with technology per se. We can make anything we want work, it's just a matter of understanding what we want to do and then doing it."

Another tunnel and another bridge. This one right through a clump of oak trees that have somehow managed to hold on when their brothers have been cut down for miles.

"Boy, was this logged over."

"Bout sixty years ago. Those days they took everythin'. They're about to reforest a lot of this land I hear."

Oaks, particularly these low, scraggly scrub oak, look like they're grasping the land, trying to climb a little higher. They never move, not even in a stiff wind that would bend most other trees. The bark is dried and tough like a lizard's back. I wonder about their sustenance: they continue to grow, but the rate of change is so slow I've never seen one bigger one year to the next. Guess I haven't lived long enough.

"This train has to do some steep grades ...?"

"Up to 8.5 percent. On the new roadbed above El Portal and over the old highway grade to Wawona and Tioga Pass. Normal trains had a diesel-electric locomotive with enough tractive effort—power delivered to the rails by motors turning the driving wheels—to pull all those unpowered cars. There's 12 wheels on a locomotive contacting the rail and pulling maybe 20 cars, each with 8 unpowered wheels. That means there's all those cars, weighing tons, without power. So the locomotive has to be heavy and powerful enough to maintain adhesion while pulling that load. Usually no more than a 5 percent grade will cause the locomotive to start slipping."

"That's what sand is for? To prevent slipping on steep grades?"

"Right. Anyway the major advantage of a train, its low friction steel wheel on steel rail, becomes a disadvantage above a certain gradient. It can't maintain traction, adhesion, like a rubber tire, which is inefficient compared to a steel wheel on rail; the tire loses a far greater amount of its transmitted energy in resistance, stickiness you might call it."

"I know, I pushed a 40-ton railroad car once; couldn't do that with a truck."

"Break your butt trying that with a truck. This train has every wheel powered so *all* the weight is on powered wheels, increasing the area of traction relative to the load carried.

"And since its power comes from stationary solar collectors, it doesn't have to carry the extra weight of fuel- and diesel-driven generators. With all wheels powered, it can climb steeper grades. And when it downgrades, instead of losing the potential energy of a falling body in the form of brake heat like a car or truck—and most trains—it reverses its motors: while braking they act as generators pumping electricity back into the rails."

In June 1909 the Knights of Columbus hired a special train for their excursion. At El Portal 68 stages pulled by 272 horses carried 601 passengers over the twelve-mile route. All the saloons were closed for the day to

"And it only uses the amount of energy it would've used had it gone steady on a flat and level track."

"Exactly."

Neat idea. I've heard it explained before, but it still astounds me. Into another tunnel.

"Sixth tunnel, only a short one."

That kid, in the third row. It is short. Right out and into a covered bridge with open sides. A station is traversed so quickly I barely can read "Split Rock Ferry." Notice only one girl in shorts deeply tanned and waving at all of us up front before turning her head to follow our passage into the next tunnel.

"Royce, you see the film George did?"

"Nope."

"He realized the potential the railroad had for Yosemite. But there'd been this National Park Service questionnaire . . . ."

"You mean the Master Plan thing in 75?"

"Yeah. There was a choice for rebuilding a railroad, but nobody in their right mind would've voted for that: a conventional railroad just had too many drawbacks. So when George and the others over in Mariposa started planning this one, they realized people didn't have any idea how to travel on trains . . . ."

"They still don't."

"So he went to Switzerland and took a lot of narrow gauge mountain railroad footage, intercut that with shots of Yosemite, sketches of the proposal, interviews with Europeans about train-riding—minimal luggage, maximum freedom—sequences of how people actually used railroads."

"People still don't know how to travel on trains. You see that crazy man this morning? Trying to board with . . . ."

Arthur cutting, practically in stitches, "that son of a bitch had three enormous suitcases and a backpack, plus a gas lantern. He kept ramming people until one cutie parked him with, 'Pack your ass right outta here!'"

I've been looking, letting my eyes wander over the near terrain. The manzanita, scrub oaks, weeds and occasional digger pines. Haven't looked up and across the river. There, up high on the canyon wall and coming out of a tributary canyon, the deep cuts and fills of what must be highway 49 meandering its way down to the river crossing. Giant scars in the mountain exposing soft gray crumbling stone and almost white sedimentary earth. Its path is ugly. The land around the highway has the look of having been heavily logged once and now left dry without its water-retention ability.

Places the majority consider "beautiful"—based on some old standard of European esthetics—we try to separate, call them national parks or wilderness areas. As if everything else is open season for the despoilers. In the past few minutes I've heard the word wasteland over and over and other pejorative de-

insure the drivers' sobriety.

scriptions of this dry, starkly wild, chapparal-dominated place. Have the stone-throwers ever got out and walked around here? Do they know the varied and bizarre life that flourishes here?

"All this makes me hungry. You care for something to eat or drink?"

Directing my question to Arthur and Royce who've been staring ahead like a couple of diehard late-movie viewers. A few other heads turn behind me. I guess everyone's a little parched by the dry view and even drier air rushing up through the ducts.

"No, thanks." Arthur reaches down to his side and picks up a small canteen holding it up. "I planned for this, knew this train would be so crowded it'd be hard to get a drink."

"A smart man. Thanks, Arthur; need more than water."

Both men rise, stretch legs folded too long and take a brief survey of the crowd behind them.

Here goes.

Through the crowd in the first car. He nods at Salli. She dances her hair at him. Thomas is surprised that she and . . . uh, Serge are still talking. They've been joined by what looks like that genuine million-dollar middle-aged newscaster with her own famous pearlhandled camera. The best in the West.

Up to his neck in the crowd in the second car. Royce right behind. "Royce, you dirty old man, how are you? How've you been? Why haven't you called me? I knew you'd be here. Is that telepathy, I ask you."

Let's see how he gets out of that octopus, one of those "prominents" who have to do with all kinds of grants and money awards. She was very helpful to the Yosemite project, if I'm placing the right person with the correct reputation.

The first open observation car, breathing fresh, clean air and a safer reality. Walking back through the train, the wind is just a bit faster. A curious combination of relative moments. We're rising on a slight grade, decelerating and I'm walking downhill. If I weren't here now, I wouldn't've believed I'd gone anywhere.

"What have you got there?"

"Some of the promotional material for this trip."

"Any good?"

"Let me see if I can find it. It was a right-hand page. I remember thinking I'd refer back to it. Now where is it? It must be in his section . . . Here it is; I thought it was at the top of a page, but it's buried in the middle, not where I remembered it at all. But anyway, here it is. From John Muir's *The Story of My Boyhood and Youth:*

> I went out and walked along the foot-board on the side of the boiler, watching the magnificent machine rushing through the landscape as if glorying in its strength like a living creature. While seated on the cow-catcher platform, I seemed to be fairly flying, and the wonderful display of power and motion was enchanting.

A lot of children on these cars, remarkably well-behaved. Now stop this age chauvinism. Remember children's rights. Another coach, the baggage car—the canoe's still secure, nobody's used it for a getaway yet—and then the dining car. Is it nine back?

On November 19, 1913 the first 25-passenger automobile stage made the run from El Portal to the valley in one hour and 35 minutes compared to the previous horse-drawn time of four hours for the trip.

```
CAR:...|........ 9/16 Inaugural Special (Pompompassos)
TIME:..|........ 1023
DATE:..|........ 3 Oct 1983
SPEED:.|........ 72 kph
DIRECTION:...... 21 degrees E/NE
GRADIENT:....... 2.1%
ALTITUDE:....... 335 m
NEWS:..|........ Nationwide energy use for the first half
                 of 1983 (Jan to June) was announced by the
                 Federal Power Commission:
                   Fossil oil...........42%
                   Solar................24
                   Fossil coal..........12
                   Wind................. 8
                   Hydroelectric........ 6
                   Wood................. 4
                   Methane (waste gas).. 2
                   Nuclear.............. 2
```

My eyes are blinking: the landscape sure is bright. Even more so than SenseSurrounda-Scope.

The placard says the buffet's in the next car. A baggage car converted. The spread runs, I'd say, about 15 m. I find I'm very hungry, lusting at the food and odors, panting from the walk back, or rather struggle back.

The white tablecloth further bleached by the sun streaming in from the clerestory and windows at the side doors: glistening copper and brass coffee urns surrounded by cream-colored cups and dishes, shining silver, light blue YR insignia and all the food from California's wild and cultivated resources. Reed baskets pouring forth luscious fruit, some still dewy after all this time. Carafes of juices, local beers and California's world-conquering wines. Pitchers of bubbly milk, cream, kefirs and other dairy products.

Then the lineup of salads, composed and vegetable, the ingredients, California's finest: tomatoes, avocadoes, celery, cucumbers, lettuces, scallions, fresh herbs.

The more substantial and cooked creations: wild turkey, venison, rabbit, chicken, pork, veal, lamb, mutton, beef in piles and slices, in tempting sauces. Plates of cracked crab, peeled shrimp, clams, oysters, scallops. Then fresh water fish from the mountain streams: whole, split, sliced, filleted, cubed, diced, minced, flaked. Varieties of casseroles, stews, quiches, crêpes, unidentifiable dishes steamy hot without infrared lamps or microwave ovens. Fresh crisp vegetables: the squashes, wild rice, tiny carrots, baby artichokes, brussels sprouts, snow peas, corn, broccoli, chestnuts, glowing onions, potatoes and all the root varieties.

Blocks of cheeses, semi-ripe to firm. Flowers intermingled with sprigs of wild herbs and plants among all this variety, this nature-given abundance that we tear at daily and yet take for granted. In the center of it all among fruit tarts and pies, a three-tier cake, pristine and unviolated. Carefully lettered on the side: "Yosemite Railway. Our First Day." On the top a rough rendering in shiny chocolate over the white frosting the front—or is it the back?—of the train, coming out of the cake.

We've passed under highway 49 after crossing over a small bridge. I caught a glimpse of a trackside sign at the edge of the bridge: "Hell Hollow, Pine Tree Mine, 2 km." Forboding place judging from a glance up the hollow.

"Your're Becky, aren't you?"

"Becky Woburn. How did you know my name?"

"The conductor—Moqui?—told me I should speak to you about working here. I'm Alicia."

"After the last few days, I'm not sure I'd recommend this."

"Is it really complicated? I've worked feeding people before."

"No, it's just that this isn't like just a job. It's more a community. You know what I mean? People sort of operating their own world. Come by tomorrow . . . I'm dead just now. We can talk it over. Show you all the legal details and stuff."

"Is it that complicated?"

"It isn't really. What it amounts to is that we have areas that need someone, and you have something to offer us that either fits those or defines other places that we haven't seen. Then we try to work it all out. You figure out what you want to do relative to what we all need. Then you propose that to the community. It's like joining a club."

"You mean you can't just move to El Portal and buy land and live there?"

"Sure you can. There aren't many more homesites available though. We're in the middle of deciding about a population ceiling now. Nobody wants a community that grows till it doesn't work anymore either. It's a real conflict."

"Can't I just come up and get a job? I don't want to get too committed until I decide if I like living here."

"Oh. Sure. You could work at one of the stores or inns. It's hard to find work though, seems like half the college population of California wants to work up here."

"How did you get involved in this?"

"Michael and I were dissatisfied. We wanted to get involved in a place. We like it in the Sierra, the climate and all.

"In June of last year we came up to see some friends in Mariposa. They talked about Yosemite Park endlessly, so we finally came up here and inquired. They needed dining car people and that's exactly what we wanted to do: run a restaurant. We had never thought, though, that it would be a rolling one."

"That's all there was to it!"

"Well, not really. We had to negotiate a contract. Only a one-year thing. It'll be longer if we want to stick around."

"And if everyone likes you!"

"And if we like them. It's a two-way street."

I remember going to the Pine Tree mine a couple of years back—1980? Had to come up here for a thing called a mining mole. It was being tested in the old gold mine between two switchbacks on highway 49's circuitous climb up this canyon.

About one-and-a-half meters long, maybe thirty centimeters in diameter, the mole looked like nothing more than a shiny, hard steel cylinder, an elongated engine piston. Its long tail of flexible steel tube in sections is like an adult version of one of those children's toys, "slinkys" I think they're called. Within the cylinder is a complex of miniaturized components. In essence there are three: a steel and titanium alloy drilling head with diamonds embedded in the surface, a spiral tube capable of carrying a slurry of water and rock and a surrounding chamber containing a pair of powerful, super-cooled electric motors, one driving the drilling bit, the other the spiral pump. Between the motors is the electronic sensing system that seeks out the ore to be mined. An operator topside views the whole operation through a camera that sees lines of information converted from sonar-

In 1915 80 percent of the 150 daily passengers during the summer were eastern visitors.

like soundings. The drilling head follows the veins and, with the help of water pumped down from the surface, sends the gritty material up via the long steel tube.

The point of all this is that the only drilling needed is the small shaft that the mole itself makes. No humans need climb down into killing subterranean caverns. And there's far less waste than usually associated with mining— particularly gold mining.

When the invention was tried in coal regions, it worked extremely well but brought about the obvious social problems. In one area, however, the vestige of a coal-miners cooperative that had failed financially decided to take advantage of it quietly. The workers formed ownership groups and proceeded to buy old mines. There was still enough coal in these mines; it just hadn't been profitable enough to continue working the old way.

Last I heard almost 15 percent of eastern coal reserves are being mined this way. Environmentalists are overjoyed. Low-sulfur-content coal is being acquired without strip-mining and the impact of giant machinery on an area. Instead, the mine co-ops are working with relatively small decentralized equipment, the money is apparently staying in the community and the result of the mining is no environmental degradation.

I've learned to be skeptical of such inventions though.

I understand the Pine Tree Mine and a number of other small gold mines have reopened using the mole. Gold is up in price again; everytime things get a little weird, gold gets more valuable. I still feel revulsion at the thought of human greed and what it can do to the Earth. However, there's hope: more kinds of materials are being recycled and that means their value is understood; there's a definite trend toward diminishing the size of industries dependent on basic ores and raw materials like forests.

An inn set back into the mountainside across the tracks from the river. Beyond the 4 rails, a border of poplars are rehearsing their waving. The owner of the South Fork Inn sits peacefully on the porch, among her friends, sipping coffee. Cool air down by the water swirling with hot air off the dark rock. River wind.

A hum of the rails barely perceivable over the river rapids. Coffee cups set on wooden railing, a flyswatter hung on a nail in the bleached white log column, this morning's *Fresno Bee* dropped on the pine floor.

Down the steps across the lawn and under the apple trees. A man stands with arms folded looking down toward the tunnel as if not believing it will come. An old man and young man stand, both with hands in back pockets.

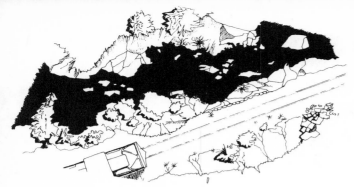

Now the train: a segmented worm, shiny aluminum. Gliding. A bridge throws a left shadow doubling the train's width. The river looks like it caused that swelling. Under digger pines or arching scrub oak, the clean train sharpness splatters with shade splotches going the other way.

Closer still, the land flutters at the train's passage. Open space between the cars pockets the wind, orchestrating the weeds and grass with its rhythm. It disappears into a tunnel: visual silence.

At 85 kph at this moment, the train's been underway for 107 minutes; she's nearing South Fork Station, 92 kilometers from Merced. She's averaged 47 kph; her highest acceleration, 95 kph; regular service runs should equal out to about 80 kph.

At South Fork after rising 317 m since leaving Merced, the train will be 365 m above the sea. The remaining climb: 854 m to the 1219 m floor of Yosemite Valley.

She's overcrowded, six cars longer than any previous local run and operating over track still in need of minor adjustment. Curves have been almost constant since Merced Falls, and she's been taking them slowly, like a cat exploring an unfamiliar back fence.

She's spanned 2 major bridges, a steel and concrete truss over the Merced and a high, double-track steel-frame village over the middle of Lake McClure. She's crossed 41 smaller stone, concrete and /or wood ones, 3 of which were rebuilt from the original railroad: those 4-by-4s last supported a train in 1945.

The 12 tunnels she's burrowed through ranged from 31 to 125 m in length. Three were hewn out of solid rock. Five cut in shifting strata and are reinforced with concrete lining. Two are concrete-lined bores completed in 1924 for the Yosemite Railroad. And 2 short ones have temporary wooden bracing since they are still unfinished.

She's passed through the platforms of 10 stations, each with an inn or attached to one. Two stations were covered bridges and 27 smaller flagstop shelters were passed.

As well as 13 double-track passing sections, 5 railroad yards—2 of which are considered major—41 switches, 53 signals, 7 electric substations. The steepest grade so far, 4.6 percent.

The train's lost about a pint of oil because of one bad seal in a main gearbox of the sixth car; the oil's caught in the drip pan beneath the seal. The air brake system has a leaking connection between the tenth and eleventh car. The servo motor on the last axle of the second baggage car is reporting 60 percent capacity; it is not yet known why. The 24 sewage tanks are almost up to capacity and will be emptied in El Portal this afternoon. A broken oak branch fell as the train passed and scratched the fourth coach's blue stripe. It has picked up thousands of pine needles, hundreds of seeds and at least twenty wildflowers.

The last scheduled run of the Yosemite Valley Railroad left Merced at 3:17 p.m. on August 24, 1945.

An old man walks gingerly from round rock to rock. About every fourth one he bends over slowly, as if he wasn't used to this, and picks a clump of bright green watercress.

Rattling of South Fork passing track switch. He looks up, holds the dripping watercress out from his body, left hand over his eyes, squints and the sun flashes off the train as it courses around past a pair of cottonwoods.

He retired in 82. Forty-five years of managing the Bakersfield branch of Consolidated Pipe and Steel, Inc. Forty-five years pushing paper, lording over I-beams and spending weekends in the Sierra. His wife died; his children live in San Diego, Houston and Wichicoomb, Florida. He let his hair grow; he doesn't take off his black, deeply scratched Chippewa boots, sort of the style of an ol' West drifter.

Last ten years he's become closer to the Merced, took it on as a hobby, then an occupation, always a friend. He's now what he calls a river steward. That's the title he offered to the Yosemite Park meeting. Lives at South Fork near the junction of the south and middle forks of the river. In his small house he keeps a book of the river: daily notations about flow rate, fish population, insects seen, water acidity/alkalinity and the general condition of an ecology he has more than his feet in.

His hand slowly arches up from his forehead and as it reaches the peak of the arc, he begins to smile. Waving with long washes of his hand. A few waves returned from the open observation cars. The train's gone behind the trees. He looks back to the mossy, sparkling water between his boots.

"There's a Yosemite toad. Pollywog tail about to fall off. First one this season. Time of change. Autumn in earnest."

People inside close to the window: sitting, slumping, talking, yawning, pointing, sneezing, laughing, wondering, watching the land. Questions unspoken. Who are those people outside, what's their life like, how do they get around, do they ride this train, why do they live here, do they like it, would I?

"What about a tour of all the inns? A night at each, getting successively closer to Yosemite. They're all so different looking and yet they have one thing in common: a kind of cozy feeling. How many are there?"

Beyond them the looser layer: up-poppers, twitchers, kneelers, crouchers, perchers, standers, slouchers, strollers, walkers, rushers. Thomas has traffic with them all on his way through the tenth car.

"When I was a kid, my old man had a 54 Buick: loved to drive on this highway," to a younger man growing into the same style.

"You mean the *old* highway? This railroad's in its place."

"Right. The old highway."

"Why'd they build the railroad on the highway?"

"Why cut another road? It would cost more and disrupt more land. When they started doing this, you could still drive alongside this road. Then they closed it for 'bout a year while the track was being laid, I think, between Briceburg and the Valley. Look, you can still see where it was: that gravel hump over there was the shoulder."

"What'd they do with the highway? I mean the actual highway."

"I don't know what they did with all'a it. But they used the concrete from the section up near Arch Rock for bridgework. The asphalt has been recycled into gravel and oil.

"The concrete road down near El Portal, it was made into stone for bridges, too. They just drew a bunch of lines like a giant piece of graph paper. Lines all over the road making the surface into 50 cm squares. Drilling holes at each corner then placing a charge into the hole. Everybody back, zap, boom, the road's all in pieces. Neat little squares of concrete scooped up with a shovel."

"Well, during that time, how'd you get into the park?"

"From Wawona and, of course, through Crane Flat. But I didn't come up there then."

The wilderness types seem to have gravitated into the twelfth car. Healthy, ruddy people digging into the gossip that extends outdoor life indoors.

"Park Service was trying to satisfy a bunch of burned-out suburbanites who'd come up here for r & r from their personal wars. They need time in warm tubs and occupational therapy, not Yosemite. Clowns can't figure out that their whole lifestyle is screwed up. And it's not the fault of the government, their job, their town or their mother."

"Yeah it even got to the point where the rangers were giving out wilderness permits. If you didn't have one, it was a 15 buck fine. Imagine some ranger pulling you over on the trail, 'Hey, buddy, lemme see your permit.' The next step was nut-gathering permits for squirrels or license plates on pumas. But why were they into that? To keep control of the number of people in the wilderness."

In 1917 the lumber railroad built by the Yosemite Lumber Company reached across the Wawona Road and into Empire Meadow, a distance of about five miles into the Park.

36

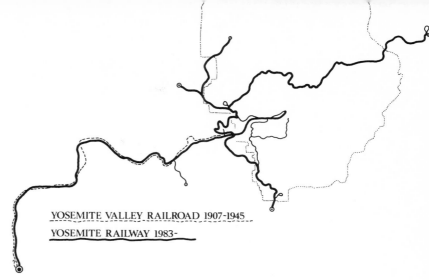

YOSEMITE VALLEY RAILROAD 1907-1945

YOSEMITE RAILWAY 1983-

"Do you get the feeling that, not literally of course, that this is like the first trip to Mars?"

"What'd'ya mean?"

"Nothing too terribly profound, only that, well, despite the indisputable fact of all that's known about the park, and all the people who have already visited it and even though it's been open to all through construction, I feel, very strongly, that what we'll find there is essentially unknown once more, something different from what we have a right to expect. You know, like the sandy plain on Mars that turned out to be, on landing, a rocky crater."

"Conductor, I hate to bother you but I'm . . . confused."

"Ma'am?"

"The program here . . . here it is, 'the first transportation system run by solar energy'?"

"Yes ma'am."

"Well curving around as much as we have, I can't see how the roof . . . ."

"No ma'am, we have four solar stations collecting the energy and transmitting it to this line where it's picked up by the train."

"Oh that's nice. Relieves my mind. But it does take away the jobs of those working in nuclear energy and hydroelectric . . . ."

"Not really ma'am."

"How can you say that? I have a cousin . . . ."

"Besides ma'am, a goodly portion of the defense budget's 23 percent cut went to solar energy collection and research. A lot of jobs. You can't look at a development from the point of view of how many people it will put out of work. That's backward. Changes always create more opportunities. And you know how good sun people have been about the reconversion. The horror stories about the changeover were fudged. The press will do anything for a story."

"You seem well-informed, young man."

"You'll notice we're doing 70 kph, smoothly, there's no pollution and the price for the ride is lower than any other system could do. I dig the efficiency of the system, ma'am, that's why I'm here."

The land is still a canyon, only now the walls are higher, more mountainous. My eyes follow the ridgeline maybe seven, eight hundred meters above the train as it snakes along the river on its belly. Patches of forest intrude on the clean desolation of grass and spread out outcroppings of dark rock. The train hasn't yet gotten to the granite for which Yosemite is famous.

Ellen replaces a flower pot that may have been tipped over by a visiting raccoon, closes the door, looks back over her little wooden house perched near the peak and starts down the stone-lined path toward the cable car.

Ellen lives in one of several houses clustered along a bare ridge near Eagle Peak, eight hundred meters above El Portal, itself 580 m above the waves. Eagle Peak is the point of a long ridge extending south from thick pine forests down a steep fall to the Merced River. The town of El Portal steps up the side of this embankment, maybe a quarter of the mountain's height.

Near the peak itself is an ecological observatory focused within a rock-and-wood structure that appears to grow out of it like a small uplift of rock. Its windward side is steeply slanted as are the roofs of the other mountain houses, covered with windblown sod.

Ellen and the others living in this aerie conduct a daily series of observations about this land. They're concerned with cloud patterns, relative to trees, to forest growth, to animal species and numbers, health, preservation, growth and learning. They watch in order to see, to begin to understand these mountains just west of Yosemite. Ellen has a particular thesis: that ecological patterns are influenced by the stars. Just how and to what degree is what she's been observing.

This morning a clear, warm early fall breeze cruises the peak, whispering winter in gust and taste. Two cumulus clouds stand off to the north over Crane Flat. The sun is cleaned by the moisture in the air. A special morning.

Ellen reaches the cable car station, a pine structure like a long garage with horizontal windows. Its steeply peaked roof in the winter will be crusted with thickly packed snow. Two CCs—the local slang still needs time to ripen—stand waiting. The first, number 14, is the one Ellen usually rides.

The horizontal track bends to a near-vertical angle that vanishes in the bushes way down there. Don leans back from his precarious perch on the front seat only meters from the edge. He folds his morning paper neatly, slips it into a pocket already holding the operator's book. "Goin' down to watch the party?"

"Yeah, thought since it was the inaugural I'd venture forth and grace the great occasion. Everybody else already gone down? Breakfast at Pinoche House?"

"Wondered where they were. I was about to start down early. Was gettin' kind of lonely up here."

Ellen gets comfortable, braces her legs routinely so she won't slide down into the wood seat. Donald engages the grip, tightens it and in a lurch they're over the edge. Headed almost straight down, aiming at the shiny roofs of the mountain-stacked houses in the town.

In 1920 the narrow gauge Hetch Hetchy Valley Railroad was constructed solely to facilitate the building of the O'Shaughnessy Dam.

Through the high rocky fields of yellow-brown grass. Into forests of stunted pine and oak. Through a dense clump of vines that yield a covey of quail, a community of sparrows. The wooden car rolls steadily, restrained by a cable that occasionally rattles beneath in its pine-needle-covered steel box.

Deer stand off in a patch of green weeds that look like they found a spring. The buck turns his head as the car passes into a forest of scrub oak.

Ellen hears the scree-scree and looks for it. Peering out the open side and up. Don points, says nothing. A falcon is trimming the treetops right behind a robin. The falcon is gaining. The robin peels out and dives into a dense crop of bushes. Falcon overshoots, turns and heads out over the immense canyon. Gliding, considering his loss or looking for something else?

"I'll walk down from here. Thanks. Goin' to the party tonight?"

"Wouldn't miss it. I'll be grippin' the upcar about 11:30."

"See ya."

Don starts over the lip just out of the station, waving back as he flies down toward the buildings of El Portal.

Ellen waves at Don and turns to look for the old man in the garden. She doesn't know him, but he's been there for months now, watering the same garden. Always waving to her as she passes. The first time he hasn't been there.

Ellen walks briskly down Foresta Road. It's a beautiful day and her step is exuberant. She doesn't know many people, having lived on Eagle Peak only through the summer, but she loves El Portal. She's continually amazed that a place so new can radiate such wonder and mystery.

Foresta Road clings to the side of the steep mountain like the other seven streets of El Portal. Its twisting, narrow course delineates each bump, outcropping of rock and narrow spring-filled creekbed that Ellen knows only as dry, rocky avenues the birds use as runways.

There's a path leading off to a yellow door in the back of a three-story inn. She can see people talking inside, bluejays scampering about outside on a leaf-swept deck. A woodpecker flashes by, an arm's reach away. Three steps more and she's between the walls. A space as wide as she's tall. Narrow vertical windows to either side above. Tiny porches surrounded with terra-cotta flower-pots. One has a railing formed by someone who enjoyed making steel look like the branches of a pine tree.

The buildings she'd come down through were on the upside of the street. On the other side only single-story structures: the top floors, decks, gardens, turrets and entrances of buildings that face out on the next street down. The sense of horizon, of distant mountains, is not cut off.

She walks into the middle of the street knowing there won't be any cars; the rail vehicles have respect for the life on the street. She walks along imagining the other end of steel her feet touch. The twists, switchbacks, bridges and tunnels between here and Mono Lake. Places in spirit only next door, yet over land distant and quite different.

The street is paved with blocks of pressed clay that've been there just long enough to display tiny weeds clinging to the surface of cracks. Down the street's center are two rails of the Crane Flat line set flush with the paving blocks. To either side of the rails, the street is wide enough for vehicles. Not the usual rubber-tired ones, but El Portal's own electric trucks and buses capable of both rail and road use. Vehicles used only in town and for local transport around the Yosemite region. Small vehicles that brighten the streets with their occasional presence.

Ellen hears a woodpecker—the same that flew by a minute ago?—hammering away almost in sync with the sound of the distant hammers pounding in nails, a team working on a house, an inn or maybe a shop? The smell of fresh coffee and sap-oozing sugar pine flavors her walk down the gentle, sloping street. Then that of freshly sawn pine.

The inns are pigeonholed with shops on the street floor, verandas over the wooden sidewalks dotted with tables where people sit out reading newspapers, drinking coffee, chatting, looking. Now only a suggestion of trees—oak, pine, cottonwood, maple, chestnut. Ellen occasionally passes beneath their shadow, affecting her rhythm and direction as much as the manmade wickets: the streets, buildings, occasional vehicles and very few people today. One oak out in the street. Two apple trees with only a few brown apples, the rest picked a month ago. Three children playing with a stick and a ball in the center of the street. Ellen smiles at the sight of children playing so simply on a railroad track.

She looks up at the multileveled, grape-arbored deck of Pinoche House. They have apparently gone down to the station, no one is sitting at customary tables. She likes the thought of having this walk to herself. She waves at Marguerite, Bill and Janey, who sit in oak chairs on the sidewalk in front of their shop, the Piton Palace, still crammed with cardboard boxes, crates and nails.

Next street down: more inns and shops. More gardens tucked in between, over and around. Buildings less complete. Bare framing still visible. Clean brick and concrete chimneys with bright, colored weathervanes standing amidst angled roofs supported by thousands of 2-by-4s studded with nail heads.

She detours past a corner of the El Portal hotel and enters the Visitor Center from the top. She always forgets how the building is, how high the multiple-trussed ceiling and huge the angled skylights. No accident the clear view to Pinoche ridge across the river.

She's almost skipping now. Past the top-level model of Yosemite as it might have been 10 million years ago. Down wood stairs yielding to a giant side window that cross-sections the newly thickening deciduous forest. Second level down: this time Yosemite with a glacier filling its valley. Ellen imagines lying down there filling the valley with her body, her arms extending up the miniature tributary canyons: Tenaya and Little Yosemite.

A third, fourth and fifth level down and Ellen stops. Looks down over a model of Yosemite as is. Bends over and leans out, letting her eyes wander over the forest landscape of ground-up green foam on brown. She looks closely at the

In the early part of this century most major US cities operated interurban rail systems. The electric railways had up to ten cars, often with dining and lounge service. By the early 30s — before the Depression and the automobile

tiny blocks of wood colored to represent the buildings of El Portal, including the one she's in. Is there a tiny Ellen in that building looking at a smaller building holding a tinier Ellen?

The human-size woman goes out the wide glass door, past a varnished sign, oak with bright red and green letters, "Visitor Center." Down a meandering path through more oak trees and past small cottage offices, she can see the station's roof through the trees and the greenspace that separates the upper part of town from the lower: railroad repair shops, community center and market. A few steps further, the main station and railroad yards come into view.

That station over near the edge of town is cleanly marked by the wide swath of white granite boulders that are the Merced's spring path. Ellen approaches the station by a wide flower-lined path paved with hardened red-gray clay: already thin cracks breaking the block form. Perpendicular to her path, the six parallel tracks, separated by young apple trees being trained to lean out over the tracks' collection of railtrucks, shuttles, dining cars, railbuses.

Ellen walks up the platform. There must be more than a thousand people in here, half El Portal's population plus a few hundred visitors. The air is vaulted in there, almost like the space in a cathedral. Looking through it she's begun to pick out familiar faces.

Ellen looks down the track. Nothing yet. She turns, looks back to see a dozen other faces also leaning over the platform edge trying to see as far down the line as she.

Everyone suddenly quiets. Whistle sounds twice, pause, then a third.

The nose reaches the end of the station slipping out from shadow into sunlight. The cars roll in the sunlight until the fifth from the end is half in, half out of the station. A sigh. The brakes. She has stopped in El Portal.

David tugs the whistle cord. A short sound. He looks at the clock between him and Lea: one minute to go. Lea leans out the side window, looks back down the train watching the people crowd up around the doors. She can feel the pressure of those boarding.

Lea pulls the bellcord. David looks back down the train; Moqui's standing at the end of the train with his left arm stretching straight out. When he drops it, they'll be clear.

Crowd's quieting down. The bell sounds louder. All the lights are now green, as well as the signal up ahead. David reaches for the throttle, fingers the red knob without moving it. Looks back again. Moqui sees him, drops his hand and yells "ALL ABOARD" at the same moment.

"Lea, clear through to valley. Take it up!" El Portal dispatcher's voice from the handset in the palm of her hand etches the crisp air.

"All clear?" David looks over. "We're ready!" Lea looks back down the train just to make sure no one or nothing is hanging loose.

put them out of business — the network was so extensive in the northeast that you could have traveled in a variety of fast, smooth, quiet, efficient electric trains from New York — through half the small towns in New

Instantly 32 motors driving 128 wheels begin to hum. Electrons that'd been roaming as static flash into copper courses, rivers of electrical phenomenon. With a whoosh of air the brake shoes release evenly. David's thumb moves another millimeter. The motors build up enough magnetism to move, barely, like a muscle vibrating under increased weight. Wheels roll forward, some creaking, some groaning before David moves it up another notch. A tight brake shoe releases. A wheel squeaks. Second car moves out into the sun, 3 kilometers per hour, 4, 6, 9, third car, fourth. The crowd moves along the platform, spilling out into the grass-bound yard tracks, climbing rocks, cliffs and promontory surrounding the train's path.

David and Lea bring her up to 15 kph, then 23 as wheels begin to get into the grade. They look to both sides, into the eyes and lenses of dozens of people standing right up next to the accelerating train. They both catch themselves waving frantically, excitedly. One second's inattention. They snap back to eyes straight ahead.

As the grade steepens, the right-of-way narrows, curves sharpen: the train is turning northeast. In a few kilometers, it'll turn almost due east for the final ascent to the valley. Up to this point the track has been tame—relatively—in gradient, curvature and landform. Now, rails are not laid through sparse grass on decipherable land, but over dozens of small leaps from stone to soil. Little depressions, valleys, clefts, cracks and notches laid over with a dense mat of leaves, dried grass, crawling vines, broken twigs, pine cones, needles, acorns, thistles, seeds and burrows.

Thomas sits in the right front corner of the nose, Arthur next to him. They both waited till practically everyone deserted the train in El Portal, using that moment to grap the best seats. Light streams in from both sides of the car, the sun is almost directly overhead.

"*That* was the best welcome yet. Banquet tonight's goin' to be some party. Is that a piece of asphalt?"

"Where?"

"Comin' up on the right, under the dogwood."

"Oh yeah." Thomas watches the chunk go by. "Bet I drove over that once. People are excited like they were when we left Merced."

"Sure is a rush of energy. I've ridden this route on the construction trains. Wasn't the same; we were all lookin' at the work to be done. This looked like a scar then, now it's healed by the leaves," Arthur comments, eyes glued to the rails ahead.

The steepest grades yet: 7 percent computed by the inclinometer in front of David. At the same time rounding curves where the vegetation and boulder-strewn land almost touches the train. Down in the canyon, the route, though circuitous, was more predictable. From the nose you could see far enough ahead to be ready for the curve, tunnel, new vista. Here the trees, scrubs, boulders and gorge walls are so close you begin to wonder if the track won't peter out in a tangle of rock, steel and roots.

Jersey, Pennsylvania, Ohio and Indiana — to Chicago.

The Merced River gorge, unlike the canyon, is a slot between two plateaus. Its sides aren't a continuous reminder to the passengers of the train's position. The forest is so thick, such a complete canopy, that only occasionally can passengers glimpse the water-stained granite hundreds of meters above.

The river flows down through the gorge in falls and rapids over jumbled white granite boulders, the largest the size of a small house. Between the white water are deep aquamarine pools, so clear and clean trout can be seen swimming into the oncoming current.

The floor of the gorge is just wide enough for the river, a ten-pine-wide forest braiding the river on the southeast side and the railroad on the northwest side. Pines growing between, around and seemingly on top of boulders as large and round as those in the river. Only these are capped with a blanket of matted pine needles, yellow-brown oak, sycamore, cottonwood, alder, poison oak or maple leaves. And stained down their sides with mottled lichens or by raindrops carrying pigment of the trees.

Between the boulders are foot-sized wyes—bowls or clefts filled with twigs, spider webs, leaves, rotting weeds, grasses dried and matted as if exhausted. Small crawl holes and tinier reaches, marked not by conspicuous openings but by half-eaten acorns strewn about on a flat granite shelf.

People in the nose aren't conversing, only trading brief observations about the terrain. Arthur and Thomas barely comment about the types of trees, what it would be like to walk across this land or how different it looks from the train than the highway.

"... that's just the point. I never saw it before."

"What, saw what?" Arthur asks pleadingly in response to a statement Thomas made while studying the passage of a small flagstop building.

"I never saw this gorge as part of the formation of Yosemite. This was where the tip of the glacier flowed. That's what left these boulders strewn about. If they'd fallen from the cliff, they'd be bunched up near the base. Only a glacier would neatly drop them like this, after grinding them round; these boulders were the glacier's feet."

"Erratics," Arthur looks up from the track.

Salli, who Thomas hadn't realized was sitting behind him, chimes in, "Might these rocks be pieces of what was once Half Dome when it was full?"

"Might. Water pouring into cracks in the granite when frozen would expand the crack until the rock broke out into the glacial ice. The rock would slowly sink down through the thick blue glacial ice which was crawling down the valley. By the time the crumbled rock arrived here, it would've looked like it'd been through a stone polisher."

"What a rush!" Arthur looks away from Thomas, back to the rails now curving around an immense black-stained boulder.

Has this passage and the anticipation of what it approaches shaken the roles out of people? Now are they all merely excited children, sharing the wonder of the view?

Before freeways, Los Angeles' interurban electric railway, called the Pacific Electric, covered nearly 2000 kilometers of Southern California. One branch ascended the snowy peaks above the San Fernando Valley allowing

The train passes slowly by Arch Rock: the old entrance to the Park where people in cars once stopped to pay their fee. George Spencemuller watches the deserted ranger station as the first observation car slides by reflected in the dirty windows.

"When I was a child," he says to his wife, "I thought the minute we paid our fee, we were in wilderness. As if the bears, rattlesnakes and deer came to this imaginary line and stopped. Step over that line, my friend, and you will be wild again. I never knew all the land we've just passed over. In a car, as a child, it was just mountains you endured until mommy and daddy said the magic word, 'Yosemite.' It never occurred to me that a park boundary is meaningless to wild animals. They wander as freely outside Yosemite as they do in it. Only highways, towns and settlements intrude on their life."

Everyone in the nose, even David and Lea in the cab above, is transfixed by the view as they round a curve: the train is reflected, foreshortened in the mirror-like glass of a bridge spanning the track between the two structures of Elephant Rock inn: towers composed of two- and three-story-high tree trunks complete with bark. Between them are panels of glass, diagonal cedar boards. The windows yield impressions of warm incandescent light in the middle of the forest's mottled light. As the train passes under the bridge, the residents wave straight down to those in the nose.

People have seen the inns, flagstops and stations that are separated now by no more than a kilometer. But they're focusing on the mysterious rocky forest; the gorge containing it; the infrequently seen mothering river; the smell of Yosemite. Nature, not man, is back in the spotlight.

David and Lea, high in the cab, see it first: the blueish, hazy form, the southwest wall of Yosemite Valley, Cathedral Spires. Salli catches two of the steeples between a ponderosa pine and an incense cedar. The view quickly disappears as the train creaks around a curve between a cut with round boulders sticking out of it and a cliff dropping to the river.

Out into the open again, where only a dying pine interferes with the view of the granite mass, a jagged silhouette looking like immense arrowheads. A few in the nose may think it's El Capitan. Others know it's Cathedral Spires with Profile Cliff beyond, the forms blending together in one shape.

Arthur points, and everyone in the nose looks up to the left. Appearing to move from the frame of one triangular panel of glass to the other is a mass of granite protruding above the forest. As the train continues it recedes back into the trees until the passenger's eyes turn back to the river.

A trickle of water almost lost between the boulders. Rapids visible then grounded behind a rock. Tree trunks: bleached, randomly tossed, balancing from boulder to cleft. Arthur and Thomas follow spiraling orange and brown leaves swirling around an eddy. On either side a smooth bowl-like depression carved in the white stone. The mark of a spring eddy.

Los Angelans to ride a streetcar to go skiing.

Royce's now on the platform of the tenth car. For a second his focus extends through swirling blue smoke to the circling leaves. Then, startling him, a family of douglas firs a meter from the train. The compressing rush of air between the train and the trees causes his tobacco to glow.

"We're almost in the valley! I think it's just . . . ."

"It is. Gorge'll start widenin' out in a second."

Becky's been sitting back in the dining car for the past five minutes, indulging in a taste of self-pity. She's mad at the dishes, the pots and pans, cups and spoons, spill and splatter, all of it.

"Get to Valley Station, we'll start in, okay?" One of the teenage girls suggests as if it'd take only ten minutes to clean up.

"Okay. If we really get at it, we can probably be done in a couple of hours," Becky sighs, gazing out the window wondering what it'll be like after dozens of trips? Hundreds?

The woman in the fur coat meanders from booth to booth gradually making her way back, doesn't seem to know which way to go. She looks at Becky. "Dear, this sure calls for a drink!" Becky smiles politely as the woman teeters to the outside of the next curve and waves at a fox with the same taste in outerwear.

"Feel that leveling? Grade's lessening; means we're gettin' close to the valley. It's widening out; see the river? Should be passing Crane Flat junction any second now . . . ."

David and Lea bring her speed down from 45 kph to 35. David smiles, chuckles.

"What's so funny?"

"Whole thing. It's so crazy it's funny. We're driving a train into Yosemite. Who'd believe . . . what the hell?"

"We just picked up a new passenger!" Lea looks right into the eyes of a startled squirrel. He bounds up onto the cab roof.

"How'd he get on?"

"Overhanging branch?"

"What's he doing now?"

Lea looks back down the train's roof. "He leaped from the end of this car to a branch, swinging upside down and climbing at the same time. Everyone's a star!"

"All the color seems to shine." Someone in the nose comments, Arthur nods, Thomas smiles and they all look up as glimpses of El Capitan become frequent.

Forest in the valley is different, gentler in a way, more level, consistent in tree height and form. A carpet over a floor of leaves and grass. In the gorge it was burlap laid over stones.

For a short time in the late 30s it was possible to ride the "Comet" electric train — a three- to five-car train with dining and open observation car from downtown San Francisco across the Bay Bridge, through the Berkeley

Entering the valley the air changes. No longer does the river dominate; it becomes only one of many influences, one of the many scents that come together in Yosemite Valley. You can taste the magic of gently mixing odors. Like smelling sugar, flour, butter, milk and eggs exploding into cake batter.

Across a wide meadow bordering the Merced River, the track curves through dense, dry meadow grass. Neither Arthur nor Thomas can see rail more than a few meters ahead. It's the first clear, open section: the valley's form is evident. El Capitan's high, near-smooth face to the left, Three Brothers standing up over the forest and Sentinel Rock dead ahead.

Two does and a young buck look up, their lower jaws moving around till the train comes within a meter. They freeze. Arthur looks at them, leaning forward as the train passes. Arthur sits back just as a yellow-bellied sapsucker streaks by.

Wheels resound over a log bridge spanning the Merced peppered with dried leaves and dead summer insects. Crossing the bridge, immediately encountering the first valley station, El Capitan, an incomplete structure standing in the forest. Seedlings have claimed the bump that was once covered with asphalt; rails over pine cones and by baby trees.

A short hill crests the train's climb from El Capitan Station to the south side of the valley. The train begins a straight, five-kilometer run, broken only by the most gradual of curves. Thick forest to the north side of the track, a lessening in density and evergreen to the south. For the first time in hours the Merced River isn't visible at all.

"After Sentinel Station we come out in the open, right?" Thomas leans over, asking Arthur as the nose seems to pierce the space between the pincushion needles of two douglas firs only centimeters away.

"Yeah, after Sentinel. A short passage of forest, then the edge of Leidig Meadow, then the station."

"Aren't the tracks different in the valley?"

"They're buried so only the tops of the rails show."

"Thought so. Not as visible as a foot trail."

I'm amazed. It's like it must've been when the Indians lived here."

The talk, what there is, has turned to the place. No mention of the party later, who's sleeping with whom or any such nonsense. Just the valley. As if people were talking about a miracle of existence that just glided into their sight. Some feel self-conscious with ecological wonder, saying things that'd sound foolish in their own homes: looking out like voyagers on Alice's trip down the rabbit hole.

"Didn't we go through another station?"

"Yeah, Sentinel. The first was El Cap and we're coming to Valley Station, it's the main one."

hills, the delta marshes by ferry and trestlework to Sacramento's downtown, and then if you wished north through fields all the way to Chico, a distance almost half the length of California.

"That's where Yosemite Village used to be?"

"Right!"

"They say there aren't any buildings but the stations now."

"None? Not even a few?"

"I don't think so."

Light floods the car as it breaks out of the short forest into Leidig Meadow at 30 kph. The train slows slightly as it slides through the slot in dry meadow grass.

Becky looks at all the faces looking around, and then looks at Michael sitting across from her. She smiles, he smiles right back. "They're getting it, aren't they?" Michael nods.

Royce puffs on his pipe, still contemplative, but now his eyelids are up a hair.

George widens his stance in the observation car. Looks up at the granite domes, walls, ridges and clefts. Feels the rush of pride at having placed his track where it is.

Hands in the nose point to a corner of Valley Station visible in the trees below the Royal Arches: a huge cliff concave where a couple of city-block-sized chunks of granite once fell out.

Nobody moves. Only a few whispering comments, a slight whirring of slowing motors, the clicking interval of rail joints. The nose quiets. The train is quiet.

Across the Merced River. Into the trees. Slowly through a sharp switch. Half Dome disappears. Crowd surrounding the train, the echo in the station. Under the roof, outside: waving, yelling, crying, laughing, talking, running, jumping. In the train: smiles turning to laughter, joyous shrieks, thumping congratulations as the last car clears the switch. Lea lets go of the bellcord, David pushes his thumb forward. The red knob has performed its function.

The train stops.

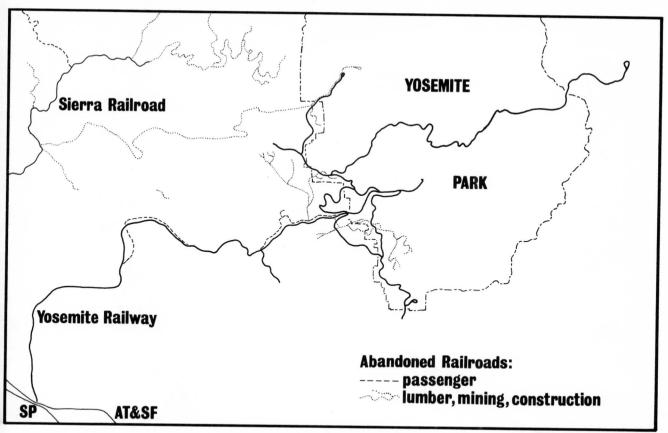

Sierra Railroad

YOSEMITE

PARK

Yosemite Railway

Abandoned Railroads:
----- passenger
~~~~~ lumber, mining, construction

SP   **AT&SF**

In 1939's World's Fair, the future of Yosemite Valley as envisioned by General Motors' Futurama exhibit had a dam at the head of the valley. The high speed highways that traversed the valley rose 4000 feet (1219 meters) in 14 miles (23.3 kilometers) without a grade of more than 4 percent so that cars could take all the curves at 50 miles per hour. A secondary road (center left) was modeled passing through El Capitan! Cars shaped like raindrops and costing as little as $200 were expected to reach speeds of 100 miles per hour on special express lanes.

SO MUCH FOR PREDICTING THE FUTURE. IT TAKES BRAVERY AND PIGHEADEDNESS TO CONTINUE.

since 1939:

WWII
COLD WAR
KOREAN WAR
Somnambulant 50s
Arab/Israeli Wars
Vietnam
60s HIPPY BLOSSOM FADES
EARTH SEEN FROM 160,000 MILES IN SPACE

LUNAR LANDING, MARS LANDING

SPUTTERING 70s
BOTTOM OF OIL BARREL
Nuclear Energy Neutralized
Solar Energy Efficiency Realized
Undeveloped Continents: NINE LOCAL WARS
CHINESE SOLAR WEAPON DEVELOPED
142,000 DEAD: Atlanta Biotoxin Accident
YOSEMITE POLICIES REVOLUTIONIZED

DOSSIER: Yosemite

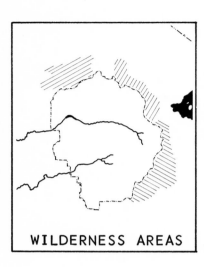

WILDERNESS AREAS

NATIONAL FORESTS

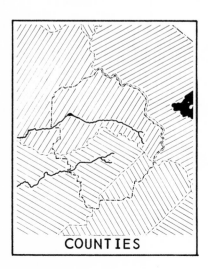

COUNTIES

1. Between the extremes of urban sprawl and wilderness is a vague twilight zone in land use. Border farmlands, the edges of suburbia, mountainous terrain, all fall into this odd category of neither used nor unused land. In these places we can see our own maladaptation to the Earth. We're not comfortable enough to allow wilderness and habitation to coexist, so these nether regions, neither fish nor fowl nor anything else, remain.

Within a radius of 93 miles (150 kilometers) from the borders of Yosemite is a thin population density; most settlements (and unfortunately the word can be used with impunity) are well below 1000 in population. The regional economy consists of tourism and the servicing of travelers to Yosemite, real estate (mostly in the vacation and retirement category), light agriculture, logging and sporadic small-scale mining.

2. National Parks reflect a splintered vision of purpose. Though the original aim for setting these areas aside was preservation, recreation has superseded that function. And that's where the dichotomy is: what exactly is the definition of recreation?

Yosemite National Park visibly demonstrates this amusement park/wilderness split: from the center of the valley you can stand in the flow of tour-guided recreators, listening to the tinny blare of the PA system mechanically blasting the shuttle's timetable while looking up and out to the wilderness still perched at the edge of the granite's sheer faces.

The valley's 25 miles (40 kilometers) of asphalt-paved roads, 350 buildings and millions of summer visitors wandering between parking lots and cafeteria are the primary but not the only blight. Tuolumne Meadows, located east of the valley and traditionally the core of the backcountry, is in danger of comparable dispoilment. Popularity of this fragile alpine environment is increasing.

3. The conditions in the two overused regions of the Park are in direct contrast with vast reaches north, south and east of the valley where the human encroachment is sparse, the terrain left only to the hardiest backpacker fleeing from the day-trippers.

4. The human impact on Yosemite is extremely difficult to measure. More can be learned from what is not seen than from what is. Land seemingly can take the cars, trail overuse, campfires, wood-gathering, general foot traffic and smog within the valley in the summer. But these human additions alter the flow of life. Animals no longer pass along their natural routes. Food chains are unlinked. Timid creatures that once entered the valley simply don't.

5. There is no clearly delineated responsibility for Yosemite National Park. Through historical hands-changing, the Park is managed by the National Park Service, a part of the Department of the Interior, based in Washington, DC. The state of California maintains a 136-mile (220-kilometer) highway system of two-lane asphalt roads in it. The state Department of Fish and Game controls fishing licenses. Four national forests surround Yosemite with private holdings and leasings managed by the federal government, through its local offices, where the multiple-use doctrine of management is under continuing--and justified--criticism. Further jurisdictional haziness exists in the functions of the local county sheriffs, small-town law enforcement districts and fire protection agencies, the national forest rangers and some of the unincorporated towns.

The Sierra Nevada is still a wilderness. Compared to other regions where human activities are more concentrated, it is relatively unchanged. Yet it is wounded. Its resources are being exploited by careless actions and unthinking encroachment. Its value to humanity is usually measured by how much we can get out of it instead of how we can get into it.

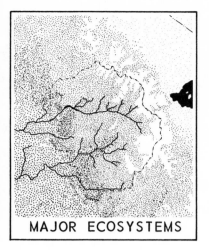
MAJOR ECOSYSTEMS

And the manmade boundaries--counties, park and forests--have no relation to the natural landform or its inhabitants' natural lifeflow. Within the Park also is the Hetch Hetchy valley which along with its watershed to the north was appropriated by San Francisco and the Modesto and Turlock irrigation districts in 1913. A dam and extensive hydro-electric facilities were constructed in that valley. Southern California Edison maintains a small hydroelectric facility just outside the Park's eastern boundary at Tioga Pass. Water flowing east from the Mt. Dana region within the Park feeds this system.

6. All of this implies that there's definitely room for improvement. Historical solutions and patch jobs needn't be institutionalized forever.

But this situation can't be altered easily: there's too much basic, fundamental rethinking and regrouping needed. And the change it would require calls for tremendous energy, creative forethought and a primal new approach.

In order for us to begin any substantive work, we have to be able to act holistically without the present constraints. Do you think we have what it takes?

Daniel C. Wiley
Daniel C. Wiley

Alfred B.J. Winjert
Alfred B.J. Winjert

Co-Organizers
SIERRA NEVADA CITIZENS
INITIATIVE COMMITTEE

January 14, 1978

AREA		CAMPSITES	
3078 sq km		2460 developed approx	
1189 sq mi		4700 capacity approx	
(approx size Rhode Island)		average per year 800,000	

VISITORS		BACKCOUNTRY	
1970	2,277,193	average per year 150,000	
71	2,416,380		
72	2,666,634	TRANSPORTATION	
73	2,339,429	car, pickup	80 %
74	2,343,123	camper truck	10 %
(75% Californians approx)		car trailer	5 %
		motorhome	2.5%
1890-1976	54,853,966	motorcycle &	
		other vehicles	1.5%
LODGING		public bus	1 %
1700 units approx			
4600 capacity approx			
average per year 500,000			

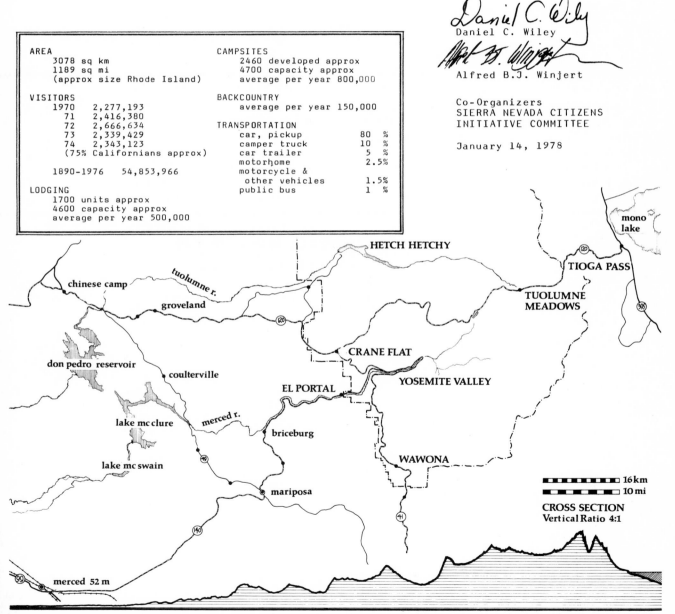

mono lake

HETCH HETCHY

TIOGA PASS

tuolumne r.

chinese camp

groveland

TUOLUMNE MEADOWS

don pedro reservoir

coulterville

CRANE FLAT

YOSEMITE VALLEY

EL PORTAL

merced r.

lake mc clure

briceburg

lake mc swain

WAWONA

mariposa

16 km
10 mi
CROSS SECTION
Vertical Ratio 4:1

merced 52 m

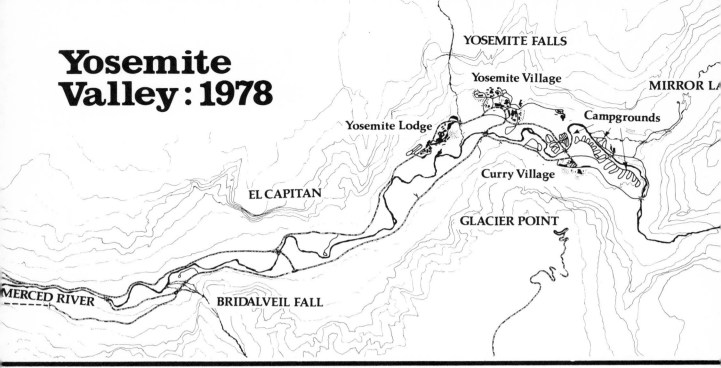

Yosemite Valley: 1978

YOSEMITE FALLS

Yosemite Village

MIRROR LA

Campgrounds

Yosemite Lodge

Curry Village

EL CAPITAN

GLACIER POINT

MERCED RIVER

BRIDALVEIL FALL

In the valley: a dentist; 5 picnic areas; 1 post office;
1 bank; 2 service stations; 1 car rental office; souvenir/
gift shops; 1 first class hotel; 1 lodge/motel with rental
cabins and tent cabins; 7 campgrounds; Park offices; fire/
police stations; 1 grade school; 3 swimming pools; 2 tennis
courts; 1 golf course; 1 grocery store ; at least 15 parking
lots; warehousing structures; employee housing; 2 cafeterias;
4 restaurants; 1 fast food stand; 1 chapel; and a hospital.

✪ A heliport at present
location of Yosemite
Village? Helicopters
are extremely expensive
to operate, noisy and
a horde of the mechanical
beasts would be necessary
to ferry the millions.

▶ All transportation in region
being eliminated with walking, horseback riding and bicycles only. It
wouldn't act to decentralize. Rather
would encourage concentric circles
of population radiating out from
disembarkation point. Would it
discourage many people from coming
at all? Hence, would the value of
the National Park to the whole
society be diminished?

○ High speed train to El
Portal; walking only from
there on? Would encourage
huge concentration of
walkers in a narrow, con-
stricted canyon.

⬤ Eliminating all camping from the Park? Placing a
series of closed-circuit television theaters in a
50-kilometer ring around the Park. Going 24 hours a
day?

HOW ABOUT?

★ Tioga Pass as primary entrance? Inaccessible
in winter. Further from population centers than other
alternatives. Road narrow and tortuous. And it's far
from the valley.

Ignoring the whole place?

◎ Turning Yosemite into an amusement park,
giving the concession rights to Disney?

⬤ Declaring the entire Park off-limits
to everyone? After a 10-year recovery
period, we can decide what to do then.

□□ Crane Flat being the
service center for the
entire Park? Would elicit
the same objections as
Wawona.

◣ Developing technology that
suits the wilderness rather
than adapting urban ways?

☆ Wawona Village being the service center
for the entire Park? Doesn't favor decentralization
because it would require main access to valley
to be one corridor within Park rather than
broken down before Park boundary. Isn't main
traffic route. Would destroy ecology of Park's
southwest region.

56

WHAT IF

we try to decentralize by taking many of the services out of the valley and relocate them along the approaches

we construct public transportation going from the nearest urban center directly to the Park

we use this system of public transportation and ban all private cars from the Park

we encourage other forms of movement within the Park: walking, cycling, horseback riding

public transportation to the Park, by concentrating access into one corridor, diminishes tourist revenues of surrounding localities

main access route relieves congestion by branching before valley

we use El Portal as the primary service town for the Park, its natural function geologically and sometimes historically

we encourage camping without cars to minimize impact on wilderness

we open up neglected areas within this large Park: Hetch Hetchy region, Wawona, Aspen Valley, Crane Flat to White Wolf, etcetera, without destroying backcountry

transportation to major urban center connects with air, rail, bus and freeway arteries

public transport system follows existing highways

public transport system follows old right-of-way from Merced to El Portal

El Portal was used as primary terminal from which radiate different routes into decentralized parts of the Park

transportation system was constructed with a compatible lighter weight system within the Park

system could carry freight as well as passengers in all weather and terrain conditions

system provides shuttle between lodging and the Park

system uses power source that's viable, efficient and nonpolluting

system is designed to take advantage of country it passes through quietly and unobtrusively rather than treating it as access corridor

environment could flourish healthily while still being visited by millions each year

campgrounds and transport system were designed to help the natural growth of the environment

the species lost to the Park were reintroduced

animals in the Park were encouraged to reinhabit the valley

trails, footbridges and other human pathways were located away from principal animal passage routes

a holistic overview concept were instituted to observe life in the Park in a complete way

The Problem Seems to Have Three Parts

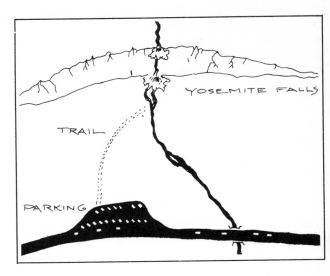

TRANSPORTATION
PRESENT METHODS ENCOURAGE CONCENTRATION
- THREE WESTERN ENTRANCES FLOOD THE VALLEY
- INTRAPARK MOVEMENT HAS TO FILTER THROUGH VALLEY
- PARKING IS CONCENTRATED NEAR POINTS OF GREATEST INTEREST
- ONLY PUBLIC TRANSPORTATION--BUSES--ARE INFREQUENT, INCONVENIENT, USED BY LESS THAN 1% OF VISITORS. WITHIN PARK IT IS LOUD, OBVIOUS AND INCONSISTENT WITH THE CHARACTER OF THE PARK

ENVIRONMENT
WHAT HAS RESULTED IS A SEVERELY DISTORTED ENVIRONMENT FOR PEOPLE TO COME TO SEE AND/OR BE IN
- THROUGH HUMAN ACTIVITIES THE AREA HAS BECOME ESTRANGED FROM THE SURROUNDING WILDERNESS
- HEALTH OF THE PARK IS IN DANGER. IT IS STILL A REVERSIBLE SITUATION BUT IT HAS THE EARMARKS OF BECOMING PERMANENT
- WILDERNESS IS BEING ERODED BY PRESENT HUMAN USE

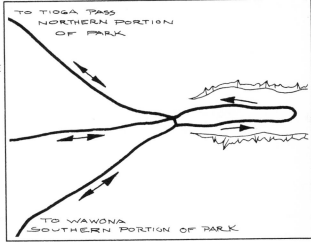

CONCENTRATION
LARGE AREA BUT TWO FOCI OF CONGESTION
- TIGHT CUL-DE-SAC VALLEY THE MAIN GOAL OF VISITOR INTEREST
- BACKCOUNTRY'S MAIN ACCESS ROAD REPEATS VALLEY PROBLEM BY CONCENTRATING VISITORS AROUND SMALL, FRAGILE MEADOW
- PERMANENT SERVICE STRUCTURES INTENSIFY PROBLEM IN VALLEY
- FOUR ENTRANCES TO PARK, THREE TO THE WEST, FUNNEL INTO VALLEY CREATING TRAFFIC RACETRACK AND COUNTERFLOW (Let's go round again, maybe this time we'll see the El Capitan exit.)
- SUMMER DENSITY: UPWARDS OF 10,000 ENTERING THE VALLEY DAILY.

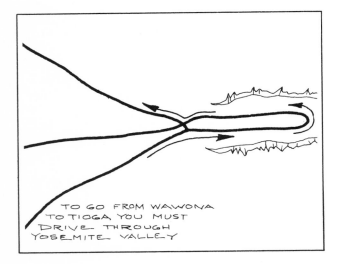

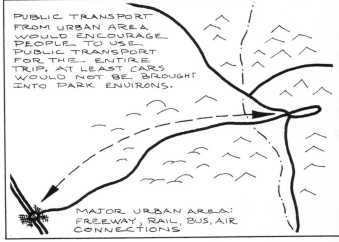

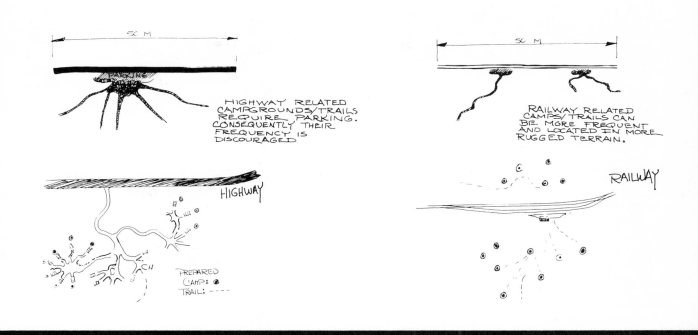

HIGHWAY RELATED CAMPGROUNDS/TRAILS REQUIRE PARKING. CONSEQUENTLY THEIR FREQUENCY IS DISCOURAGED

RAILWAY RELATED CAMPS/TRAILS CAN BE MORE FREQUENT AND LOCATED IN MORE RUGGED TERRAIN.

HIGHWAY

PREPARED
CAMP: ⊘
TRAIL: ----

RAILWAY

VALLEY

EL PORTAL

CONCENTRATION OF SERVICES IN VALLEY: 1978

DECENTRALIZATION OF SERVICES

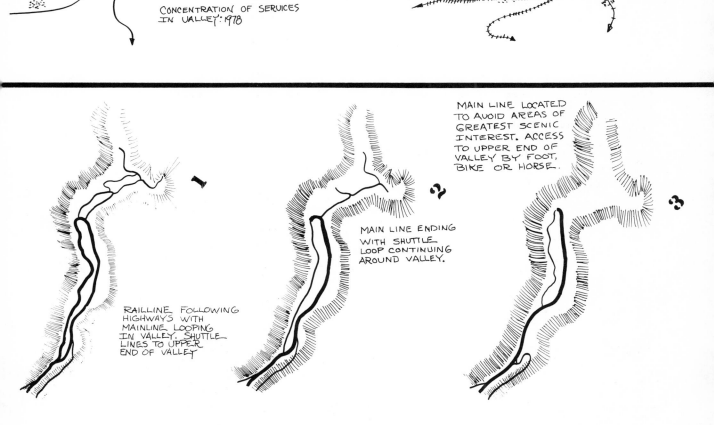

1

RAILLINE FOLLOWING HIGHWAYS WITH MAINLINE LOOPING IN VALLEY. SHUTTLE LINES TO UPPER END OF VALLEY

2

MAIN LINE ENDING WITH SHUTTLE LOOP CONTINUING AROUND VALLEY.

MAIN LINE LOCATED TO AVOID AREAS OF GREATEST SCENIC INTEREST. ACCESS TO UPPER END OF VALLEY BY FOOT, BIKE OR HORSE.

3

ROAD AND TRACK

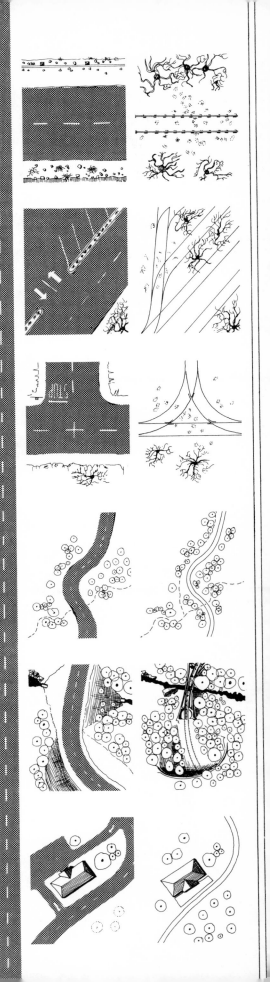

Practically everyone drives to Yosemite. Less than 1 percent don't. Though automobile pollution is lessening — when exhaust is measured — noise, particularly tire on pavement, and heat pollution will continue. Costs of this vehicle transportation are rising steadily and show no signs of stabilizing. Facilities for parking within the Park, especially within the valley, are already used to capacity; these areas already require an excessive amount of space within the valley's small area. Car camping requires campgrounds that require access roads. The area is then dominated by the sheer presence of cars, camper trucks and recreation vehicles. Roads have been turned into highways where speeding is commonplace. The dependence on individual transportation detracts from the wilderness experience. Automobiles are violating the peace of the valley.

The only public transportation into the Park is a bus service from Merced operated by the Yosemite Transportation Company. However, this line is used by less than 1 percent of the visitors.

The National Park Service operates propane-powered shuttle and touring buses within the valley. Although this service has eliminated auto use on some roads, the buses are loud, large and free.

In the interests of general energy use reduction and continued economical access to wilderness, there must be a cheap alternative to this excessive automobile impact: a system that can interconnect with existing public transportation outside the Park.

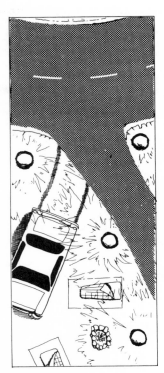

HIGHWAY

Surface: usually asphalt, a material made of oil, a diminishing resource. Virtually nonporous, asphalt needs a drainage system which concentrates runoff causing erosion. Grading and contouring reforms land to accept right-of-way. Geological movement or settling roadbed shifts emphasized by passing vehicles.
Vehicles wander between white line and shoulder
Act as barrier to natural animal paths.
Pollution limits growth of paralleling vegetation as well as limiting species.
Weather: dangerous in rain, snow, fog and particularly ice. Dangerous and expensive to plow.

CONVENTIONAL RAILROAD

Surface: composition of steel rail, wooden ties and gravel ballast. Ballast is needed to spread water and transfer it to soil beneath. Drainage ditches and culverts are also needed. Requires large-scale grading and contouring to conform land to right-of-way.
Vehicles travel known, rigid paths and do not wander.
Act as barrier to natural animal paths.
Pollution from diesel/electric locomotives limits growth of paralleling vegetation as well as neighboring animal species.
Can carry trucks, cars, buses, though gen-
Weather: less affected by bad weather than highways.

PROPOSED RAILROAD

Surface: composition of steel rail, concrete, wood or stone supports. No drainage system needed. Using existing highway grades would not require extensive cuts and fills.
If frequent bridges are provided would only impair movement of larger beasts: deer, bears, coyotes, etcetera.
If electric, it would not limit the growth of surrounding plants or favor certain species.
Will carry buses, cars and trucks.
Even less affected by bad weather than contemporary railroads.

OPENING A CAN OF

What impact will this plan have on the back-country?

What is a limit, ecologically, on the back-country?

Are we opening previously protected areas to destruction?

What is the population limit for newly opened areas? The Park as a whole?

Can population limits be defined for a certain area? At certain times? By whom? And who is the guard?

Historically, the back-country is northeast of the valley. Traditionally regarded as limited access, any public transport system must maintain the integrity of this region.

EL PORTAL/BISHOPS CREEK TO WAWONA

Inns: 3 capacity 290
Flagstops: 9
Trailheads: existing 2, proposed 4
Campgrounds: proposed 7 capacity 130-55
    Brand new route climbing the Merced River canyon south of El Portal, through narrow canyon and tunnel before turning into Merced River's South Fork canyon.

HODGDON MEADOW/CRANE FLAT TO YOSEMITE VALLEY

Inns: 15 capacity 1200
Flagstops: 22
Trailheads: existing 7, proposed 5
Campgrounds: existing 4, proposed 12
               capacity 275-90
    Extensive scenic views west to coast range. Geology city: granite domes, cliffs and faces older than those in Yosemite Valley.

EL PORTAL/FORESTA TO CRANE FLAT LINE

Inns: 5 capacity 470
Flagstops: 13
Trailheads: existing 5, proposed 4
Campgrounds: existing 2, proposed 8
               capacity 340-65
    After a spectacular climb above El Portal, the new route parallels and replaces old dirt road to Foresta; crosses numerous bridges over cascading creeks, and forests that range from oak/chapparal lowland to high chapparal to sugar pine.

CRANE FLAT/TIOGA PASS TO LEE VINING

Inns: 7 capacity 275
Flagstops: 31
Trailheads: existing 14, proposed 7
Campgrounds: existing 8, proposed 9
               capacity 375-400
    Between White Wolf and Tioga Pass is where most existing campgrounds are located, and the origin of most present backpacking. Proposed camps would concentrate between Crane Flat and White Wolf turnoff.

EL PORTAL TO YOSEMITE VALLEY

Inns: 4 capacity 475
Flagstops: 10
Trailheads: existing 1, proposed 6
Campgrounds: existing 0, proposed 10 along river, 11 above or inside gorge
               capacity 250-75
    Previously the Wawona road along the south rim, the Crane road along the north and the El Portal along the river turned this region of water- and rockfalls, granite domes, intricate forests and river cascades into a corridor unexplored, unappreciated and unpopulated.

FISH CAMP/WAWONA TO YOSEMITE VALLEY

Inns: 11 capacity 1000
Flagstops: 20
Campgrounds: existing 1, proposed 13 (not counting Wawona campgrounds)
               capacity 160-85
    Below Chinquapin, approaching Yosemite Valley, there are spectacular views of the Merced Gorge, the San Joaquin Valley and the coast range.

YOSEMITE PARK VISITOR USE PATTERNS

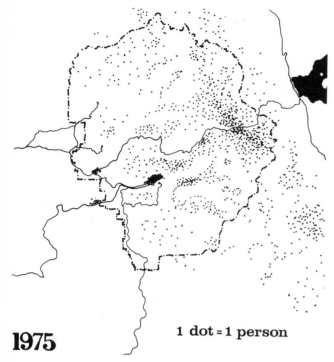

1975

1 dot = 1 person

Concentration of cars in valley, Wawona, Crane Flat and Tuolumne Meadows campgrounds almost equal to the number of people. Lack of parking space along El Portal, Wawona, Tioga and Crane Flat highways is intentional deterrent to camping.

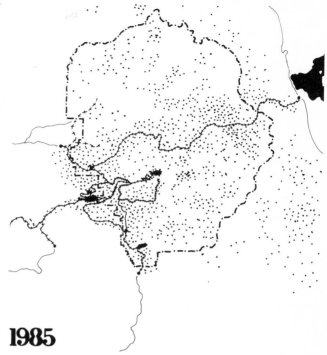

1985

Spread greater over entire Park. Yosemite Valley and Tuolumne still major concentrations although congestion relieved by expansion of El Portal and the removal of lodging and services out of those areas. The interest in camping on National Forest land outside Park's western boundaries expected to diminish as interest in these new areas wears off.

Visitor distribution by year. Horizontal lines are 100,000 divisions. By 1989 visitor use is expected to stabilize around 3,000,000 per year.

Vertical lines are quarter year divisions. Horizontal lines are 50,000 increments.

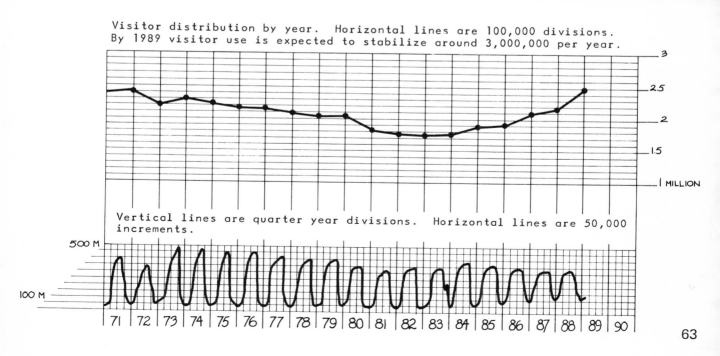

WILL AHWANHEE SURVIVE YOSEMITE PARK?

(Jan. 7, 1984) Yosemite's Ahwanhee hotel has been the bone of controversy between opposing groups supporting different plans for the venerable old stone structure.

Despite the radical changes in the Valley, many feel the style embodied by the Ahwanhee, opened on Bastille Day in 1927, should be maintained as the only luxury hotel of its kind, and preserved as carefully as the Valley itself.

Others, seemingly in the majority, find it inconsistent to offer luxury accommodations when all other lodging was relocated outside the Valley, primarily in El Portal. It smacked of "favoring the nest of the rich," while others had to sleep outside or on the ground, one spokeswoman commented. "It should be torn down or at least disassembled and rebuilt in El Portal or some other Valley approach."

The controversy about the sprawling old hotel delayed its being taken apart by the meticulously zealous razing crews: there isn't a scrap of plastic where Yosemite Lodge used to be.

Now the Ahwanhee stands as a lonely citadel, speaking of another era. It has had continuous business lately from those driving the Crane or Wawona roads to witness the changes. Opposing locals have described these onlookers as viewing the situation with "morbid fascination" and being "fatalistic like surviving European royalty."

Despite the efficiency of last year's "trash summer," most of those who took apart the buildings voiced respect for the Ahwanhee's unique blend of mountain architecture and traditional service.

Although the three new railway stations are capable of holding all the normal Valley services, they were not planned to hold what is becoming a larger aspect of the whole project: the indigenous ecological studies now being undertaken in the Valley. Some of the foremost naturalists in the world are living in the squalid group of remaining Camp Curry cabin tents. It has been suggested that the Ahwanhee might be used for offices, libraries and small labs for these wildlife

studies. The public spaces, and maybe a restaurant, could continue to operate or be altered to accommodate conferences and related activities.

Though no decision must be made immediately, all lodging has to be out of the Valley by the summer of this year according to the 81 policy statement. The question remains whether that fiat be followed to the letter. Right now friends of the Ahwanhee are doubtful about presenting this issue to the community meetings. As one leader put it, "I just don't think we have enough strength against the revisionists."

Notice

AHWANHEE HOTEL July 7, 1984: As of Monday we will no longer be offering hotel services. Conversion to offices will commence the 19th. The dining room will continue to function according to its present high standards.

GRASS RAIL NEWSLETTER

Volume 2   August 84

—— A group of concerned citizens, many of them long-time Ahwanhee patrons, have put together an investment package for the construction of the Hotel Del Portal. Planned as a two-hundred-room luxury hotel on El Portal's Sugar Street, it will offer services comparable to the old Ahwanhee, as well as expanded conference facilities, extensive terraces and gardens to take advantage of the spectacular view from so high in El Portal.

The group, which grew out of the wide-spread "Save the Ahwanhee" movement, has asked that the public that is interested view their plans on exhibition at the El Portal station. They will be making their initial presentation at the town meeting on August 27. This is of vital interest to the town because, if built, it would have a great impact on our town.   —WYG

Objects found in Yosemite Valley

6 human skeletons (partial)
51 kg animal bones
487 pairs or parts of glasses, 43 with rhine- or other stones
3 car bodies, a 1921 Reo, 1934 Graham Paige and a 1952 Nash Rambler
4 full-size kitchen stoves, gas burners
1 Wedgewood woodburner stove
2 upright electric refrigerators, one with freezer
109 single shoes, boots, sneakers, slippers, wedgies, springelators
3 pairs hiking boots
41 wristwatches, one from the Pan-Pacific Exposition
23 cufflinks, singles
2 bolo ties, one with clip
1 steamer trunk, empty
16 toupees or partial hairpieces
4 full wigs, one turquoise
422 flea collars
36 automobile, bus, tractor and airplane tires
1 pair baby shoes, bronzed
4½ bins (3 x 2 x 3 m) cigarette stubs, filters, matches and match books
6,423 pencils
1,015 pens
14 erasers
2 bins paper products
1¼ bins assorted rusting metal objects, nuts, bolts, etcetera
3 bins assorted paper and other wood pulp
2½ metric tons of rags and articles of clothing
2 separate statues of Jesus, made of plastic
143 kg coins, subway tokens and other unidentifiable pocket metal
13 assorted neck chains, two of gold 18 and 10 karat respectively
36 dog or other animal collars, one inscribed, "To Baby with love from Daddy"
2 dozen stamp coupon books
1 gas rationing book, circa World War II
123 tape cassettes
5 tape cassette recorders
41 portable radios
1 console model radio
389 sets of keys
10,688 hair combs
2 television sets
1 bin of film cartridges
22 cameras including one 1931 stereo-scopic with undeveloped film in it
enough used Polaroid filmbacks to stretch from here to Rochester
14 bins of poptop pull-tabs
25 bins of tin and aluminum beer and soda cans
1¼ bins of suntan lotion
3 bins of mosquito and other insect repellant
enough eatable garbage to increase the bear population five-fold
342 compacts
4028 lipstick dispensers
495 eyebrow pencils
102 tubes of mascara
31 snakebite kits

41 sleeping bags intact, 14 of them mummy bags
1 extension telephone
4 television antennas
2 electric heaters
1 bathtub
19 carpets, one unrolled 24 x 26 m wall-to-wall shag
1 rhinestone tiara
7 bags of cement, 20-pounders un-mixed
2 church pews with cushions
56 kg feathers
13 bins of bottles and broken glass
4 typewriters, one with a Tagalog keyboard
72 45 records
167 long playing record albums
1 78 recording of Debussy's "Afternoon of a Faun"
6 fans, one electric overhead
1 35mm movie projector with one reel of "The Little Foxes"
a completely intact World War II para-chute
8 full-size flags, including one of the Republic of Lithuania

recycled:

MATERIAL	WEIGHT: METRIC TONS
asphalt	448,372
concrete	47,921
gravel	202,041
glass	24
steel	97
iron	7
aluminum	9
bronze	.35
plastic	.13
tile	.29
copper	1.12
wood	25,098,193 meters

ITEM	NUMBER FOUND
toilet	211
sink	397
kitchen items	57
urinal	89
window	393
door	427
furniture	1121

UNSTRUCTURING

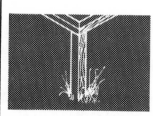

or taking a building apart:

First, take the roof off if it's shingles. We can use em so be careful.
Siding's next: that's outside. Inside siding, but not the frame. Get the picture?
Dismember the roof's ribs: keep in mind they often hold the side supports together.
If two stories consider the top floor a roof.
Keep on going this way till you hit bottom: rock, earth, sand, gravel, whatever.
Report all corpses and other found objects to the social director or your mother. Which-ever is closer.
Anybody found taking it out on the buildings or getting too many kicks out of destruction will be volunteered to the construction crew!

ORGANIZATION CHART

Each of the flowerlike shapes represents one of the three companies: Yosemite Overview (lower left), Yosemite Railway (upper right) and Yosemite Inns (lower right). Each company is divided into three groups. Overview consists of Park Service, railway/transport and accommodations. Each of these is composed of teams (represented by the tiny globules). Teams are made up of different numbers (usually between three and twelve) depending on time of year and other factors. The surrounding petal is internal communication and/or energy, the darker band is the interchange between teams. The triangular shape between the groups represents the interface of communication and understanding. The dark center of each flower is the core of evolution, the continual discourse and argument. At this particular time the graphic shows the beginning of a major conflict in Yosemite Inns (lower right) that involves the other companies as shown by the dark explosion centered between their stems. Conflict contributed by the outside community is represented by the three spiraling clouds from outside the circle. As a certain amount of energy is expended by the members of the three companies, it bounces off and is spewed into the atmosphere as shown by the streams radiating out of the center. The surrounding ring of mountains symbolizes the enveloping wilderness of the Sierra Nevada on the activities of Yosemite Park.

credit: "Flowering of Sierra Self-Government," a television documentary presented on Sierra Community CCT, April 14, 1984 and nationwide on September 26, 1984.

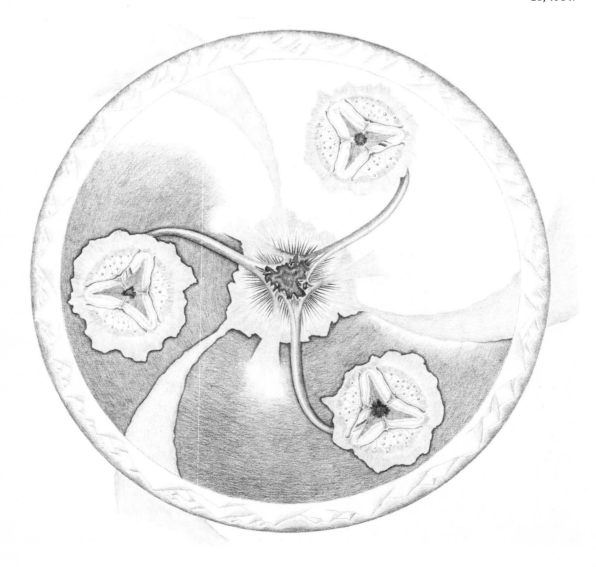

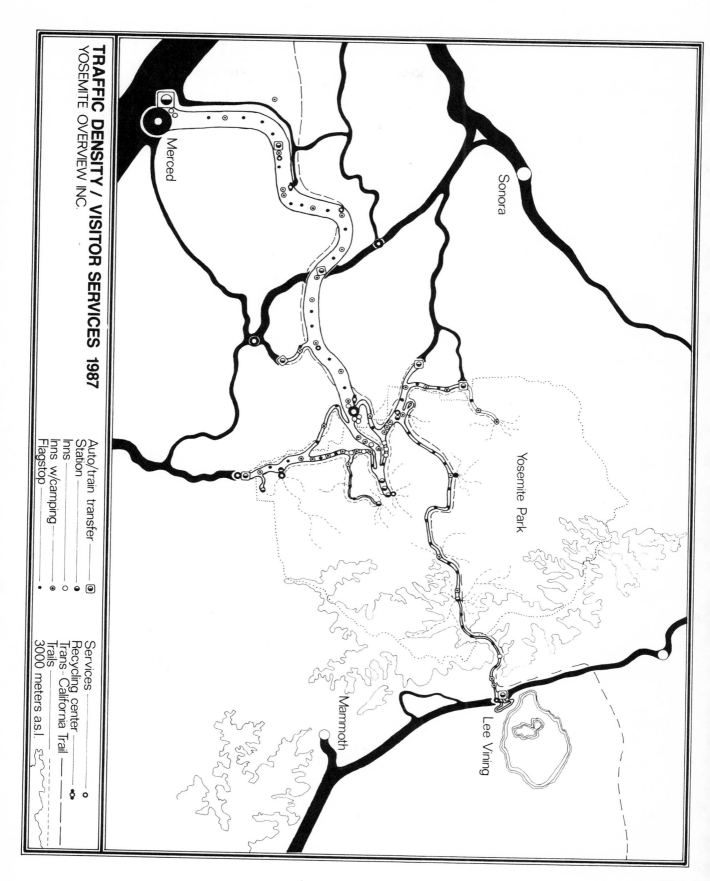

TRAFFIC DENSITY / VISITOR SERVICES 1987
YOSEMITE OVERVIEW INC.

Auto/train transfer
Station
Inns
Inns w/camping
Flagstop

Services
Recycling center
Trans.-California Trail
Trails
3000 meters a.s.l.

Merced

Sonora

Yosemite Park

Mammoth

Lee Vining

67

YOSEMITE VALLEY · POST RAILWAY

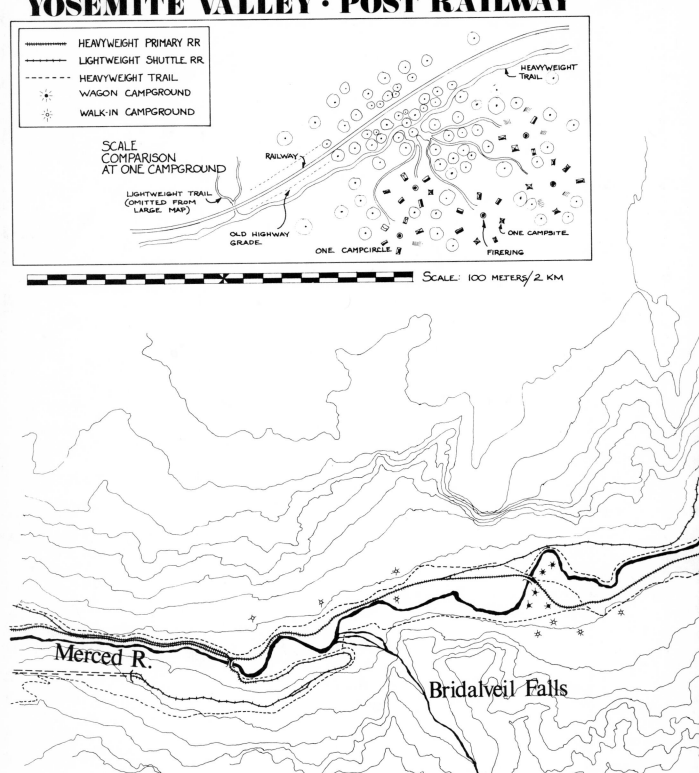

HEAVYWEIGHT PRIMARY RR
LIGHTWEIGHT SHUTTLE RR
HEAVYWEIGHT TRAIL
WAGON CAMPGROUND
WALK-IN CAMPGROUND

SCALE COMPARISON AT ONE CAMPGROUND

LIGHTWEIGHT TRAIL (OMITTED FROM LARGE MAP)

OLD HIGHWAY GRADE

RAILWAY

HEAVYWEIGHT TRAIL

ONE CAMPCIRCLE

FIRERING

ONE CAMPSITE

SCALE: 100 METERS / 2 KM

Merced R.

Bridalveil Falls

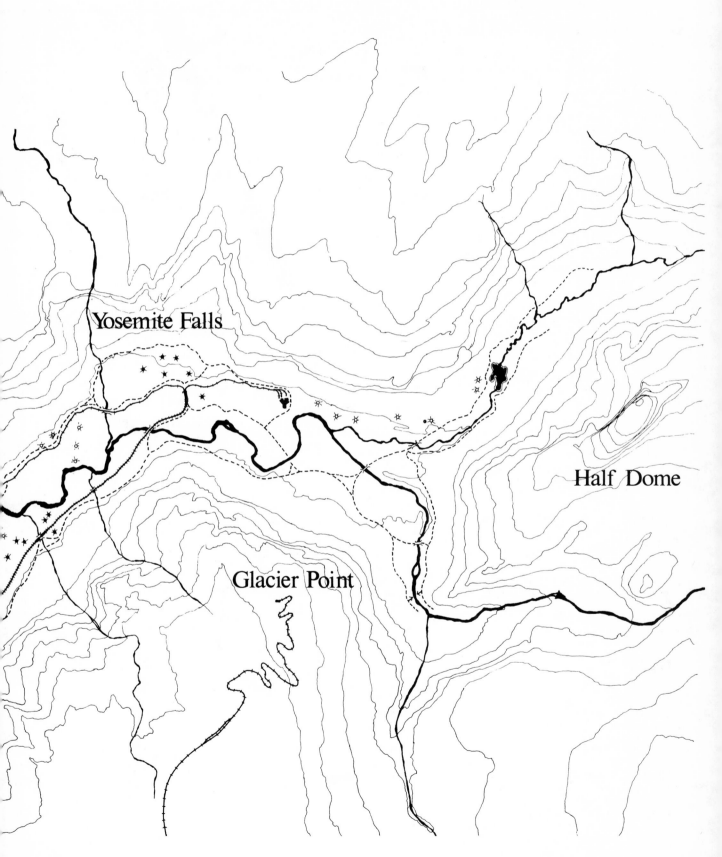

Yosemite Falls

Half Dome

Glacier Point

Three Stations In Yosemite Valley

Each station shed accommodates primary line and shuttle trains, contains access ramps for the handicapped and has a data board containing continuous, up-to-the-minute schedule information. Laminated wooden arches support the sod-covered roof punctuated with skylights. Redwagons are stored in the station's ceiling where the arches meet the platform. The rammed earth platforms have granite borders and retaining walls. Walls and interior structure is wood, some recycled from previous valley buildings.

There are no exterior souces of energy. The solarskins and auxiliary batteries supply the shed's energy needs as well as heating the restaurants and service structures.

The service buildings house the ranger offices, emergency medical clinic, equipment rental, essentials shop, information, message and map center, lockers, showers and bathrooms.

Surrounding each of the stations is a ring of water monitors augmenting the interior fire sprinkler system. In a wildfire a light mist is sprayed over the buildings to dampen the wood and cool the air.

El Capitan

Covered bridge spans the Merced, the curved train shed spans two tracks, the services are housed to the right, the restaurant to the left, the plaza along the river. Primary line from El Portal and Merced crosses bridge after splitting into two tracks. The lightweight shuttle line enters the primary line just west of the bridge. All four buildings are designed to withstand the river's periodic flooding.

Sentinel

Two train sheds span track with Sentinel Creek flowing between. The services structure is at the upper right, the restaurant at lower left is two stories with a second-story veranda for outdoor dining over the track. The two wye tracks store ambulance and fire truck emergency equipment.

Valley

The largest station in the valley is located on the approximate site of the former Yosemite Village grocery. Spanning three tracks it functions as the center of valley activities as well as the terminus of the railway. The shuttle line to the Ahwanhee is at the upper right, the lower right shows the restaurant, middle right the minor maintenance and main firehouse. The T-shaped service building maintains a small inn for employees and rangers on night duty. The bell tower to the right of the service building can be used in emergencies to contact everyone in the valley.

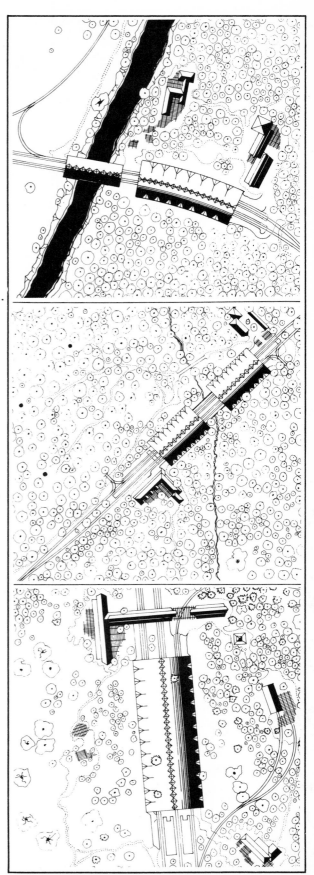

South elevation

VALLEY STATION

20 ft.

10m

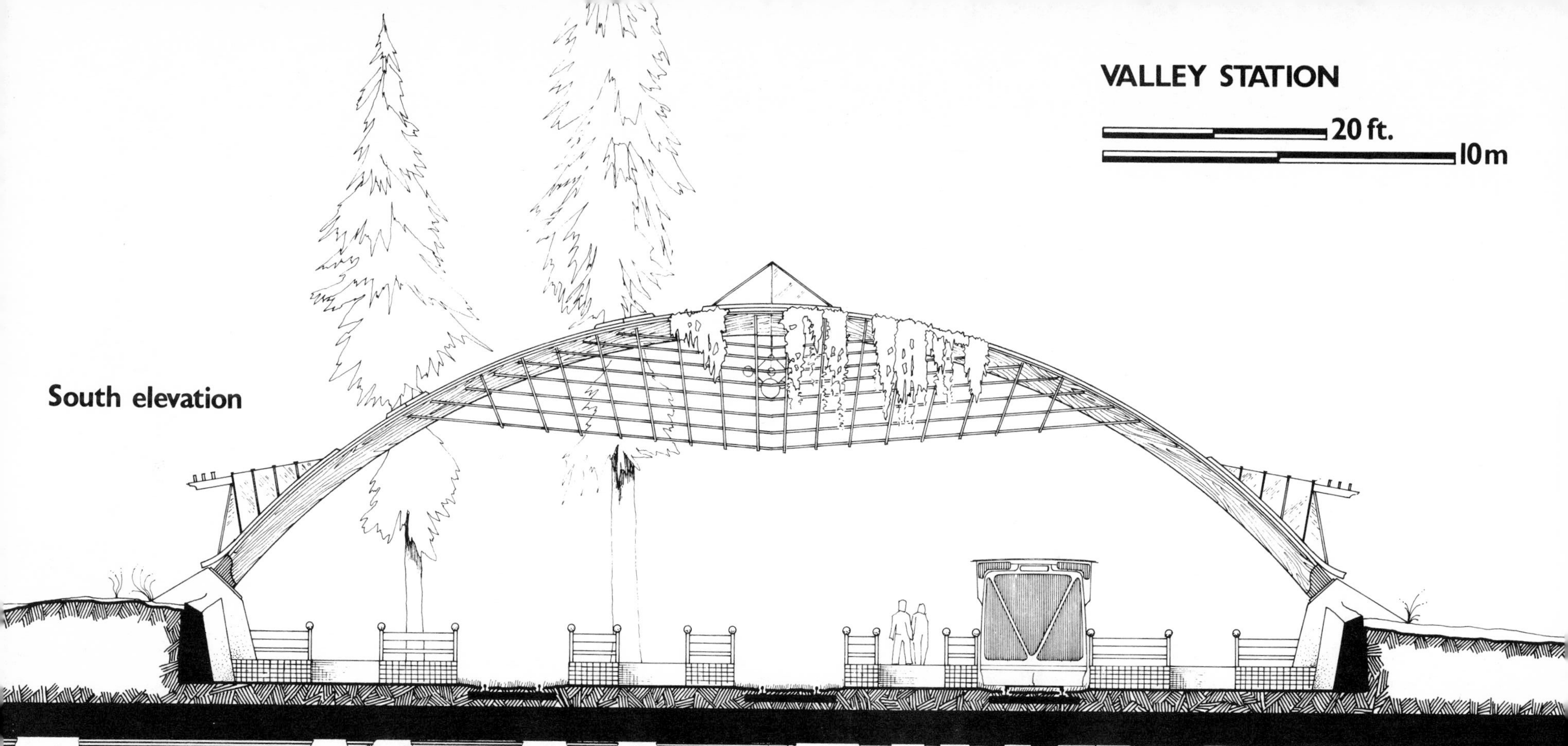

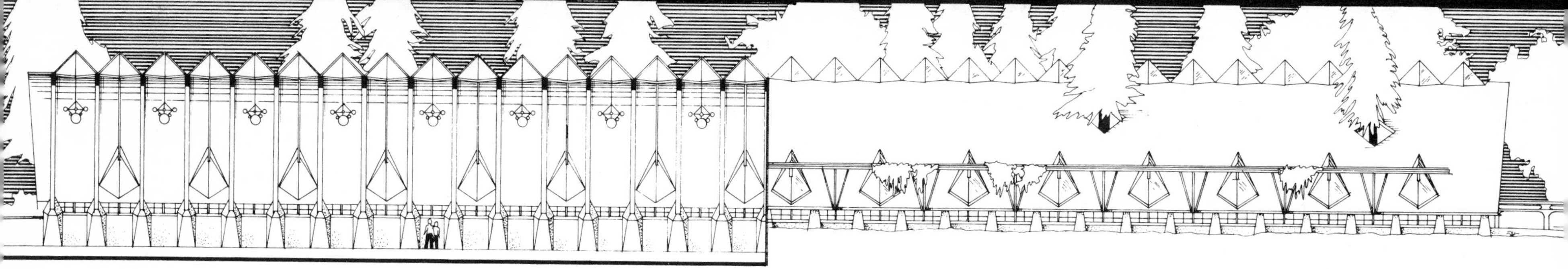

Cross section

West elevation

50 ft.

20m

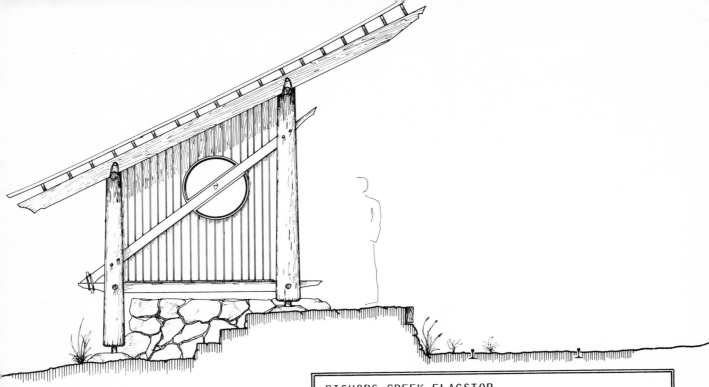

FLAGSTOP

FUNCTION: Secondary train
station as well as wilderness
shelter. Approximately 50
scattered along entire rail
line.

DETAILS: Constructed with indigenous materials where possible. Where building contacts
ground, steel pipe is used as
the connection between post
and stone footing. If the region
were temporarily closed or the
position of the flagstop proved to be undesirable, the whole
structure could easily be moved.
Gently graded ramps lead to all
the platforms to allow wheel-
chairs access on and off the
trains. Powered equipment
consists of emergency telephone,
databoard and low voltage overhead inside light. The roof
solarskin and auxiliary fuel
cells provide the energy for
these minimal devices.

BISHOPS CREEK FLAGSTOP

TOUCH THE SCREEN WITH THE PALM OF YOUR HAND.

AT THIS TIME OF YEAR THE TRAILS, WATER AND
WOOD SUPPLIES AROUND BISHOPS CREEK CAN AC-
COMMODATE 27 PERSONS. MORE THAN THAT WILL
UNBALANCE THE ECOLOGY HERE.

THERE ARE NOW **28** PEOPLE IN THIS REGION.

PLEASE CHOOSE ANOTHER AREA.
THE NEAREST DOWN THE LINE: ELEVENMILE CREEK
                    UP THE LINE: ALDER CREEK

ALDER CREEK FLAGSTOP

TOUCH THE SCREEN WITH THE PALM OF YOUR HAND.

AT THIS TIME OF YEAR THE TRAILS, WATER AND
WOOD SUPPLIES AROUND ALDER CREEK CAN ACCOM-
MODATE 71 PERSONS. MORE THAN THAT WILL UN-
BALANCE THE ECOLOGY HERE.

THERE ARE NOW **57** PEOPLE IN THIS AREA.
THIS IS A TOPOGRAPHICAL MAP OF ALDER CREEK:

PLEASE HAVE EVERYONE IN YOUR GROUP PRESS THE
KEY FOR THE NUMBER OF DAYS YOU INTEND TO
STAY IN THIS REGION.

                    HAVE A GOOD TRIP.

Redwagon

Redwagons are used in all the inns and stations
as baggage/utility carts. In the stations they
hang by their tongues from the ceiling. They
rent for a very nominal fee, so give the guy
some money and get your wagon.

Throw in your junk, take it to the store: besides other junk food, you can get ice for the
wagon's icebox, perishables like milk, fruit
and vegetables, and with all of this, you can
walk to the campsite.

The valley has two kinds of prepared campsites:
redwagon and backpack. The first are within
ten minutes of the stations, the others radiate
out from there. All sites rotate on a bi-yearly
basis. The trails from the stations are built
of rammed eart blocks only as far as the redwagon camps.

The top of the icechest can seat two small children, so it can be used as a stroller for as
many as four children under six.
The top of the icebox has two unfolding panels
that act as a table.
The wagon itself can hold two to three suitcases and the usual variety of assorted bags,
clothing and other possessions.
A lockable compartment behind the icechest can
hold two handbags and/or a camera. The redwagon
comes with a chain and lock for security--if you
need it.
The rear flat area can hold one reclining adult
or two children in the event of emergency.
A cookstove attachment will fit the top of the
icebox as well as a tent that is attached to
the tongue for unfolding when it is placed in
an upright position.

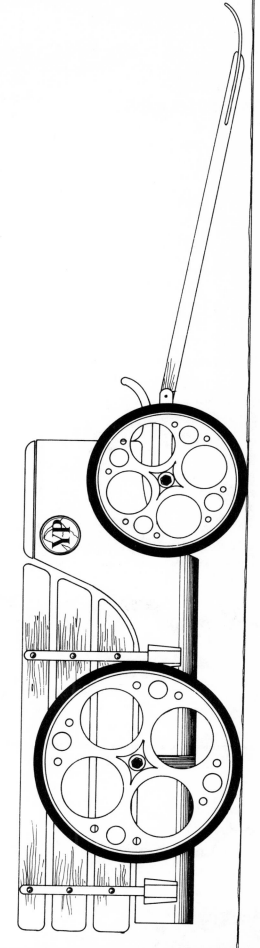

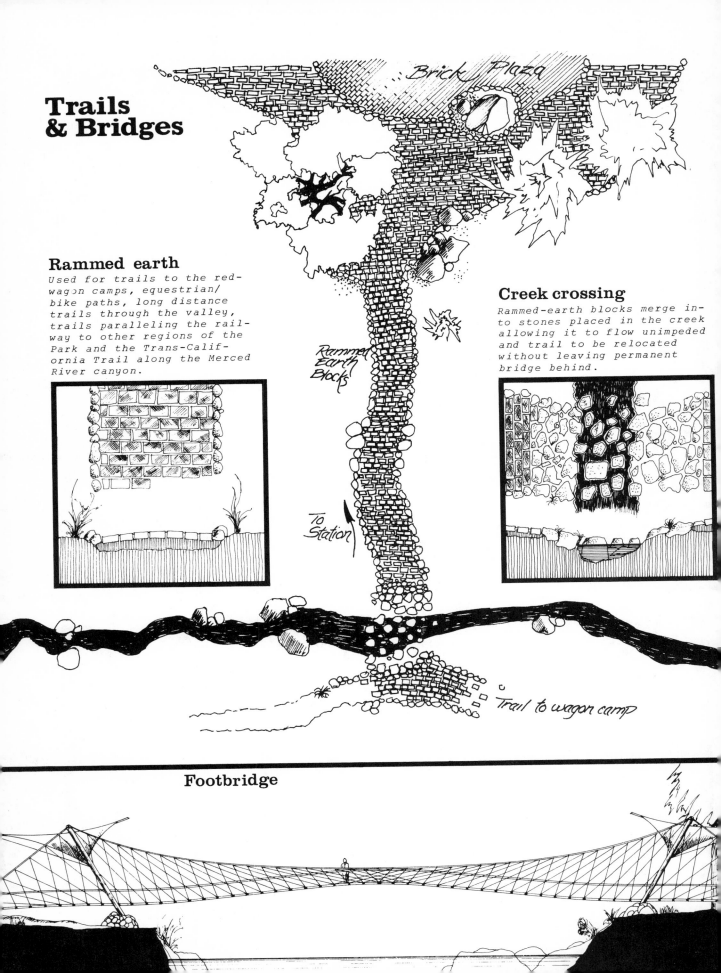

Trails & Bridges

Brick Plaza

Rammed Earth Blocks

To Station

Trail to wagon camp

Rammed earth

Used for trails to the red-wagon camps, equestrian/bike paths, long distance trails through the valley, trails paralleling the railway to other regions of the Park and the Trans-California Trail along the Merced River canyon.

Creek crossing

Rammed-earth blocks merge into stones placed in the creek allowing it to flow unimpeded and trail to be relocated without leaving permanent bridge behind.

Footbridge

Redwagon Camp

Fire ring

Redwagon camps tend to have heavier impact on the land then walk-in camps, so rotation is more frequent. Designed for family camping, they offer larger fire rings made from reinforced concrete pads with stone walls.

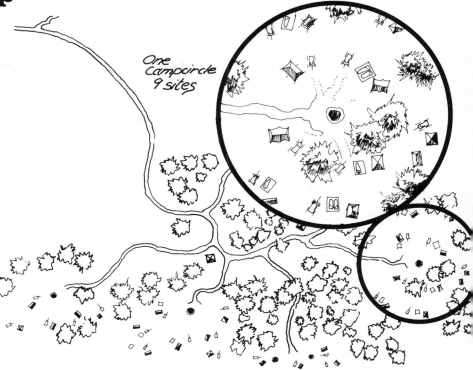

One Campcircle 9 sites

OVERNIGHT IN YOSEMITE VALLEY

1978: Approximately 960 camping sites in seven campgrounds.
One campground for people with pets.
One group campground.
Two walk-in campgrounds, the rest designed for people with vehicles.
Also, Curry Village tent camps, Yosemite Lodge motel and the Ahwanhee hotel.

1984: Approximately 1800 camping sites in 40 campgrounds.
Any campground can be used for groups.
Twenty-three walk-in campgrounds with an average of 36 campsites each.
Seventeen redwagon campgrounds averaging 62 campsites.
Also, lodging trains for charter.

Walk-in Camp

Service booth

Portable wood structure: waterless toilet(s) telephone, drinking water and washbasin. Local trail and emergency information listed on the outside.

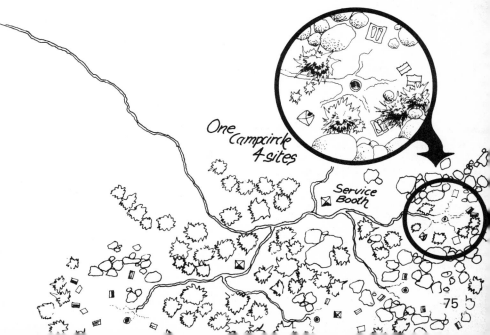

One Campcircle 4 sites

Service Booth

BREAKING THROUGH SMOKEY THE BEAR'S SMOKESCREEN

A wild forest is one untouched. Where the evolution of species continues as it has immemorially. Where fire burns unnoticed by human eyes. Where the relationship between fire and forest still smolders.

A wildfire can occur only in a wild forest. A wildfire is a fire caused by lightning. Storms and forests are in continual co-evolutionary dialogue. The ancillary exchanges like dry air, ion concentration, exposed rock configurations, canopy moisture and all the other variables are too interwoven to extract an exact interaction formula. However, in a particle of a second, the mix is perfect: a fire combusts.

Most of Earth's forests have been domesticated, wildness tamed into orderly, managed behavior. Domestication--in much of the Sierra Nevada but not Yosemite-- introduced species suitable for lumber to build civilization. To a forest this means the prevention of wildfires. Other ways of collecting downed wood, thinning undergrowth and general grooming must be instituted.

Managed fires are common in domesticated forests. In Yosemite, the National Park Service allows wildfire in about 60 percent of the Park. Uncontrolled fires in managed forests can reach conflagration--a fire so hot it sucks in air, in effect creating its own wind--or become a crown fire--a fire so completely fueled by the uncollected undergrowth that it reaches the upper branches and kills the tree.

Clean-burning fires of these varieties almost never occur in wild forests with the exception of unusual regions of dense undergrowth somehow untouched by small, smoldering fires, or with concentrations of certain species like white fir which tend to burn completely.

I.   FIRE IS DESIRABLE BECAUSE IT:

1. removes undergrowth including dead branches of otherwise healthy trees
2. burns off dead growth
3. kills diseased bark, branches or whole trees, preventing the spread of disease
4. rebalances insect populations, frequently getting rid of tree-dwelling insects that would otherwise kill trees and forests if uncontrolled
5. burns up ground cover whose thickness and acidity prevent the growth of seedlings, wildflowers, grasses and shrubs
6. produces ash components that are easily absorbed by soil to enrich it
7. controls the too-rapid growth and proliferation of shade-tolerant species
8. germinates some tree species, like the knobcone pine whose cones open only through heat
9. encourages the growth of grasses, shrubs and seedlings which increases the presence of browsing animals which attracts predator animals
10. alters rooting and branching patterns of trees, enlivening previous shade-affected slow growers
11. moderates microclimate by allowing reduced maximum and increased minimum air temperatures
12. encourages increased air circulation under canopies
13. brings about an increase in humidity which encourages ground-hugging plants and seedlings
14. acts to enliven and strengthen every wild forest. It is a cleansing of the body forest

II.   FIRE DOES NOT OCCUR IN YOSEMITE VALLEY BECAUSE:

1. people are afraid of fire, a concept based on the devastation it produces in domestic forests
2. until recently fire was considered detrimental to all forests, since it damag- the product: lumber
3. human habitations and settlements were threatened by forest fires
4. antiforest fire propaganda worked very well, even blanketing attempts to put things in a clearer prospective

III. THE COMPONENTS OF WILDFIRE:

1. slow, small flame, low heat groundfire
2. expands outward from central ignition point
3. rarely affects overstory trees, a few species of fir being the main exceptions
4. little effect on water souces and does not pollute streams or lakes
5. kills insects but not many mammals who are frequently back foraging for seeds exposed by the fire while the ground is still smoking
6. saturates the air with large particles of rich nutrients and so spreads them over wide areas
7. has no primary patterns but can smolder for weeks and months or burn out within a few hours

IV.   WILDFIRE IN YOSEMITE VALLEY:

1. would be a direct factor in returning the valley to wilderness
2. bring back more deciduous trees and healthy meadowland
3. discourage the domination of pines, a relatively recent phenomena
4. encourage diversification along the southern rim of the valley by clearing the undergrowth to allow more sunlight to warm canopy-held air
5. increase the growth of wildflowers, shrubs and grasses
6. owing to the valley's bowl shape, smoke might be trapped by higher air layers for days or weeks, a mild pollution that could produce side affects like unusual sunsets and other visual displays

WILDFIRE IN DOMESTIC FOREST BURNS THE DENSE UNDERSTORY GROWTH. HIGH FLAMES CAUSE CROWN FIRES.

WILDFIRE IN WILD FOREST BURNS THE GROUND COVER PRODUCING LOW FLAMES.

WILDFIRE POLICY PROPOSAL

Continue fire research and monitoring. Continue managed fires in regions of the Park where accumulated forest fuels make wildfire a dangerous possibility. Remove dense coniferous undergrowth within Sequoia groves (Mariposa and Tuolumne primarily) by low impact logging. Develop managed fire programs in National Forest and Wilderness lands bordering Park (particularly in El Portal region of Merced River canyon because of high level, dangerous accumulation of chapparal).

Modify existing and develop new firefighting equipment capable of traveling on and off railway. Develop lightweight fire trucks capable of traveling over all terrain without disrupting the surface.

Design a public information system, available to all Park visitors, detailing the differences between domestic and wild forest fires and specifying what to do in the event of fire.

Design building fire protection systems--sprinklers, emergency water sources, exterior monitor nozzles--so that structures may withstand wildfires. Develop evacuation plans as well as means of allowing visitors to watch wildfires and under- stand these fires as natural and not disaster occurrences.

ANIMALS IN THE HUMAN ZOO

1. LOCAL CREATURES WE KNOW WE HAVE AFFECTED

TROUT   Brown, Golden and Rainbow. Information about their habits confused because of man's tampering since the 1870s. For example, the stocking of high Sierra lakes many of which were previously fishless. Evidence beginning to show that hybrid species raised in hatcheries do not survive more than one or two generations. They are stocked only for fishing.

CARPENTER ANT   Increasing numbers of carpenter ants live in--and eat--more trees around campgrounds than those even four meters away. Does our litter encourage their presence?

SIERRA GROUND SQUIRREL   Greater numbers congregate around campgrounds: people like to feed them peanuts and just about everything else. The Merriam chipmunk, habitat 1200 meters, is experiencing a similar population explosion.

STELLER'S (BLUE FRONTED) JAY   Population has increased due to garbage scavenging and people feeding them. Their presence in some areas overwhelms the sighting of other birds.

CALIFORNIA MULE DEER   Elimination of wildfire throughout much of the Park and surrounding land has increased the undergrowth, making movement difficult for these creatures.

CALIFORNIA BLACK BEAR   The human-food dependency of Yosemite's 250-400 bear population led to a widely publicized public information policy and the introduction of "bear-proof" trash cans. The human-fostered attitude of bears is more visibly aggressive, but no more harmful, than that of the jays, the small rodents or the ants.

GRIZZLY BEAR   The namesake of Yosemite, the grizzly was the largest animal in the Sierra, the standing adult male reaching more than three meters. By the early 20s the species was extinct in the Sierra and almost so throughout the West with the exception of the Rockies from Yellowstone north into Canada.

BIGHORN SHEEP   Hunting almost eliminated this animal in the Sierra. Approximately two hundred remain between Olanche Peak and Sawmill Pass (near Mt. Whitney and the eastern edge of Sequoia National Park).

WOLF   Once common species is extinct in the Sierra. A similar species inhabits the Cascades, the Rockies and other western ranges.

GOLDEN EAGLE   A species once flew in the Sierra similar to those now limited to the northern coast of Canada and southern Alaska. Unsubstantiated sitings have been reported, however, in the northern Sierra.

COYOTE   Remarkably well-adapted to the presence of humans, the coyote is surviving in increasing numbers after being once hunted almost to extinction. Believed to be a killer of sheep, it still is hunted in the Sierra foothills.

2. WHAT WE KNOW ABOUT THE REST

We know the sizes and weights and dimensions of many species, the numbers of young born, family structure, what they eat, general social habits including seasonal changes and approximate distribution throughout the Park.

We know the types of animals living in Yosemite and, very roughly, what their relationship (affect) is on other animals, areas, particular plants and plant chains, and something about how they are part of the ecosystem.

We know what we know about animals and plants in Yosemite, but only how it is within the presence of human beings.

3. ANIMALS WE KNOW ALMOST NOTHING ABOUT

RING-TAILED CAT   A shy, retiring creature who looks like a cross between a raccoon and a tabby cat. How much of its habitat has been restricted by the presence of humans?

PRONGHORN ANTELOPE   The size of an adolescent mule deer, this species exists in the arid, mountainous regions of Montana, Idaho, Wyoming, New Mexico, Arizona and Southern California under protected status. It probably lived in the Sierra foothills (east and west slopes) before being hunted almost to extinction. Is reintroduction to the Sierra even a possibility?

MOUNTAIN LION (PUMA)   The largest wildcat in North America, its numbers have been increasing since becoming protected after being hunted for eighty years. Their natural range is unknown, as well as to what extent their reclusive nature is due to an understandable fear of man. Will protection mean that one day they will be a common sight?

WOLVERINE   Looks like a small black bear, but only about one meter long. It has the reputation of being an extremely savage carnivore. The relationship between food sources, competing species like the coyote and the wolf is unknown. And how would the reintroduction of wolves change the wolverine population?

4. WHAT WE DON'T KNOW ABOUT ANIMALS

Behavior of all animals in groups and groups of other animals.
Structures and patterns of communication.
Patterns of movement relative to seasons, wildfire, floods, water and human activity.
How the migration of extinction of various species has affected the area. Are niches filled, left vacant or otherwise affected?
Is it possible for a species to reintroduce itself into a region once their own territory?
How do animals alter the vegetative patterns? How does the flora influence the fauna?
How are wild animals affected by people? Do different human behaviors affect animals differently? Do loud groups have a different effect from quieter ones? Do people afraid of wilderness attract predators? What are the interactions?

5. ORGANIZING THE PROBLEMS

We have created a dependency cycle--one of pushers and addicts--between ourselves and animals like bears, squirrels, chipmunks, jays, ants, deer.
Those animals that were able to respond to our behavior by adaptive and aggressive behavior are favorably influenced by us: their population increases and they achieve the ability to remain in a human-dominated environment.
Those less aggressive tend to stay away from where we and our quasi-pets congregate.
Current animal research is highly specialized and is usually focused on individual problems of specific species out of any context.
We have the most data on the most observable animals.
A crisis situation, like the bear problem, brings results, but only after the fact and in the nature of a cleanup.
BEYOND NOT INTERFERING AND EMPHASIZING MORE EXTENSIVE, HOLISTIC STUDIES OF THE AREA AND ITS VARIABLES AND INTERACTIONS, IS THERE ANY POSITIVE ACTION WE CAN TAKE?
The peculiarity of physical events that go beyond our comprehension constantly startles us. Particles that don't go where the "laws of nature" prescribe they're supposed to. Species that don't follow the "laws" of natural selection. Electronics freaks talk of electrons that wander. And engineers in their fine world of delicate judgments notice phenomena for which there is no explanation. The explanation? The laws don't work? Of course they don't. It isn't law. It's it.
Civilization is now looking to the lab, still. The world, the wilderness is out the door, back behind the barn, way out there. We keep trying to see the whole thing through the eyes of the myriads of people who are each concentrating on one thing. How can the total of all these studies add up to a complete picture? How can even a million nails describe a house?
Let the scientist stay in his lab if that's where he's happy. But we have to realize that all he's doing is gathering new information, not putting together a picture.
What we want to know about is Yosemite, the whole area, what it's about. Why it's a region, what makes it a region and what's going on and off there.

SPECIFICALLY: We can locate campgrounds away from principal animal habitats and paths of movement. Near the base of El Capitan, west of Mirror Lake, there are boulder-strewn areas with flat bases. The hollows are ideal for small campsites. Other areas like these could be located, areas chosen for animal convenience and noninterference as well as human comfort.
Culverts now under highway fill can be returned to natural creekbeds. The railway bridges can be built in high, open-frame arched forms that allow light to penetrate, the creek's life system to reestablish itself and animals to pass beneath our own form of transportation.
Encourage, even support naturalists to live in and study the wilderness. The intricate ecology of the Sierra needs this kind of all-encompassing survey of the way life exists here.

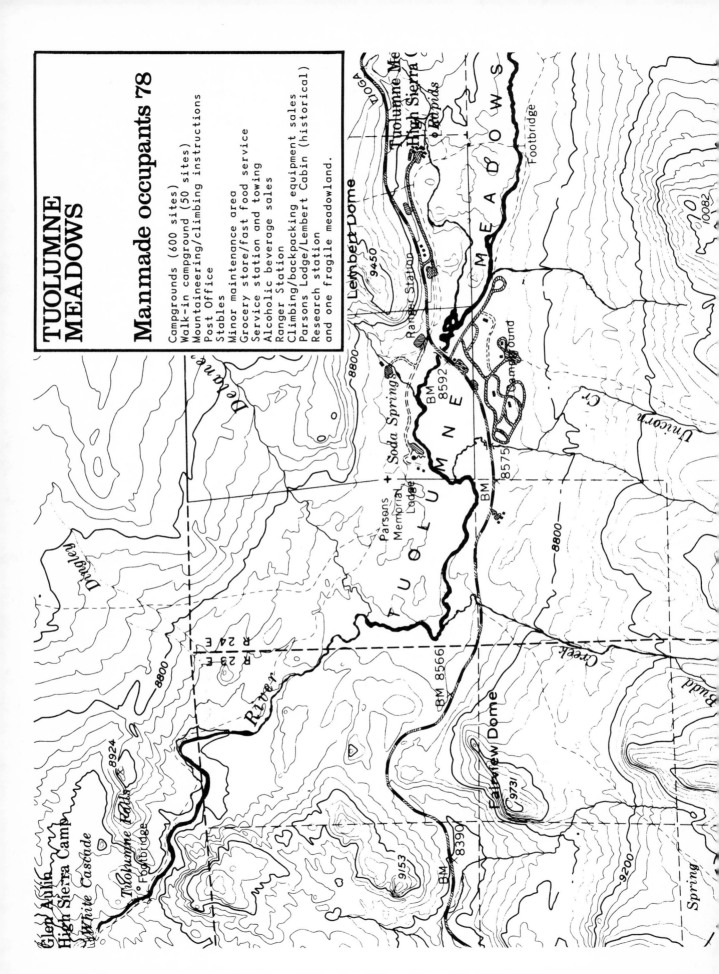

TUOLUMNE MEADOWS

Manmade occupants '78

Campgrounds (600 sites)
Walk-in campground (50 sites)
Mountaineering/climbing instructions
Post Office
Stables
Minor maintenance area
Grocery store/fast food service
Service station and towing
Alcoholic beverage sales
Ranger Station
Climbing/backpacking equipment sales
Parsons Lodge/Lembert Cabin (historical)
Research station
and one fragile meadowland.

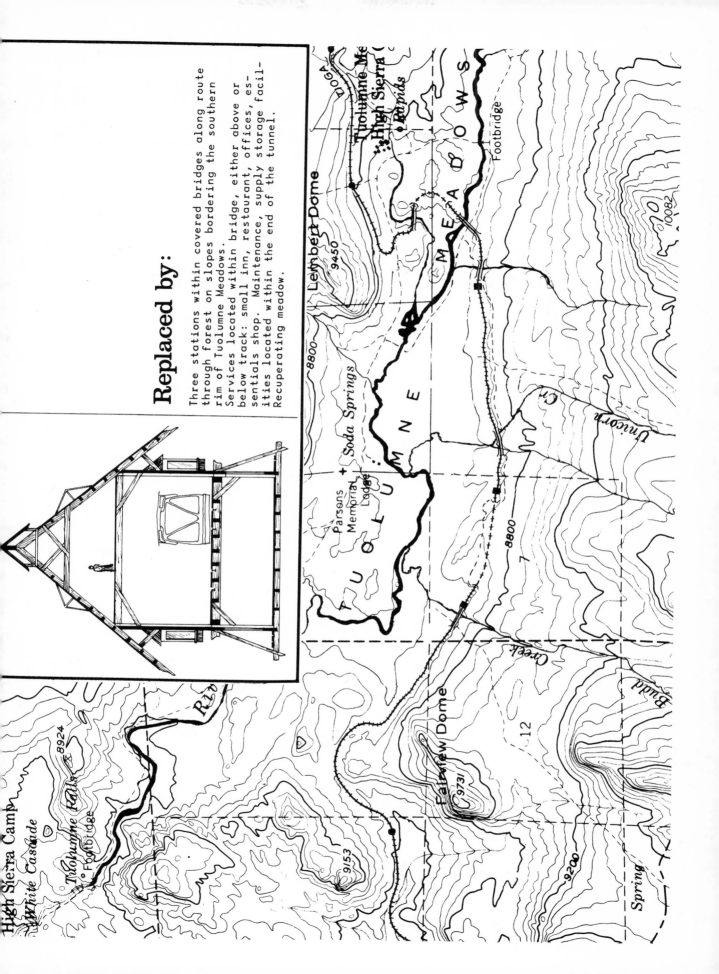

Replaced by:

Three stations within covered bridges along route through forest on slopes bordering the southern rim of Tuolumne Meadows. Services located within bridge, either above or below track: small inn, restaurant, offices, essentials shop. Maintenance, supply storage facilities located within the end of the tunnel. Recuperating meadow.

High Sierra Camp

White Cascade

Tuolumne Falls

8924

Footbridge

9153

RIV

Fairview Dome

9731

Budd

Creek

Spring

9200

12

Lembert Dome

9450

Soda Springs

Parsons Memorial Lodge

TUOLUMNE

8800

MEADOWS

Unicorn Cr.

8800

Footbridge

Lembert Dome

Tuolumne Me

High Sierra

Rapids

TIOGA

10082

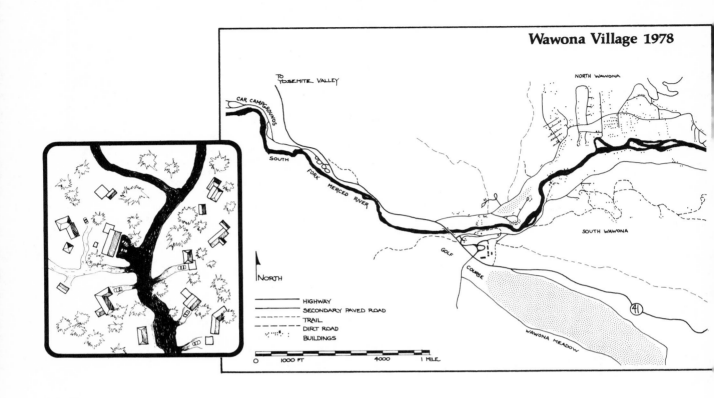

Wawona Village 1978

TO YOSEMITE VALLEY

NORTH WAWONA

CAR CAMPGROUNDS

SOUTH FORK MERCED RIVER

SOUTH WAWONA

GOLF COURSE

41

WAWONA MEADOW

NORTH

HIGHWAY
SECONDARY PAVED ROAD
TRAIL
DIRT ROAD
BUILDINGS

0   1000 FT   4000   1 MILE

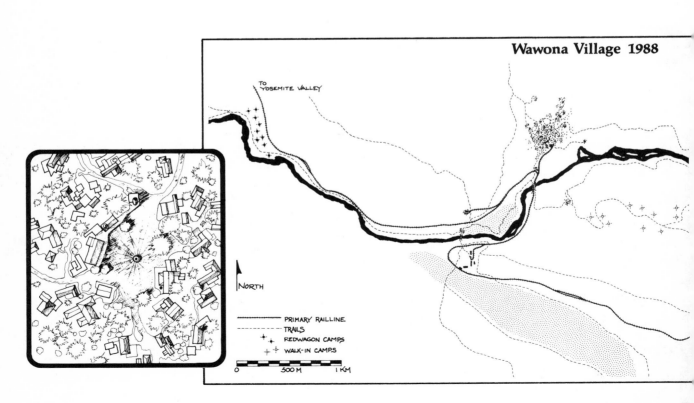

Wawona Village 1988

TO YOSEMITE VALLEY

NORTH

PRIMARY RAILLINE
TRAILS
REDWAGON CAMPS
WALK-IN CAMPS

0   500 M   1 KM

1978

CRANE
FLAT

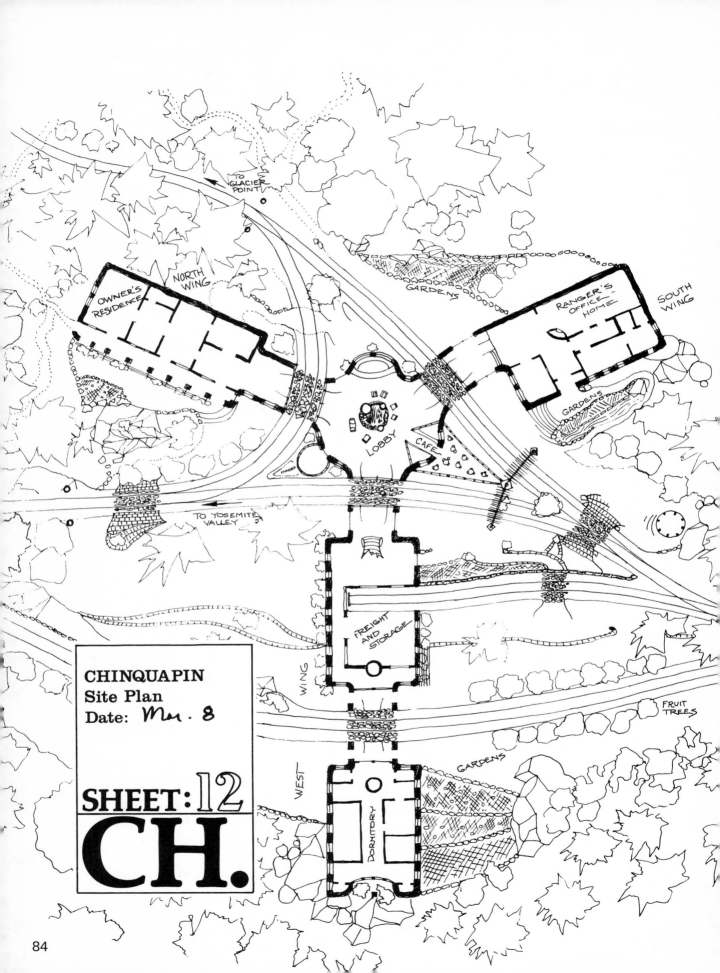

TO
GLACIER
POINT

OWNER'S
RESIDENCE

NORTH
WING

GARDENS

RANGER'S
OFFICE
HOME

SOUTH
WING

GARDENS

LOBBY

CAFE

TO YOSEMITE
VALLEY

FREIGHT
AND
STORAGE

WING

FRUIT
TREES

WEST

DORMITORY

GARDENS

CHINQUAPIN
Site Plan
Date: Mu. 8

SHEET:12
CH.

84

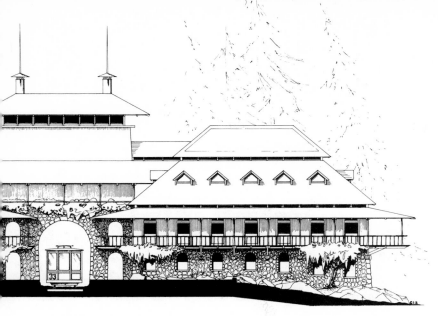

Elevation

Center section tunnels the Wawona shuttle line, contains third floor locker space and top floor lounge. Wing to the right contains 14 third floor single rooms, 14 second floor double rooms and 26-person first floor dormitory.

CHINQUAPIN
Cross section of west wing

Top floor greenhouse contains eight 1.5 meter square plant beds hung beneath glass roof. Left side top floor, small beds tucked under roof. Dwarf fruit and nut trees in center, vines growing between. Trapdoor in floor for raising and lowering of plants and materials to rail and plaza levels. Third floor dormer rooms have connecting doors for doubling. Small garden bed is under window. Second floor doubles have folding bunk bed for two children or one adult. Bottom floor provides dormitory and storage. Pipes along eaves are for rainwater collection.

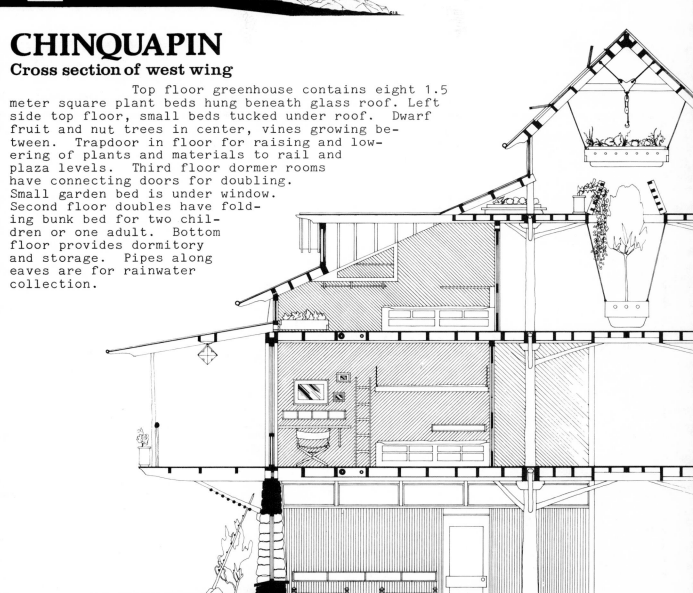

85

Lettuce Bed

*Suspended planting box:
1.5 m square. Soil: earth,
ash and decaying vegetable
matter on pebbles and sand.
Spongy soil encourages roots
to grow down, allowing more
plants to grow closer, encouraging natural symbiotic
relationships. Water,
through the tubes at the top
and draining down the pyramid-
al supports, sprays through
small holes. Drain pan tube
can also admit water for roots'
capillary action. Infrared
lamp (top center) prevents
freezing in cold weather.*

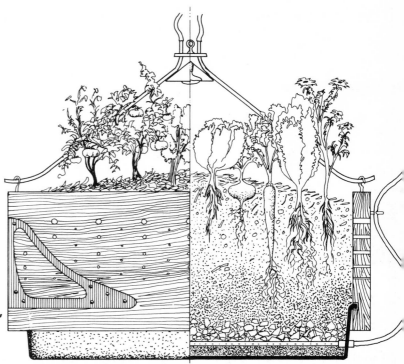

Garden Design

*One of the most extensive gardens is around the creek and under the
first floor lobby/restaurant at Annie's Rest Inn. The center of the
building is a greenhouse with a creek running through. Terraced gardens
take advantage of the creek's natural drainage while orchards on the
lower terraces benefit from the rainwater storage pools above them.
The gardens are the outdoor equivalent of the garden bed principle
illustrated above.*

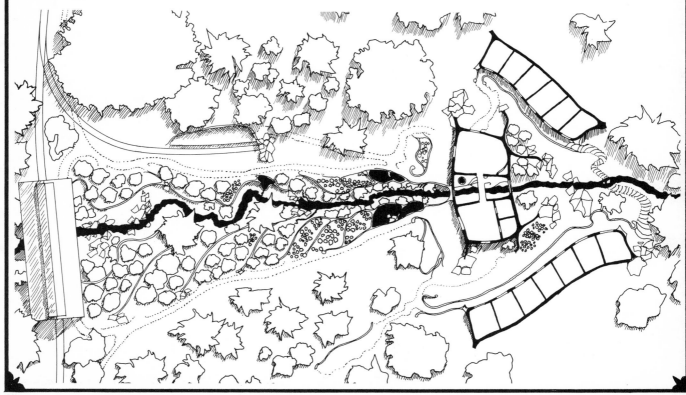

SUN & LEAVES

SUMMER: Sun deflected by leaves. Air cooled by damp plants passes into building. Warmer air rises through roof vents.

WINTER: Sun penetrates bare branches to warm building. Warm interior air is maintained by cooler outside air trapped by bushes.

Avalanche Inn garden, like all the gardens surrounding the inns, creates a natural transition from wild to manmade spaces. Because of the terraces and the judicious placement of thick bushes, deer and other grazers cannot sample the garden.

Green Places

A typical railway garden: Merced Falls repair shop and storage yard. Orchard between storage tracks helps cool the equipment besides being fruitful.

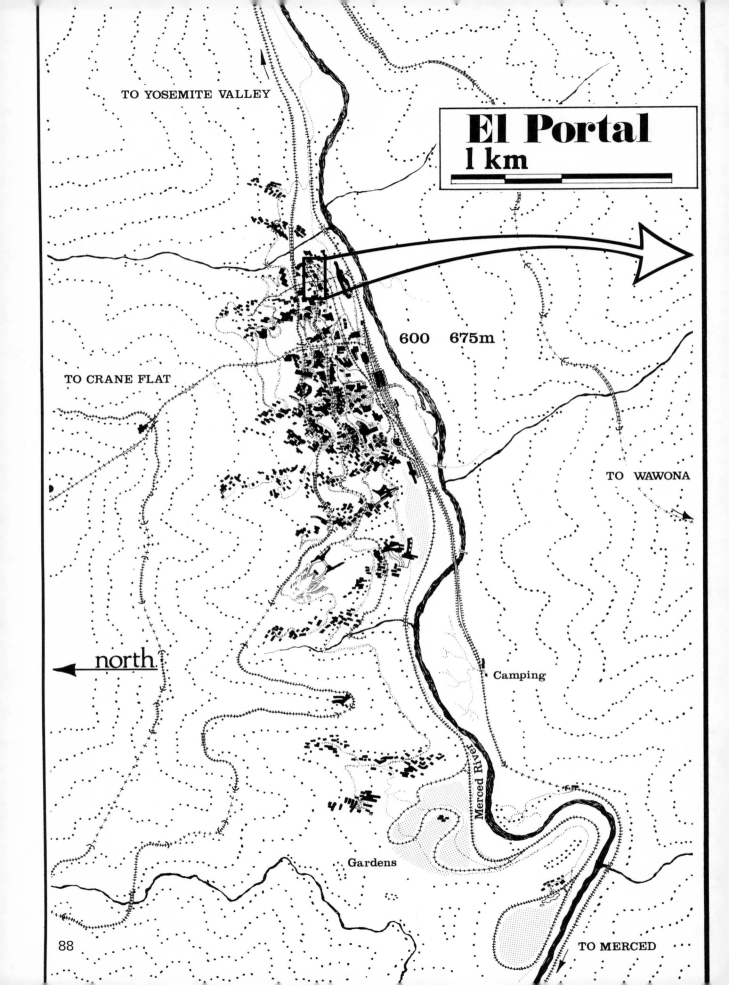

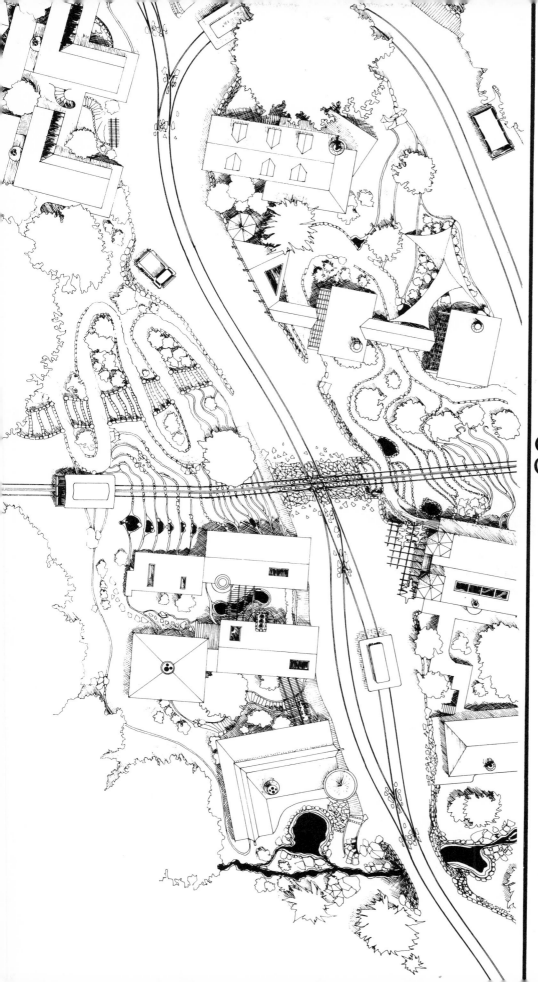

Gardens
Cable car

Projects Under Way in El Portal

1. Erosion: how to plant gardens and wildlife corridors to absorb flow of rainwater runoff.
2. Wildlife paths: how to develop and maintain pathways for wild animals through town.
3. Use of mountain plants as gathered crops.
4. Demanagement of wildlife: planning unplanning schedules.
5. Mountain medicine: study of effects of prolonged exposure and related problems of backpackers, mountain climbers and ill-adapted urban people.
6. Psychology of mountain living, a long range study to determine the differences, their causes and results.
7. History of Sierra Indian tribes, combining archaeology and compilations of 19th-century oral transmission, folklore, etcetera.
8. Astrological, lunar and human cycles: determining patterns experienced by people living in proximity; how the understanding of these cycles can maximize health.
9. Evolution of mountain mythology: extracting Indian, 19th-century gold miner, lumberjack and early settler stories and tales.
10. Simplified techniques for the design and construction of owner-built homes.

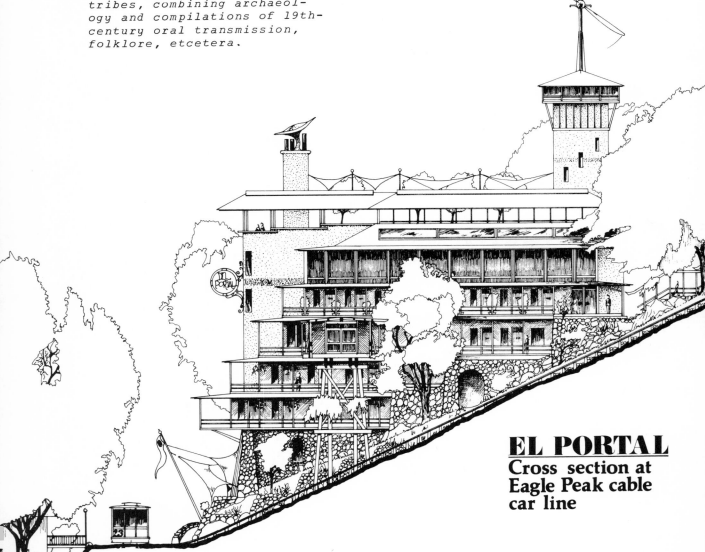

EL PORTAL
Cross section at Eagle Peak cable car line

Sugar St.

Fairs

Spring and Autumn Equinox Fairs
Winter and Summer Solstice Follies
July 4 kayak and water sphere races
October 3 Opening Day dinner.
George Orwell Week, last full week
*   in September*

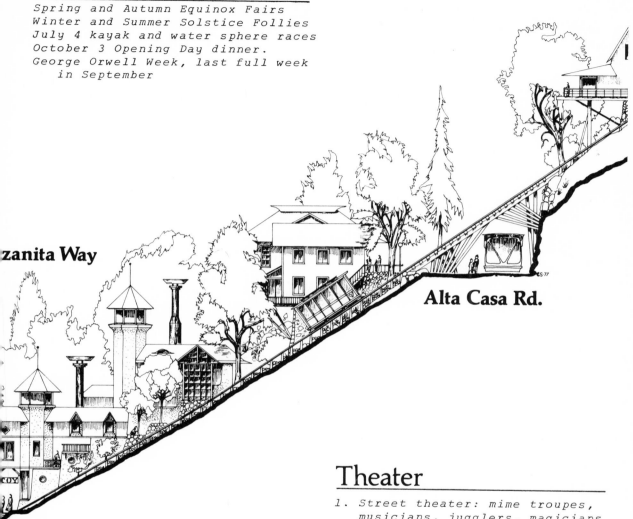

zanita Way

Alta Casa Rd.

Athletics

1. *Soccer frequently played on large field near main station.*
2. *Basketball nets and half-courts scattered throughout town.*
3. *Melees, self-defense games between two teams of up to fifty members, in the forest above El Portal.*
4. *Yearly Queen of the Mountain, medicine-ball-over-the-hill game played between El Portal and Wawona on Pinoche Ridge.*
5. *Loggers' games taking place in El Portal and Mariposa: tree-climbing, log-lifting by balloon, cable rigging, etcetera.*

Theater

1. *Street theater: mime troupes, musicians, jugglers, magicians, etcetera.*
2. *El Portal amphitheater: summer plays and concerts performed at the open amphitheater seating 1800, while another thousand or so can watch from decks and streets above.*
3. *Concerts given in the Del Portal during the year and on special occasions in Yosemite Valley.*
4. *Impromptu concerts and theater occurring in town inns and cafes. Performers play for room and board.*

Visitors' Center

Continuing activities: interpretive displays, slides, movies, lectures, tours, camping, backpacking, climbing classes.

30 m| 15 m

Cross section of early model utility core in typical El Portal residence. Core is constructed of standard concrete blocks, but other material can be used for this structural building part. Opposite page: schematic shows the functions, cross section d-d is through the bottom of the core.

CORE RINGS: Junction for piping and electric circuitry. Top ring's main function is the differential pump's drawing heat off chimney or solar-heated water. Middle ring is primarily for electrical distribution and hydrogen/oxygen storage. Bottom ring is primarily plumbing drains.

DIFFERENTIAL PUMPS: Top ring shuttles water through the system, the one in the middle ring pumps hydrogen/oxygen into storage tanks. Both operate off either cold or hot water, needing at least a ten degree difference from ambient air temperature.

HEATING: Differential pump in the top ring draws cool water up, circulating it through the solarskin. Water heated by the solarskin is channeled to the top ring. Heated water is also stored in core wall cavities giving off heat into the rooms. Fireplaces are auxiliary heating sources, warming air in rooms as well as water within core.

ELECTRICITY: Solarskin can either generate electricity directly or crack water into its components. The stored hydrogen and oxygen can be drawn upon on demand, admitted to a fuel cell where they recombine into pure water, giving off electricity in the process. Tanks are automatically vented in the event of fire.

SHOWERS/SINKS: Pure water is pumped or gravity-fed from storage tanks in core walls. When not heated by the sun, water can be heated on demand by electric heaters surrounding the pipes. Gray water drains into storage tanks at the base of the core. Heavy particles settle in stone and gravel base, and the water is gradually recycled up through a filter (cleaned once a year) into the solarskin. Water lost by leakage and evaporation is replenished by rain.

REFRIGERATION: Both the refrigerator and the freezer (not shown) are operated off stored oxygen. During the summer when heat, hence electricity, is abundant, the oxygen tank is under its highest compression and lowest temperature.

TOILET: Water spray bidet type. Shit, pee and a small amount of water drop into the digesting tank which surrounds gray water storage tank. The heat accelerates digestion of organic matter. During winter the sludge, usually greater in quantity because people eat more, maintains heat in the gray water storage tank thereby contributing to heating the house. Prime fertilizer is collected periodically from the digesting tank.

KITCHEN: Organic garbage can be dropped down the chute into the digesting tank. The stove operates off hydrogen and/or methane. An electric pump circulates solar or electrically heated water for the combination dishwasher/clotheswasher.

UTILITY CORE

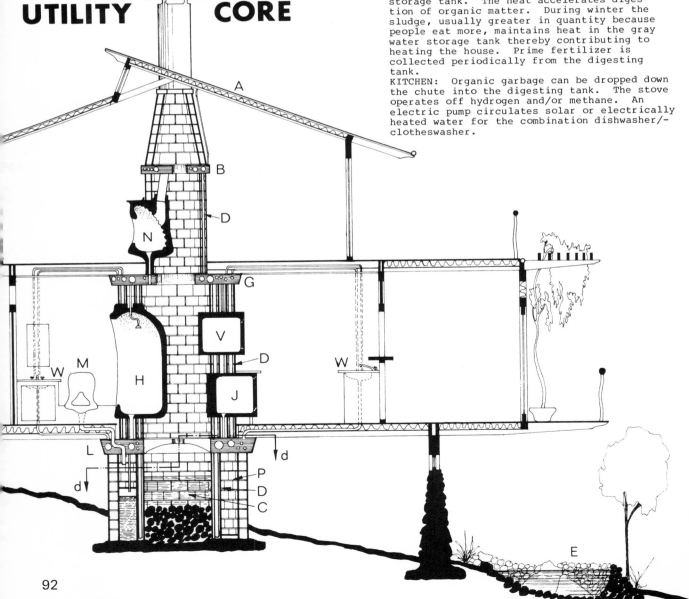

SCHEMATIC

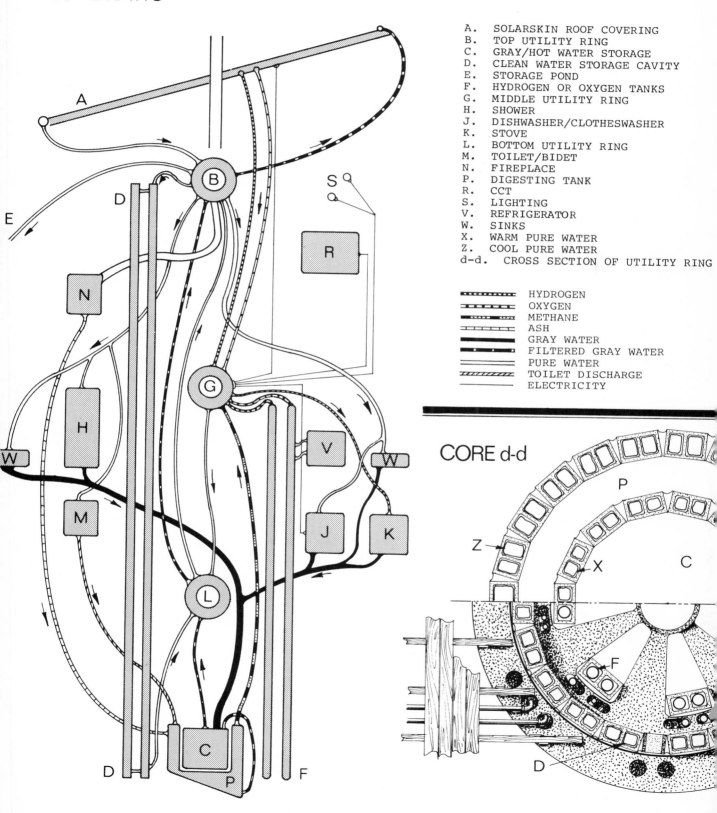

A. SOLARSKIN ROOF COVERING
B. TOP UTILITY RING
C. GRAY/HOT WATER STORAGE
D. CLEAN WATER STORAGE CAVITY
E. STORAGE POND
F. HYDROGEN OR OXYGEN TANKS
G. MIDDLE UTILITY RING
H. SHOWER
J. DISHWASHER/CLOTHESWASHER
K. STOVE
L. BOTTOM UTILITY RING
M. TOILET/BIDET
N. FIREPLACE
P. DIGESTING TANK
R. CCT
S. LIGHTING
V. REFRIGERATOR
W. SINKS
X. WARM PURE WATER
Z. COOL PURE WATER
d-d. CROSS SECTION OF UTILITY RING

HYDROGEN
OXYGEN
METHANE
ASH
GRAY WATER
FILTERED GRAY WATER
PURE WATER
TOILET DISCHARGE
ELECTRICITY

CORE d-d

GAUGE : 1.44 m

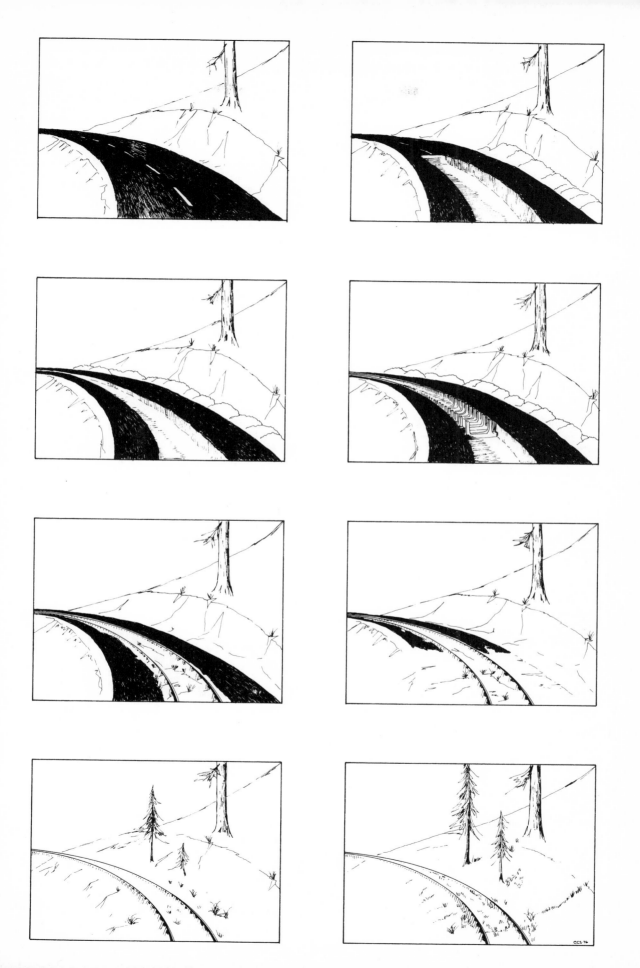

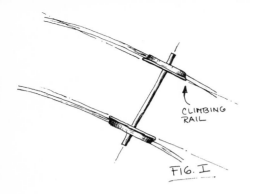

CLIMBING RAIL

FIG. I.

I. Conventional railroad equipment cannot negotiate tight curves without excessive wear and loud squealing. When the wheels, connected to a solid axle, enter a curve the flange on the wheel to the outside tends to bite and climb the rail, causing squealing. The outside wheel actually has to travel further--owing to the greater radius--so it tends to lag behind the wheel riding the inside rail.

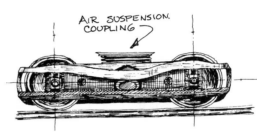

AIR SUSPENSION COUPLING

FIG. II

TYPICAL PASSENGER CAR WHEELSET

II. To minimize environmental damage, Yosemite Railway equipment was designed to follow curves and grades of existing highway routes, which have steeper grades and tighter curves than conventional railroads. That necessitated the design of a new wheelset.

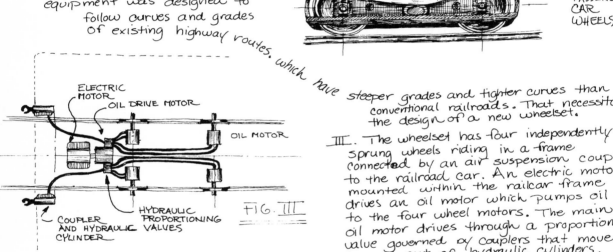

ELECTRIC MOTOR
OIL DRIVE MOTOR
OIL MOTOR
COUPLER AND HYDRAULIC CYLINDER
HYDRAULIC PROPORTIONING VALVES
FIG. III

III. The wheelset has four independently sprung wheels riding in a frame connected by an air suspension coupling to the railroad car. An electric motor mounted within the railcar frame drives an oil motor which pumps oil to the four wheel motors. The main oil motor drives through a proportioning valve governed by couplers that move in and out of hydraulic cylinders.

IV. A typical train is headed by a cab unit carrying a laser-sighting device that computes the degree of curvature the train is entering to proportion the oil --and therefore power -- to flow to the two wheels on the outside of the curve. Once the laser has initiated the process each pair of couplers translates the motion from car to car.

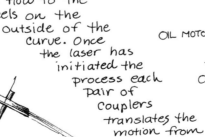

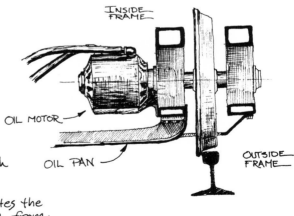

INSIDE FRAME
OIL MOTOR
OIL PAN
OUTSIDE FRAME

WHEEL WORKINGS 5

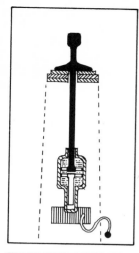

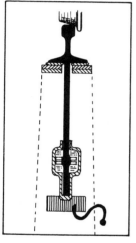

not to scale

Rails are in 50-, 70- or 90-meter blocks. When a train approaches a given section, its weight depresses a rubber cushion beneath the rail in turn depressing a short steel rod down within an insulated tube. The rod is connected to a piston moving within an oil-filled cylinder. The oil prevents arcing across the contacts. Full weight of the passing train (or shuttle car) makes contact. Power flows from feeder cable through switch into rail, wheels and energizes the motors; it returns via the opposite rail to ground. The oil switches (three per 50-meter section) are sealed in a waterproof chamber within a special concrete tie.

TRACK WORKINGS

The typical railroad right-of-way--mostly gravel and creosoted wood--tends to produce dust and dirt as well as collect it. The track always looks dirty.

The YR track is remarkably clean, even after three years' use. When the track-laying was completed, the topsoil was replaced--or added in the instances where track was laid on the old highway grades-- and reseeded. Since it became so completely surrounded by grass and wildflowers and weeds, it's difficult to see anything more than the shiny tops of the rails.

The engineering department was concerned about the track's safety. Would the switches always work? Was there any possibility of anyone's being electrocuted standing on the rail? And what about the effects of ice and snow?

The test track became the guinea pig. It was battered, flooded, pounded, run into, and one afternoon half the engineering team stood on it and the low voltage was turned on. Thirty-five people jumping up and down weren't enough to open up the circuit, even though one woman fell off and broke her arm.

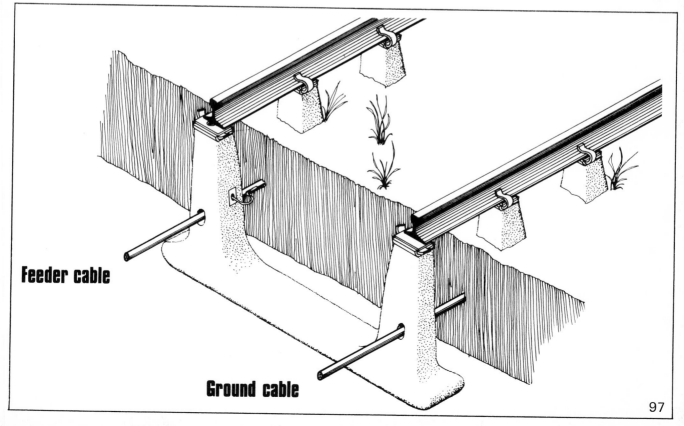

Feeder cable

Ground cable

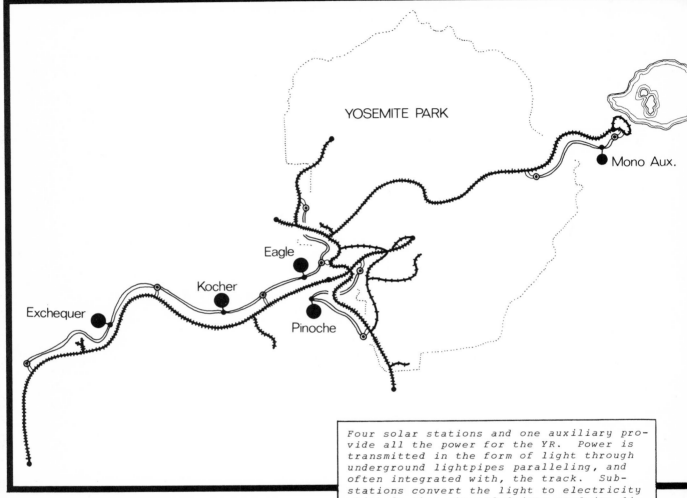

YOSEMITE PARK

Mono Aux.

Eagle

Kocher

Exchequer

Pinoche

*Four solar stations and one auxiliary pro-
vide all the power for the YR. Power is
transmitted in the form of light through
underground lightpipes paralleling, and
often integrated with, the track. Substations convert the light to electricity
which is then channeled into conduits directly beneath the rail. Decelerating
trains generate power which is pumped
back into the system via the substation
and then fed back into the conduit to
power trains accelerating or climbing the
grade. Or it can be returned to the
solar station in the form of light pulses
which are converted to hydrogen and oxygen for storage.*

SOLAR STATION

*Exchequer Solar Station's 25 m diameter double walled glass solar collection sphere.
Between the outer walls is an inert gas filled with microscopic particles of glass/
aluminum fiber. As the sun rises through the day, a magnetic web of wires is
energized. The magnetic field set up causes the particles to line up like millions
of mirrors. Sunlight bouncing off each particle focuses on the Crysol, a crystal-
line focusing sphere which converts it into coherent laser light. The beam travels
through a lightpipe to the light terminal tunnel where it is dispersed into dozens
of photovoltaic cells cracking water into hydrogen and oxygen to be stored underground for cloudy and evening periods when it can be recombined giving off elec-
trcity. If the tanks are full, the light is transmitted to substations where it
is directly converted into electricity.*

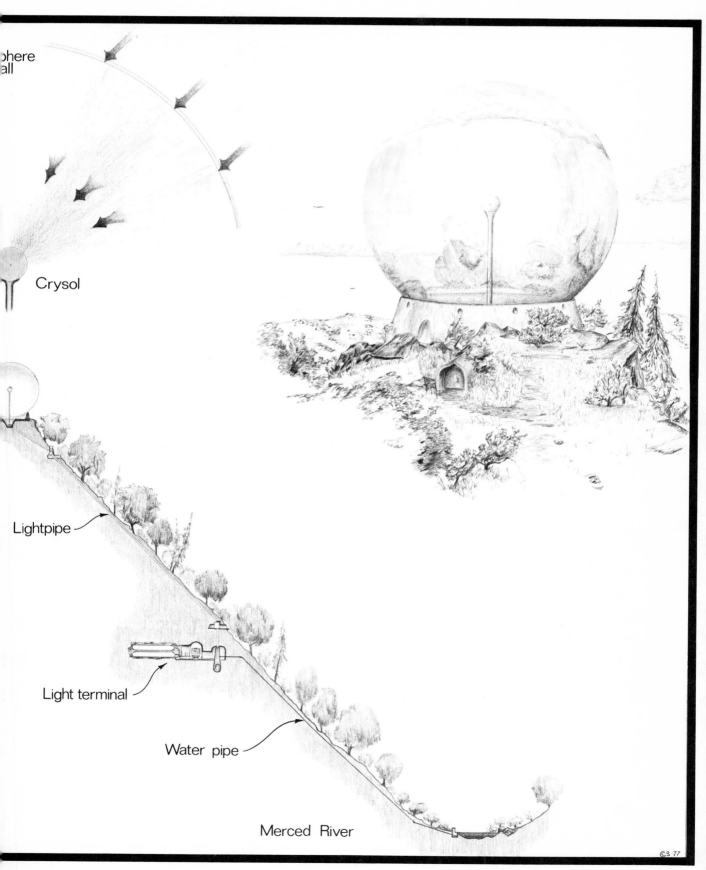

phere
all

Crysol

Lightpipe

Light terminal

Water pipe

Merced River

©S·77

COACHBUILDING

Designing railway cars is peculiar. The language of architecture--as old as civilization--used in rolling, not stationary forms. Like conceiving a long hall in a rococo palace, only instead of mirrors reflecting tromp l'oeil, we have the living landscape passing by.

In architecture as well as industrial design, there is what is know as the *hidden dimension*. Beyond the specifics of height, width, length, color and texture, there is the unquantifiable vagueness of the space itself; it can only be experienced. That's why the train's interiors were modeled in full scale before the prototypes were built. We wanted to feel what was hidden within the space.

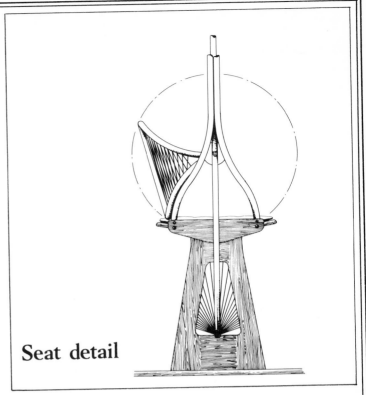

Seat detail

Open shuttle car

Uses same wheel size, motor, drive and control systems as gravity cars. Hard pine frame is steel reinforced. Floor, roof framing and end walls are hardwood--California black oak, maple with walnut trim or redwood with cherrywood trim--depending on builder and wood available. Seats are hardwood supports, plywood seat, weatherproof "breathing" vinyl cover over foam, reversible aluminum tube and cord netting back. Railings are polished aluminum, curved at the top to hook baggage. Double-paned sandwich safety glass and incandescent low wattage are used. No heat in open cars. All the body parts including nuts and bolts as well as the undercarriage parts are on-the-shelf items of hardware, metal supply stores and lumberyards. Life expectancy is between 25 to 35 years for these cars.
Operation is bi-directional. Operator sits at left of seat separated from passengers by low partition.

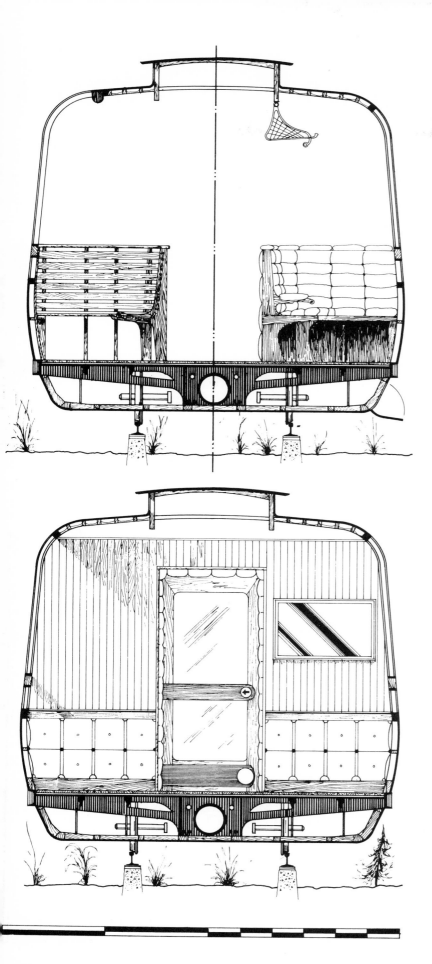

RAILWAY CAR INNARDS

LEFT: Open observation car.
Seating: oak frames, pine slats.
Weather protection: sandwiched mylar
and reinforced vinyl shade that rolls
into box above opening.

RIGHT: Typical coach.
Seating: oak and bent plywood frame.
Aisle side is cloth upholstered foam.
Seat and back is cloth-covered gra-
dated density foam.   Luggage storage
beneath seats, racks of polished aluminum tubing and white nylon cord above.

BOTH: Indirect fluorescent lighting
in clerestory.   Reading lights (not
shown) on adjustable tubes pulled
out of seatback and bent to focus.
Electric forced air heating/cooling
system beneath floor (not shown).
Power drawn from rail and roof solar cells.
Open door, lower right, access to
control, heating/cooling and communication modules not shown to display structure.

TYPICAL COACH, OBSERVATION, DINING
OR LOUNGE UNIT.
Mainframe: central steel torsion
tube.   Steel outrigger limbs longitudinally braced with V-section
steel ribs.
Subframe: hardwood ribs sheathed in
rusting steel.
Floor : sandwich of steel underplate,
lead sound barrier, foam vibration
damping and hard pine planking.
Carpet used only on center aisle.
Side walls: box section steel tubes
between windows, continuously welded
into roll cage and longitudinally
connected with box section tubes and
hardwood ribs.
Exterior skin: polished aluminum
sandwiched with thin pressboard
below windows.   Cloth upholstered
foam panels set within hardwood ribs
cover interior wall under windows.
Glass: double-pane untinted safety
glass; lower panel two sliding panes.
Clerestory: framed with hardwood,
sheathed in aluminum, designed to
collapse in the event of roll-over.
End wall: plywood. Lower portion
trimmed with oak or other hardwood
and covered with cloth upholstered
foam.   Middle portion finished in
oak veneer. Top covered with light
blue cotton print fabric.
Door Frame: oak, edged with tufted
upholstered foam.
Sliding door: hard pine and safety
glass, oak crossbar with red plexiglass actuation button.
Bottom kick panel: polished aluminum
with plexiglass actuation button.
Databoard is to the right of door.

ODDITIES

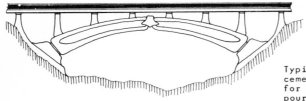

Typical railway bridge using precast ferro-cement steel reinforced components. Used for spans up to ten meters long. Footings: poured in place concrete or local stone.

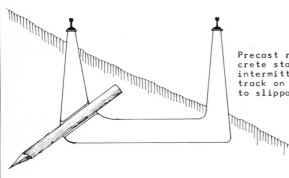

Precast reinforced concrete stabilizing tie for intermittent use with track on steep slopes prone to slippage.

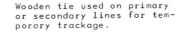

Cable car ties for short straight grades steeper than 15 percent. Cable box: rolled Cor-ten steel, carrier pulleys spaced at ten meter intervals.

TIE TYPES

Standard tie (precast reinforced concrete). Used on most primary lines. Designed for footing on bedrock.

Shorter standard tie (precast reinforced concrete). Used on primary line where soil is shallow, bedrock or broken rock close to surface.

Lightweight standard tie (precast concrete). For sidings and infrequently used passing tracks.

Standard tie (ferro-cement) used for secondary shuttle lines. Requires ballast footing.

Dressed stone footing for secondary shuttle lines. Used for short passages of exposed rock.

Wooden tie used on primary or secondary lines for temporary trackage.

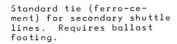

"X" tie (precast reinforced concrete) used on primary or secondary lines in areas of extreme soil instability.

"Saddle" tie (thin wall mesh reinforced ferro-cement) used on primary or secondary lines through talus or loose sedimentary rock.

Concrete poured in place supports used on primary or secondary lines over pieces of bare rock.

Excess baggage

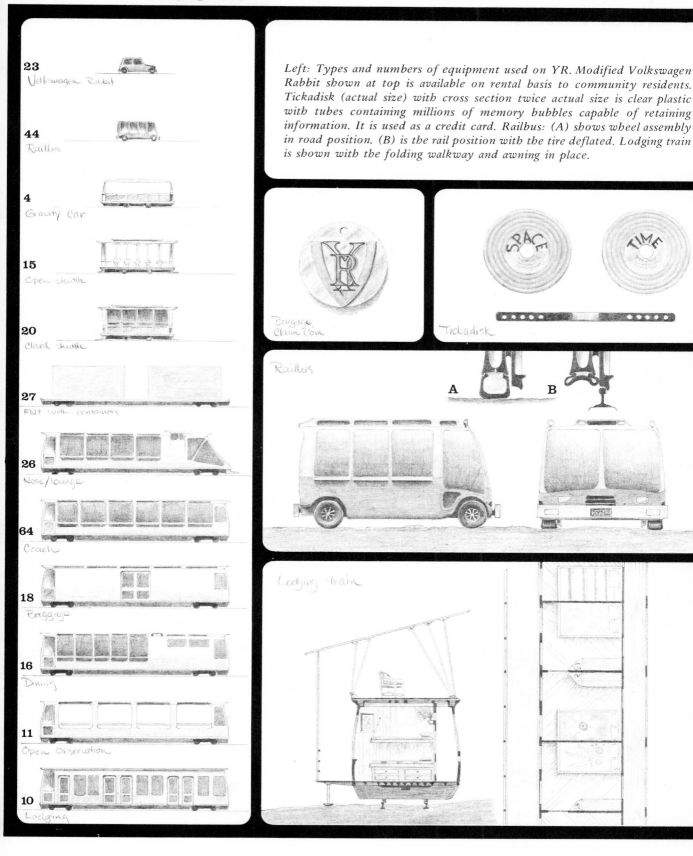

23 Volkswagen Rabbit

44 Railbus

4 Gravity Car

15 Open shuttle

20 Closed shuttle

27 Flat with containers

26 Nose/lounge

64 Coach

18 Baggage

16 Dining

11 Open Observation

10 Lodging

Left: Types and numbers of equipment used on YR. Modified Volkswagen Rabbit shown at top is available on rental basis to community residents. Tickadisk (actual size) with cross section twice actual size is clear plastic with tubes containing millions of memory bubbles capable of retaining information. It is used as a credit card. Railbus: (A) shows wheel assembly in road position. (B) is the rail position with the tire deflated. Lodging train is shown with the folding walkway and awning in place.

Baggage Claim Coin

Tickadisk

SPACE TIME

Railbus

A   B

Lodging train

Yosemite Park Chronology

● **1978 WINTER**

Region: Yosemite Valley Plan referendum; approved by Mono, Merced, Mariposa, Tuolumne counties.

Statewide initiative passed.

First bond issue passed at the same time.

Congress passes experiment plan (YVP).

Special charter committee of Park Service formed.

Work plan of Yosemite Planning team initiated.

Yosemite Valley Plan divides into Three Companies: Yosemite Railway (YR), Yosemite Overview (YO), Yosemite Inns (YI).

Foothill residents demonstrate objections in Merced.

Annual visitors: 2,221,854

● **1979 SPRING**

Railway: Construction teams — track and bridge — begin work.

YR vehicle prototype tests.

Track construction equipment delivered after two-month strike delay.

Temporary precast concrete plant (for ties) erected near Merced.

Exchequer experimental solar station construction begins.

Region: Eco-restoration, first phase: whole systems, defining impact of construction, how to minimize damage.

Annual visitors: 2,150,972

● **1980 SUMMER**

Railway: Test track revised into prototype.

Heavyweight train and railbus prototype construction.

Temporary shop facilities completed at Merced Falls and El Portal.

Region: Animal territory studies: mountain lion, wolverine, deer, bighorn sheep, golden eagle, bear and coyote.

Experimental lumber mill and aerial logging project in Mather.

First foothill grass fire study near Hornitos.

Annual visitors: 1,871,654

● **1981 SPRING**

Railway: Merced city system; Merced to Barrett.

Highway from El Portal to valley removed (other two remain open).

First heavyweight trains delivered.

Fire train delivered (four-car train).

Assembly dome completed in Merced Falls.

Exchequer solar station powers first section of track.

Region: El Portal reconstruction design underway.

Valley material recycling program initiated.

Groveland furniture shop opens.

Mariposa economic panic; loss of business is complaint.

Pine Tree Gold Mine reopens.

Annual visitors: 1,721,333

● **1981 FALL**

Railway: Merced city system complete; Merced to El Portal operating construction trains over temporary track.

Snowslides delay Lee Vining to Tioga construction.

Merced main station open.

Bagby solar station operational.

Fire damages Barrett bridge.

Inns: Barrett station/inn/bridge opened.

Merced Falls inn opened.

Region: Former employee housing removed from Yosemite Valley.

Foothill ecology lab at Briceburg.

San Francisco recycled water system construction begun.

● **1982 SUMMER**

Railway: El Portal to valley operating construction trains on temporary track.

Valley to Chinquapin under construction.

Shuttle cars delivered.

Second order of heavyweight trains delivered.

Wawona road removed.

Inns: Five small inns opened in Merced River canyon.

Region: Eagle Peak solar station operational.

Eagle Peak observatory (Sierra Astronomer's Assocation).

Wawona trails surveyed.

Crane Flat region: new trails and campgrounds surveyed.

Yosemite Lodge removed.

Oakhurst, Mariposa and Foresta experimental dairy farms set up.

Three design awards: Merced River railway bridges.

CCT network established in El Portal.

Solarskins incorporated in El Portal structures.

Annual visitors: 1,765,921

● **1983 FALL**

Railway: Primary line from Merced to valley opened, October 3.

Valley shuttle system operating.

Valley to Hodgdon Meadow, highway removed.

Crane Flat to Tenaya, highway removed.

El Portal to Wawona.

Chinquapin to Glacier Point operating.

Ackerson solar station operational.

Final heavyweight trains delivered.

El Portal station completed.

Inns: All Merced River canyon inns opened.

Crane Flat inn opened.

Chinquapin inn opened.

Glacier Point station/lodge opened.

Region: Camp Curry removed.
Big Trees wildfire study.
Wawona Wilderness Labs opened.
El Portal amphitheater.
Power line to valley dismantled.

Annual visitors: 1,801,987

● 1984 SPRING

Railway: El Portal to Fish Camp, El Portal to Lee
Vining (Tioga) all operating.
Big Trees and Badger Pass branches operating.
Yosemite Valley stations completed.
Fish Camp station and parking facility finished.
Inns: Wawona line inns all opened.
Ellery Lake inn opened.
Region: Fish, water health study begun.
Golden trout habitat restoration study.
Sierra Stream Beer Company opens in Mariposa.

Annual visitors: 1,976,982

● 1985 FALL

Railway: New connecting rail service begins from Los
Angeles/San Francisco to Merced.
YR designs railcars for Lake Tahoe Peripheral
Railway.
Region: Wawona trails completed.
El Portal reaches maximum estimated population.
Crane Flat trails and campgrounds completed.
Trans-California trail complete from Big Sur to
Mono Lake.
15 lightning fires; 3120 acres involved.
First sighting of golden eagle confirmed.

Annual visitors: 1,998,565

● 1986 SPRING

Railway: Seven temporary bridges replaced on Tioga
and Wawona lines.
Two three-car laboratories delivered: ecological and
geological.
Consulting agreement undertaken with Catalina
Island Eco-restoration Project.
Inns: Inn campgrounds completed.
Fire destroys Wolfback inn, reconstruction underway.
Region: New campcircles completed in valley.
Lodging trains moved out of valley (temporary worker
housing).
San Francisco water recycling system complete.
Higher animal population recorded in Yosemite
Valley.
Coulterville restoration and light industry project.
Windships begin flights over valley.
Coyote population increasing in foothills.
One group of wolves introduced near Lake Eleanor.

Annual visitors: 2,190,329

● 1986 FALL

Railway: Three temporary bridges replaced on Merced
canyon line.
Region: Golden trout restocking project successful.

Wildfire experiments: definite relationship to deer
and predator populations found.
Bobcat population mysteriously rises.
Five grizzlies introduced in Matterhorn Peak region.
First valley wildfire, Sept. 5.

● 1987 FALL

Railway: June Lake loop extension surveyed.
Final design of gambling railcars accepted by Lake
Tahoe Peripheral Railway.
Region: Pacific to Continental Divide trail completed.
International Conference on Eco-restoration hosted
by Three Companies held in El Portal.
Flood in Merced River canyon damages track; service
restored three hours after water subsides.
Park wolf population increased by four; spread south
to Hetch Hetchy.
Dwarf elk, pronghorn antelope and wild grassland
studies underway near Warnersville (north of Tuo-
lumne delta).

Annual visitors: 2,421,125

● 1988 SUMMER

Railway: First bonds retired, first dividends to
stockholders.
Hetch Hetchy branch operating.
Two new trains constructed.
Five new railbuses also.
30 percent of core group (1st three years) still
involved, 20 percent of secondary group (three to
five years) and 43 percent of tertiary group (after
fifth year).
Region: Planting begun upper end of Hetch Hetchy
Valley.
Research project and contest: names for places in
Hetch Hetchy Valley.
Bighorn reintroduction successful.
Wolf sighted east of Mono Lake.
Delta flood/garden project underway near La Grange.
Mono Lake water level subsidence stopped.
Mono named National Monument on March 13.
Mammoth Mountain access railway and eco-resoration
under discussion.
Hetch Hetchy reservoir draining begun, animal and
plant restoration project begun.
Chinquapin and Bishop Creeks inns survive wildfire;
water cooling protection system successful.
Grizzly population spreading north.

Annual visitors: 2,547,597

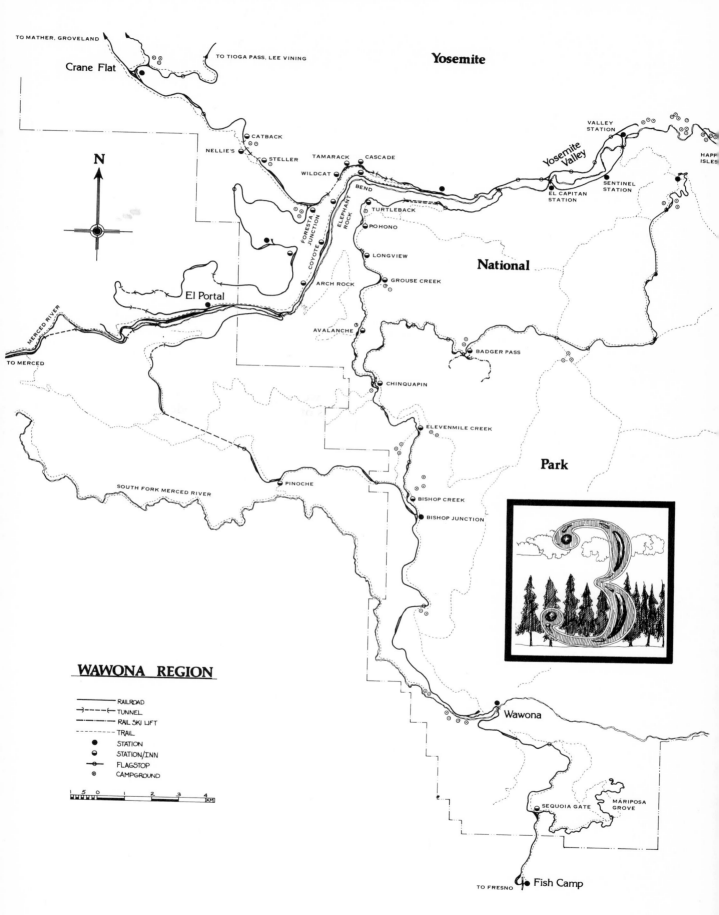

Yosemite

Yosemite Valley

TO MATHER, GROVELAND

Crane Flat

TO TIOGA PASS, LEE VINING

VALLEY
STATION

CATBACK

NELLIE'S

STELLER

TAMARACK   CASCADE

WILDCAT

BEND

FORESTA
JUNCTION

COYOTE

ELEPHANT
ROCK

TURTLEBACK

PO HONO

LONGVIEW

ARCH ROCK

GROUSE CREEK

EL CAPITAN
STATION

SENTINEL
STATION

HAPPY
ISLES

National

El Portal

MERCED RIVER

AVALANCHE

BADGER PASS

TO MERCED

CHINQUAPIN

ELEVENMILE CREEK

Park

SOUTH FORK MERCED RIVER

PINOCHE

BISHOP CREEK

BISHOP JUNCTION

Wawona

WAWONA REGION

RAILROAD
TUNNEL
RAIL SKI LIFT
TRAIL
●   STATION
◐   STATION/INN
⊶   FLAGSTOP
⊙   CAMPGROUND

5 0   1   2   3   4
KM

SEQUOIA GATE

MARIPOSA
GROVE

TO FRESNO   Fish Camp

SETTING UP

Yosemite Park is unique both as a technological and social statement. Still an evolving experiment, it is difficult to gauge the overall or long-term results of the effort, but thinking how it came together, it all seems like a flash now and coherent, the way it wasn't.

People concerned, those were the movers. Allied with locals — a lot of whom smelled profit, or at least a kind of recognition — but who were also sick of outside agencies and corporations appropriating their lumber and water and resources, leaving them with a pittance in exchange. The feudal attitude, nobles clopping and galloping through peasants' fields. Absentee management no matter how benevolent is inimical to the self-determination of any region. Community sovereignty just doesn't fit in with either business dividends or government regional summaries.

The employees of MCA — the conglomerate that owned a controlling interest in Yosemite Park and Curry Company — entered the picture because they were disturbed by management's insensitivity to the problems and needs of the area. All they needed was a real alternative. The idea of the railroad organized into the first company, the Yosemite Railway, gave the quiet agitation the heat it needed: meetings, petitions, grievances–the first move.

At the same time, the federal government and the new Department of Natural Resources (partly formed out of the old Interior Department) was grappling with the general concept of a legislated experiment. They could accept the idea of a community retaining its wealth rather than cycling it through Washington and getting only a token back in revenue sharing. They could even accept the necessity of such an experiment. But they questioned whether an area impoverished as long as the Sierra foothills could take up the reins. Also it was charged that making the Yosemite region a separate "experimental zone," as the red-tapers called it, would further confuse the role of the Park Service. But the Park Service had already resolved to maintain its role as steward — with a few policy changes. Surprisingly, or maybe not so, they encouraged the participation of the community, as well as a new and greater interaction.

After New York and Buffalo, Baltimore suddenly collapsed. Events three thousand miles apart affected one another. Drastic steps could no longer be avoided. The economic revitalization the city needed called for local initiative and participation. And through the mumblings in Congress, the connection between the two problems emerged and the special revitalization projects were allowed a green light; the pigeonhole was cleared.

Grass roots it was, and as such got the go-ahead. Who would have believed it was so easy? That of course was just the beginning. The railroad began: proposals, plans, surveying, architect and engineering teams, local lobbyists and groups and interested spectators. But the Yosemite Railway had a conventional organization — at least sort of conventional: a loose conglomeration of local contractors scraped from the hills and nearby industrial parks. But soon that kind of nepotism revealed itself: too weak, unimaginative, disruptive, it verged on the counterproductive.

This is not a recording. This is a follow-up call. Am I talking to Steven Q. Leveritt, Yosemite Park Overview purchasing team?

That's right. Who's this?

I thought by now you would recognize my voice. We don't all sound alike! I am Glass Bubble Analyzing Computer, Model 8420 C, Number 6245-389 G18.

Oh, Bubbles! Sorry I didn't recognize your voice. What can I do for ya'?

I'm inquiring whether or not you have decided about using my services.

As I've told you, Bubbles, we already use your microcomputer family for our mechanical operations--traffic, billing and so on. And we're going to stand on not extending computer use to human areas. Not to hurt your feeling, you understand, but we feel your services just wouldn't fit in.

Could you explain why, please? Wait one second. Now, record.

Our concern is the possible shifting of responsibility from people to the machine. After all, your capacity is so great.

You would have more control over variables than you do now.

Some kind of cohesion was necessary, a responsibility for a new direction. All the alternatives you could think of were suggested: the railway operated and subsidized through government, county- or state-level. Federal supervision. Conventional management-structured companies. Town councils for policy-making. Even a transportation czar. And it's not that any of these wouldn't have worked. It's just that they were what we were getting away from. More of what we'd all had enough of. We wanted something new and fresh, a way of participating in decisions that wouldn't become fossilized and co-opted. An ongoing process that wouldn't rigormortize into a product.

You can imagine what we went through! One at a time we'd go through each possibility and how it would work, until late at night, when those left could hardly move anymore. There were the advocates of community corporations, those who just wanted things to develop — just what had gotten us here to begin with, we repeated over and over — and the others who wanted to avoid all the problems and let THEM do it. There were all kinds of suggestions that the organization was already there: all we had to do was plug in to the existing structures. But we finally got it across that that was precisely what we were rejecting, leaving the real problems in the hands of bureaucrats whose ineptitude had kept us sleepwalking long enough.

MCA didn't resign graciously. They commissioned feasibility studies about buying or taking over the railway, but even three studies couldn't extract profit anywhere. After intensive negotiations a second new company emerged — Yosemite Inns — bought out the controlling interest in Yosemite Park and Curry Company and aligned itself with the Yosemite Railway. MCA left without hurting in its pocket, but with the conviction that national parks weren't good business.

The only real opposition came from the locals: the regional Park Service offices and the surrounding counties. They couldn't acknowledge how their power was eroding, and they doubted the efficiency of what was happening. The bureaucracy didn't think it would work.

Yosemite Railway was, of course, responsible for the railroad, its building and maintenance, with the exception of the track which is owned by the state of California and leased to YR. Yosemite Inns is an amalgamation of the individuals operating the inns and other Park services. Representatives from these two structures as well as the Park Service and various local factions were formed into the last company, Yosemite Overview. Members of this combination private foundation and think tank are elected in, and out. There are no fixed terms. So after what seemed then like hundreds of years in purgatory, and now a short period of confusion, we finally evolved a working solution. People were organized into teams, each responsible to Overview whose function was to make sure it all worked together. That method in combination with a kind of constitution of working principles we called the Game Book worked pretty well — for a while.

Many cultures develop rituals, social mortar intended to codify interfacing with the forces that shape life. The Game Book was intended to be that sort of guide. A relatively small pamphlet with a series of outlined procedures. It communicated in remarkably clear language — remarkable considering how many people worked on it and how many drafts there were — reasonable and pragmatic ways to go about accomplishing goals and tasks. How things fit in the whole system, where the links were, what tools and services could be tapped, what to be alert for, etcetera. Even to the edge of pinpointing the problem, the goal.

That's fine for congloms satisfied to make the same mistakes over and over. We're not trying for that rigidity. We're not interested in control. People and places are more than quantifiable information bits here. We aren't trying to develop a flawless social machine. We don't want to overlook the organic wholeness, the randomness of life. We want space for the healthy surges of wildness and creativity that are human.

You can plug in changes and constant variations, even by season if you like. This would free people from day-to-day decisions.

What does that mean, Bubbles?

Humans would not have to go through the same actions repetitively.

We buy you and we're free?

I am rented on an hourly basis.

Bubbles, we believe that people freed from such decisions, even trivial ones, lose autonomy, tend to forget value. Strengthening people's sense of their own value is part of what this project is about. Why do something to diminish that? Not to mention discouraging the flashes of insight that're always too rare.

I am sorry I am unable to serve you at this time, but if you change your decision, and I calculate that that is a likely possibility, I will be here. I hope you will not object to my making periodical calls reassessing your position?

Not at all. I really like talking to computers. And if I'm busy or annoyed I can use a technique endemic to all thinking machines: the binary yes/no. I can hang up.

At first it was taken extremely seriously, more a rule book than a game plan. Then as people got over their early doubts, self-deprecation, and got to know one another in a working situation, they realized it was a game as well as a survival manual. The organization moved from a rapid-growth, inner-directed stage — the building and planning — to a steadier/state, slower outer-directed period — geared more to environmental changes and visitor input. In the beginning all the real questions were about technology, how to use it, apply it, understand it, not overuse it, what to expect from it. Once the railway was built and functioning and everyone began settling in, they were able to see themselves more clearly as well as the visitors and most of all the environment that was being both altered and left alone: Yosemite in transition.

The Game Book was very specific about process. Just flip it open to the Contents page and you can get an idea of what it was like. At the beginning: Game Book spells out the techniques and processes of doing most tasks. Since the great majority are repetitive, it's easy to categorize and run down the action required. This makes the whole thing more fluid: people who know certain processes don't have to do them forever or be the only ones who can make these things work. One down for institutionalization.

Game Book provides the team makeups. How the tasks and the teams fit together, skills, numbers, time, priorities. How to organize groups to do certain tasks and in what order (a lot of this was culled from systems analysis procedures worked out by NASA in the 60s). Basic training like how to select those who would play leader roles. How to assign responsibility to those with less experience, kind of a self-teaching process really. The psychology of games mixed with a little Robert's Rules of Order.

Game Book delineates precisely how to deal with emergencies: large and small fires, earthquakes, land- and snowslides, train wrecks, group trauma, etcetera. It maps out the circuits of response, the paths of decision where people in one area — say El Portal — can be aware of a decision or incident in Wawona Village.

Game Book defines the role and powers of the arbiter. The relationship of the project to the outside: what can be decided locally — almost always the preferred solution — without county, state or federal intervention. Sometimes it's like having your own lawyer between the covers. (Too bad we can't do that with dentists.) Oh, and also the basic service contracts and how they work.

The legislative experiment plan is included as well as the act of the state of California and approved by special act of Congress. And an analysis of the concept so that the principles wouldn't be overwhelmed by the details. And an update sheet or two every two months.

But that's just the overview. I don't think we've gotten to the guts yet. How long-winded it sounds. Here, maybe the contents page will do it:

GAME BOOK
TABLE OF CONTENTS

During the organization meetings a lot of importance was placed on simplicity. The interchanges were to be uncomplicated, understandable, workable. So after the team relationships were defined, everyone went back to what they were doing and applied those standards. It seemed to work. In fact more often than not, what had been defined was what was being done all along anyway, but it helped to clear things up.

The meeting brought another factor to the fore, one rarely considered: ecological holding limits. There are certain tangibles — primarily water, arable land, animal populations and factors directly relating to settlement like optimum sewer development — that the region defines. Ignoring these natural limits places an unmeasurable strain on the land. The classic example in California is Los Angeles whose population, style of building construction, use of resources and way of life is severely out of touch with the arid ecology of Southern California.

As people up here recognized the holding capacities of particular eco-systems, they also began to see how far we are from sources of food and the knowledge of food production. This understanding grew out of a gradual re-awakening of self-awareness and self-reliance. In cities you lose this perception except in massive breakdowns. Then energy fade-outs, massive municipal strikes, sudden economic shortages of essentials or weather emergencies are some of the catastrophes that open eyes to the real dependencies technological institutions foster.

Even though the Game Book was quite an asset, there were problems: newer people who hadn't participated in the thinking-out process began to regard the book as company rules, rather than a process and activity guide. The old authority thing appeared in a flash, even though this time they referred to IT rather than THEM. Once again it looked like the end of participatory democracy because the setting down of statements of agreement between us became regarded as law. Instead of seeing how the game works and acting in a way that optimizes participation in the game, people began to use it as a rigid pattern rather than a growing manual.

We tried to allow an elaborate order that could cover all contingencies. We tried to make it organic but nevertheless ordered. That was our mistake. We didn't remember that the spirit of something is destroyed when it's institutionalized. Our mistake was in thinking we could make a Game Book or any other structure that would take care of the problems. Our mistake was that we really didn't want to have to worry about these decisions once we thought them thought out.

Our mistake was in thinking there's an answer.

Tourist Watching 1984

Quiet at Valley station. Looking up at the arches, at the trees above the skylights and hearing the roar of Yosemite Falls to the north.

Traffic one May afternoon: four main line trains from Merced via El Portal, one four-car local from Tioga Pass and Lee Vining whose clerestory is covered with snow, about a dozen shuttles coming and going and two or three railbuses with National Park Service emblems on their doors.

Merced trains come in quietly, only one bell ringing. People get off with little luggage, most people anyway. Train's still a new thrill for most of them so their excited, alive faces are looking around and in a matter of seconds practically everyone heard, then sees Yosemite Falls.

First ones you see are Three Company employees and park rangers whose steps indicate they have business in the valley. They're usually young, crisper looking and more intent than most of the visitors; they also wear small gold pins with a cloisonné YR, YO or YI in blue, green or red. The packers dress in eminently practical Levis, khakis or corduroys. They stride toward the opening doors of the baggage cars, collect their packs and swing them aboard their shoulders. They walk away briskly adjusting their various straps and belts as well as their perception to what's beyond the platform. Families group, begin to make decisions about where they're going, how to do it, whether to rent a redwagon and where's the john? Some of them comment about the freedom of not having a car. Older folks filter through, intent on strolling around and then returning on the train for early dinner in El Portal. A few of them walk across the platform to a waiting shuttle car, others meander around the platform, mingling with the families, with the huddled people pointing to the huge map of the valley or staring out in the open-ended station arch at Yosemite Falls. They're in no rush, they know they can see the whole universe in a leaf. But nobody hangs out too long: there're no manmade amusements to hold attention. People are here because they want to be in the valley.

The last out of the train--as the drivers step down from their cab and wash the front windows, adjust the headlamps or check the front wheel bearings--are a

few odd ones who haltingly survey the station then walk off as if on some mission of unknown import.

Platform traders have been actively seeking business with alert eyes and low-keyed hawking; their wares are such things as mountain climbing tools, children's flutes made of chinquapin twigs, or fruits and vegetables and other food. Between trains they've walked away for something to drink or relieve themselves or to stroll around or else they've stayed for the latest installment of the day's happenings. Today a group of them questioned the conductor as he was chipping the ice off the couplers of the Lee Vining local, gossiping about snow in May and the dangers of piloting a tiny train through a slot in the high Sierra snowpack.

The Merced train's been still for five minutes and the dispersed comers are being replaced by the congregating departers. Old people gather first, reminiscing about the way it was when they camped in '43 or where they'd parked their RV in '69. They comment on today's lack of exhaust fumes and car noises, the number of birds and wildflowers and little bright things they didn't remember seeing before. Clustering families, children asking when the train is going to start, parents measuring how far apart the campgrounds were and where the old ones were. Or they talk about the discovery of old building sites or highway grades now overgrowing with seedlings. Then the packers stalk in as if proud they can still walk before allowing themselves the relaxation of public transportation. They talk quietly among themselves, usually apart from the families, noting how clean it is, how much fun camping in the valley is once more.

All chaotically begin to board the train, funneling into lines at the end of each car. Many predict how much they're going to see on the way down the canyon, how much more than they saw on the way up. Or mentioning the sound of water, everyone seems to notice the sound of water.

ALL ABOARD! Gates close behind the last, a park ranger hurriedly catches the train on his way home to El Portal for dinner. Brakes hiss and the single bell begins to ring. A shuttle moves off in the opposite direction as a puff of dust is raised by the slowly departing train, now out in the fading sunlight.

OVERHEARD AT WAWONA STATION, SPRING, 1984

"You've just got to be a little neater! It's really very simple. Knowing that I'm going by train makes me consider everything I take. So I tend to bring just what I need, no excess crap. You just pack it all into one or two neat little bags, maybe a backpack. Then when I get to the station, I check it in the baggage car and walk through the train unencumbered. Minute I sit down I feel like I just cut the umbilical cord. The only thing that reminds me of the car is the key in my pocket."

"But when you get there...."

"Yeah, when you get where you're going, you just get off without a thought about the car, about the things you thought you needed. That's so far away, there isn't anything you can do about it. You just get off and walk into...."

113

For comparison with pre-RR traffic patterns

MERCED-EL PORTAL: Seven 10-car trains (14 cab units, 7 dining, 3 observation, 39 coach, 7 baggage): three east-, four westbound. Two eastbound railtrucks (meat and poultry, grains). Two westbound railtrucks (fruit trees, furniture). Railbus (county sheriff) stopped at South Fork. Eastbound railbus (fisherman's special).

EL PORTAL-CRANE FLAT-HODGDON MEADOW: One southbound 6-car local (2 cabs, 3 coaches, one dining, 2 baggage). One 8-car local (2 cab units, 3 coaches, one baggage). chartered by handicapped Las Vegans) stopped at Crane Flat. Northbound railbus (park service ranger) on patrol.

FORESTA JUNCTION-YOSEMITE VALLEY: Railtruck (maintenance on Cascade Creek bridge). Four shuttle cars (one chartered by Sierra Club pack trip group): three north-, one southbound. Two railbuses (regular passenger/mail service): one northbound, one stopped at Foresta Junction. Northbound railbus (park service ranger) on patrol.

CRANE FLAT-LEE VINING: Eastbound 8-car local (2 cab units, 4 coaches, one baggage, one flatcar with portable donkey stables). Shuttle car (circulating Mono Lake loop/Lee Vining). Two shuttle cars westbound, two shuttle cars eastbound. Three railbuses: one east-, two westbound. Two railbuses (park service ranger): one eastbound, one off-track near Sunrise Lake.

TUOLUMNE GROVE BRANCH: One railtruck off rails: maintenance of bathrooms. Two open shuttle cars on tour service.

EL PORTAL-FISH CAMP: Two 8-car locals (4 cab units, 5 coaches, one dining, 3 open observation, 2 baggage, one flatcar with produce container): one east-bound, the other stopped at Pinoche Inn.

BISHOP JUNCTION-YOSEMITE VALLEY: Eight shuttle cars: five north-, three south-bound. Three railbuses: One south-, two northbound. Northbound railbus (park service ranger) off-rail near Chinquapin.

VALLEY STATION-VALLEY SHUTTLE: One 10-car train (2 cab units, 5 coaches, one dining, one observation, one baggage) at station. Two westbound shuttles, two open shuttles eastbound. Two westbound railbuses (park service rangers) on mainline.

GLACIER POINT BRANCH: One railtruck (flatcar carrying rail parts): maintenance at Bridalveil Creek bridge. One shuttle car eastbound, two open shuttle cars: one westbound, one at Glacier Point Lodge.

MARIPOSA GROVE BRANCH: Four open shuttle cars: two east from Sequoia Gate Inn, two west from Mariposa Grove.

MIDPINES BRANCH: Three gravity cars: weekend service for Mariposa residents to Merced river for swimming and fishing.

MERCED FALLS YARD: Eleven flatcars: two under repair. Two open observation cars under construction. Five coaches in storage: two being washed. Six dining cars: four being readied for dinner train, two in storage. Four baggage cars in storage: one being refitted for carrying horses, one having motors replaced. Three railtrucks: one used for gardening, two others for use in yard. Snow-plows in storage.

EL PORTAL YARD: One gravity car being repainted. Two shuttle cars being washed. Two 5-car lodging trains used for overflow guests attending Water and Logging Conference at the Del Portal Hotel. Seven railbuses: one being lubed. Four flatcars loaded with produce in market siding. Fire train (8 cars) idle.

MERCED TRANSFER YARD: Eight flatcars being loaded. Two railtrucks being loaded.

OFF-RAIL/ON-HIGHWAY: One railtruck loading furniture in Groveland. One rail-truck in Mariposa, leased to Sierra Stream Beer for deliveries. Four railbuses two north-, two south on highway 120. Three railbuses westbound on highway 140. Three railbuses northbound on highway 41.

1984

George Orwell
INDEPENDENCE DAY

It started as kind of a joke in recognition that this year didn't turn out the way Orwell predicted. Maybe because he saw it so strongly was why it didn't happen that way.

Anyway we had a picnic up at Little Nellie Falls, about fifty of us who appreciated the joke. It was followed with a tribute by Herb and Marvin Ingersoll who did the CCT program on the effect of Yosemite Park on the Groveland area. They put together a collage of events and happenings since the publication of 1984 in 49 culled from stills, movies, headlines, old tapes and songs, television kinescopes, video tapes and films, CB and CCT tapes, slides from local collections including some shots of the old firefall and things like people in front of station wagons on the old Tioga road. One shot seemed to sum up the whole thing: a 58 Mercury parked at Glacier Point on a startlingly clear afternoon with a blond model sheathed in floor-length black contrasting with the bright yellow car. The legend: "Luxury and Control with Mercury."

During the next days talk returned incessantly to the preponderance of technology in those years. The passage of seasons in the 50s, 60s and 70s was less vivid than the remembrance of favorite machinery. Closer to home was a kind of overall realization of how obsessed we'd become with tools during the Park's reconstruction and now, even though much work was still to be completed, interest had turned toward the wildlife and less in the tools and methods of getting to it. Someone, we don't remember who, suggested a no-machine week following Orwell's birthday and that's when we found out Orwell hadn't known his date of birth in Bengal.

The week required hectic preparation--notifications that there'd be no train service, inns and other services not accepting new visitors and how to slow down with those already there. Generally, Yosemite Park would be on low volume.

Not that you could tell from the parties and get-togethers and celebrations that started it off, but we all had to walk from event to event. The streets in El Portal were full and crowded, and the town took on a Brazilian carnival flavor; sharing with people who hadn't prepared fostered a crazy, let's-throw-everything-in-the-salad spirit. Then things kind of settled down, became quieter, even introspective. There was much sharing of experiences, a kind of sober magic even in places like the Cosmo and up at Andromeda House not usually frequented by locals because they had felt like visitor places.

The biggest revelation was the wildness of Yosemite that seemed to surge over us like a presence we had somehow missed. Despite even the low vibration level we had kept the tech at, its absence made us realize how we'd been locked into the duality of stewarding the land and the tech we used on it. The Ingersolls' program started thought about how machines had dominated our sense of the passing decades, but the week without the railway and the CCTs drove it home. Since birth we'd been caught up in a dialogue with confusion. Planes soaring overhead, cars and trucks and bikes all around, the constant buzz everywhere. The base growl of a culture moving on grinding machinery.

That week we were quiet and open enough to see how this confusion led to confusion about tools, confusion about the environment, confusion about what to do. People afraid of the life they had made, making more machines and pressure and sound to drown out their fear. Machines are a crutch. But a week of independence showed us we could still walk.

Candy Wrapper Stops Train

(El Portal, June 15, 1984) Cassius Gallio, 47, of Saginaw, Michigan stopped service on the Wawona line of the Yosemite Railway for 15 minutes this morning. The passenger was seen by conductor Moqui Q. Saranon throwing a candy wrapper from the platform of the 0810 local to the valley. The conductor later reported that upon observing the action he spoke to Mr Gallio, insisting that the vacationer get off at the next flagstop, return along the track and retrieve his discarded property.

Gallio told reporters later in El Portal that he refused. "I never heard such nonsense in my life! That guy must be crazy!"

Witnesses report that a disagreement broke out between the two men and, as passengers attempted to break it up, the train was stopped.

According to passengers, Conductor Saranon insisted that he would not let the train "budge one millimeter" until the offense was corrected. An argument, or brawl — depending on which witness you talk to — ensued, with an undetermined number of passengers taking part. Finally, at the insistence of the conductor and two other passengers, Gallio was persuaded to walk back and pick up the offending litter. When he returned to the train, service was resumed.

Gallio vociferously threatened to sue both the railway and the conductor. "Why don't they get someone to clean those miserable tracks?" he questioned arbiter Leonora Hepple who met the train in Valley Station. "Why should I have to do their dirty work for them?"

Hepple stated that she countered Gallio's argument by itemizing the cost of services he had used in the Park, showing him where all the money went and then estimating the same cost with clean up and other customizing services added on. The total was more than double what his Tickadisk amounted to. "Nuts," was Gallio's final comment. "I'm not coming back here!"

Almost on Time

Bill and I were walking along one of the creeks that feeds the Tuolumne river. Nice sunny morning. Frost still shivered in the shady spots. Trail wound along the water. Matted earth and green grass, exposed roots from high water and an occasional jumble of piled tree trunks.

Came to a turn, almost a right-angle bend in the creek. Couldn't help noticing that the creek was almost filled--covered really--by four or five firs that'd fallen in from the undercut bank at the outside of the bend. We stood for a moment, just looking at the trees. Bill noticed the soil surrounding the roots. It was soft and crumbly. Small pieces were still falling off into the water.

"Hey, we just missed the sound of five trees falling into that water. By no more than a few hours!"

Yosemite Journal
May 21, 1984

SAWMILL. IT SEES ME

Walked up from El Portal on a half-completed trail that kept crisscrossing Indian Creek. Must be a million Indian Creeks in the United States. Up there to see what I could from the new trail — always wanted to get into this area — and take a look at the inn being constructed at Chinquapin. I carried ten kilos of equipment and by the time I reached the construction site, used to be a ranger station and I think a gas station, I was dripping with sweat.

"Sure go ahead, look around; but you better ask Mike first. He's sort of boss around here. That guy over there, the one in the blue shirt."

I scattered bluejays crossing the work area, smelling green pine and September scents, passing five men in blue or green workshirts. Looking up through the framing, I saw flickering, strobe-like in the sun. Moving faster than I was: it took me a minute to figure out a two-bladed wind generator was fixed on a white granite tower within the light-yellow framing. I stood over near the portable sawmill waiting for Mike to finish shutting the thing down. Blades, wheels, belts, levers, sparks gradually, sporadically, coming to a stop. Slash brushed off the table, dust blown by the breeze in my direction, my eyes squinting to keep the tiny bits out.

"What are you doin' up here anyway? Writin' a book or somethin'?" Mike had turned around.

"You got it. A book on the Park, the railroad, all the changes around here. Nonfiction. The real experience."

Mike brushed the dust off his sleeves. "When's it comin' out?"

"Jesus, I haven't the slightest idea. Pretty far behind original deadline. Enough material here for ten books. But maybe less than a year."

"Listen, you put me in that book and . . . and I'll give you a guided tour," he laughed at the value he put on immortality.

"You're on!"

I didn't even get my pack off before he began to explain the knotty-gritty of the sawmill. I love to interview people like Mike; they do all your work for you, give you the grabbers, underline the jokes and square the Ts. I sort of stood there and taped as he talked. I just agreed, "No, I don't know how that works either." He pointed and explained and made the connections as if I didn't know shit about cutting logs. So I played dumb reporter, letting the questions get more and more basic, questions he probably didn't hear. After just a few minutes in his kindergarten, I had it down about how a four-car sawmill operation worked. Still a remarkable happening, no matter how simply or painstakingly it's explained. You simply pop a log in at one end and the other end spits out all the 2x4s, 2x6s and 2x8s you need at any one time, or any other measure you want.

Mike and his small crew had been building the whole inn out of trees cut right around the site. "You gotta clear an area for the building anyway." They'd cut the trees, skid them to the mill with horses and cut them into the frame-work, all in a matter of weeks. No bulldozers here.

He emphasized how this saved on lumber and transportation costs. I think he'd already been talked at by more avid conservationists: he spoke with a tinge of defensiveness. Since the trees were cut and milled here, they used the whole tree, everything but the needles and cones. "They're used for campfire kindling." Bark would become mulch for the gardens, branches were held out for bannisters and trimming details, heartwood would finish up as interior panels and the rest was cut up for framing members.

Granite for the first floor walls was carried up by railtruck from Pinoche tunnel excavation on the Wawona line. And plaza paving material was made from decomposed granite along one side of the site. The gain from this judicious use of local materials? Only specific mechanical components like door and window hardware, plumbing and electrical supplies had to be brought in from outside. Virtually the entire building sprang from the place, literally and esthetically. I can even imagine it finally slumping, rotting back into the land to continue the cycle.

We got to the center of the building, next to the stone tower that will finally be used as the utility core: pipes, wires and sewage tanks all capped with the still spinning, shining windmill.

"I'm proud of it," Mike said. "It may be the best buildin' I've ever built. Before I was doin' all kinds of small contractin', mostly solar conversion of private houses in the foothills or restorations in the gold towns. Never had the freedom to breathe like we have on this one. 'Stead of being faced with a complete set of strict plans, we were brought in early and consulted on some of the technical things. The designers encouraged us to modify and change things. Results got kind'a direct, but with a kind of rough grace and at least one or two ideas I've never seen anywhere else!"

We walked around to the stone stairs that led to the second floor. Out on the sugar-pine-planked veranda he pointed to the railing between the columns, a series of branches stripped of bark and shined with preservative. He began pulling on the railing, "to make sure the notch connections are tight enough." He looked up at me. "You know, I used to take lumber for granted. I'd just go to the lumberyard and pick out what I needed or fill out a purchase order on the job. I never gave it a second thought. Here," he pointed around the structure, "here I'm involved with pickin' and cuttin' the trees. Even to where I'll find a gnarled old fir about to die and we'll put it out of its misery and into so much flooring, using the twisted grain — that most mills grind up for plastics — for walls. It wasn't long before I started arguin' with the miller, Leroy Johnson," he was pointing in the general direction of the train on the track from El Portal, "when he picked the trees."

We both laughed, and he stood up. "Yeah, I would look at the one he chose, and it was usually a beauty. Leroy has a good eye. And I would say, 'Do we have to cut that one?' And Leroy would laugh and say to me, 'Son, it takes trees to get wood.' And I was the one who used to make jokes about all those crazy tree lovers! I used to think they didn't know anything about wood. Took me awhile to get it into my head I didn't know nothin' 'bout it either."

He pointed to a neatly stacked pile of darker wood near the tracks, small branchlike logs, more delicate and graceful than the pines and oak that were now shelter. "Madrone and scrub oak for furniture, some interior stuff too. Furniture train due here in a couple of weeks, a complete rolling miniature factory. Just like the sawmill here, only different."

He was pointing at me now, tapping his fingers against my open-shirted chest. "In the country 'round here, they cut down forests like so many tooth-picks. You know, bet'cha anything if the people that built things had to cut the lumber or watch it cut, they wouldn't waste it anywhere as much and," his fingers rested on one of my ribs, "neither would those who write books either."

ARCHITECT'S NOTES 1982·84

Hooray! What a revelation. All of a sudden a building without parking lots, without public spaces walled off from street noise, without a designed separation between the building and the way in which you get to it. In Chinquapin the tracks go right through the building within ten meters of rooms where people sleep. Other inns are railway bridges. And instead of parking lots, we can have gardens and green plazas.

It was a matter of specialism. The old way was to segregate lodging space from campgrounds and campers with cars from campers with backpacks and so on. Everyone was divided up into categories relative to their particular preferences. Such a way of relating to the wilderness divided people in the one place where they ought to be communing.

The passing trains will add a whole new dimension to the idea of sitting in the lounge and people-watching. You'll be able to sit there and observe those coming in, getting off the shuttle cars, waiting out on the platform. All without the constant noise that would accompany automobiles.

The site of Chinquapin--where the Glacier Point road turns--was once occupied by a ranger station and gas station. Then it was a straightforward and pragmatic connection of two roads. Now it's a junction of two raillines forming a wye. We've designed the building to accentuate this: the plaza will be shaped to fit within the wye and the building itself will bridge the lightweight line up to Wawona. It will announce the fact of this junction.

We've kind of decentralized the tourist facilities by removing them from the valley and scattering them all over the place. You walk along the Wawona trail and every so often, at convenient intervals, are those little outposts of civilization. The inns are really like diving boards into the wilderness.

The whole garden plan was something I thought strange at first. The idea of gardens in all that wilderness, in Yosemite. Then right in the middle of a meeting Adele said, "Have you ever considered how strange buildings and machines are?" I forgot my qualms about gardens in Yosemite.

A garden fanatic. She helped us lay out the garden plan and it already looks as if it's going to be

a veritable wonder of ecological
sense. On the outer edges of the
site, Adele's planning indigenous
trees and shrubs to prevent people
from casually wandering off into
the woods without respect to trails.
Within that circle will be the wild-
est nut trees and flowering shrubs.
In planters scattered around the
plaza, she's suggesting vegetables
like chard and wild onions be grown
under dwarf fruit trees. Close
under the veranda of the inn, where
they'll help warm the building, are
the tomato and pea vines. And
scattered around the plaza
scattered all around are various
species of wildflowers, so the
strangers will feel right at home.
She hasn't laid out the top floor
greenhouse yet, but I'm sure that
under her hand it'll be seething
with tasteful life.

The use of madrone in the railings
is indicative of the whole style of
the inns. The locally available
wood is naturally shiny, appealing
to the touch. The wire-wrapped and
doweled joints gently creak as the
building heats and cools; it seems
as if alive.

We can economize on materials and
construction costs by placing a few
larger bathrooms down the corridor
instead of providing toilets with
every room. And the central bathing
space can become what no small bathroom could be: sauna and communal
bath as well as the usual private
toilets and showers.

Lighting electricity is generated by
the solarskin augmented by a wind
generator above the building. The
combined electrical output of both
sources is used to light the building directly while a portion is
stored via a hydrogen fuel-cell for
periods of cloudy weather or wind-
less nights. Heated water from the
roof passes down via a central utility tower. It flows around the
chimney of the main fireplace. Then
it's collected in a heat storage
well beneath the building. Temperature differential pumps are used to
recirculate the hot water through
underfloor radiators located throughout the building.

Each inn will include a campground
as part of its accommodations. You
will be able to take a train to the
inn, bring or rent what you need and
camp nearby. For dinner you could
cook at the campground or walk over
to the inn and share dinner at a
table with others. Or you could
stay at the inn, in a single or
double or communal room, and walk
out to the campground for a quiet
evening by a campfire. Or you
could simply pack along the trail,
stopping at an inn only long enough
to do some laundry and have a bite
to eat. Everyone shares the inn,
however different their way of doing
things. It's a station, restaurant,
bathhouse, laundry, social center,
refuge in a storm, place to sleep
and above all a focal point.

The walls and flooring are of sugar
pine available in the immediate vicinity. We can move the railcar
sawmill in and mill it right on
site. The granite will probably
come from a tunnel being built
nearby. And even the furniture
will be built up near Groveland.
All we have to bring into the
region is glass, pipe, wire, cement
and special manufactured fixtures.

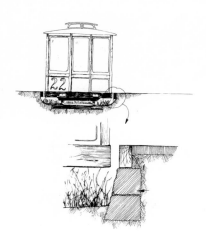

We ended up with a room about 3 by 4 meters, small by American motel standards, but adequate. Each room will have a sliding glass door leading out to a sheltered deck and/or a skylit corridor. In this way the possible claustrophobic effect is offset by the outward views.

The bed is the basic piece of furniture in each room. The headboard shelves store personal items, and two drawers for towels, bedding and luggage are under the bed; the larger drawer can hold a whole open suitcase or pack. Out of sight and out of the way, just open the drawer and there it is. And the bed is high enough to be above the colder air and usable as a seat. The other furniture is a counter along one wall and a single director's chair. A closet is at one end of the counter and a sink with cold running water at the other.

Some critics have called the proposed inns, Chinquapin included, Neo-Regionalistic. It is true that the inns show a return to some old and traditional ideas in the area. But the basic intention was to create simple, economical, pleasant, safe and warm buildings that don't jar the landscape. Early in the preliminary design stages we'd considered many freeform shapes: buildings that were plastic in their expression of function. But we realized after a few months that the buildings themselves weren't the point. What is is the way people feel in them.

Adele suggested we design the greenhouse windows to open outward with the hinge at the bottom. She just loves the idea of a greenhouse being open to the rain.

Rammed earth should be used for paving on the plaza. It's much easier on our legs and spines. Concrete or rock is too hard. Doesn't absorb shocks like earth.

The sprinkler system: rainwater is collected via a system of gutters and downspouts. It goes into the central tank which is also used as the heating water reservoir. Pipes are laid down the halls and along the eaves and peak of the roof. Then, outside and away from the building are five monitors, giant nozzles that can spray water over the whole structure. In a wildfire, we just turn on the water (or it goes on automatically). We figure this would at least minimize damage to the inn if not prevent it entirely. Borate and water bombers are our ace in the hole. But the system should allow people to stay in the inn as the fire passes. Though I don't know if anyone would.

Travel Logged at Chinquapin

Choosing among the inns bringing you nearer day-by-day to John Muir's beloved valley--if you walked in like he did--I decided to start with the best. The inns have so far achieved a European reputation: very simple, very small, but solidly based places, harmonious with the land, comfortable, practical and enjoyable. Not the splash of a Tahoe ski resort or the equally false note of imposed rustic simplicity. This kind of pragmatic hostelry has never been popular in America and the fact that it was apparently flourishing here in the midst of a re-seeding wilderness was a temptation not to be missed in its still formative days.

The world-praised, grade-defying train, plummeting towards the inn, allows just a glimpse or two of the place before you're upon it, comfortably along side it, then headed straight into it as if it were a tunnel. The train slowed and stopped inside, dead within it, swallowed up in it.

The infrastructure like an old-fashioned English Empire station was bathed in diffused light and more like a lobby bisected by cross-ible tracks than a depot. By the time you've gotten your luggage and are beginning to realize you take care of yourself here, you're aware that all along your scurried awkwardness has had the attention of all the sippers in the platform cafe in the chilly spring afternoon.

122

There's no reception desk. After consulting the databoard, you just go to your room where your key is in the door. But after the appropriate few minutes David, of your hosts David and Charles, comes along to see how you're doing and in gentle terms describes the ways of this inn. Even more than the physical plunge inwards, you are now at the core of Chinquapin. If you don't have a reservation or wandered in from the trails, your inquiring energy would I'm sure attract the notice of the hosts, who are all attention. Not that it's necessarily creepy or too much of an anomaly, it's just that they're so relentlessly cheerful, the inn is so much their life, they want you to take advantage of it all, feel comfortable at once, appreciate every last detail immediately. And yes, maybe more than that, maybe begin carrying your share immediately, undertaking right from the start your part of the load.

Let me try to be more specific. Coming directly from Merced, carried along that magnificent river valley by that marvel of unobtrusiveness, catching just a glimpse of El Portal's plateaus, a hint of the changes in the valley, I was confronted with the obvious differences that had taken place. And by the substance of the Yosemite feeling, I think I can safely call it, in those connected with the ride and its mechanism. The intensity of their dedication was almost religious and yet that's an unfair analogy. Charles was painstaking, he was resilient but persistent. How did I find the trip, what was my impression of El Portal, was the elevation comfortable, what did I think of the view, isn't it unbelievable so many facets of this Park used to be taken for granted before?

Before what? Oh, the way things are being seen now. Yes, there's no hot water in any of the rooms, only a cold water tap. Old-fashioned jugs and basins (maybe I'll be able to break ice on the water surface tomorrow morning) make using the baths and accompanying goodies--sauna, steam, hot tub, showers--so much more inviting. There's quite a bit more that can be pooled for everyone when you don't have to separate it out individually.

Some people are taken back at first, not quite used to this approach, especially in so fine a hotel--inn, really only about fifty rooms, that's about one hundred capacity without counting the dormitory accommodations. We can feed nearly three times that number-- "chance," in hotel slang--so it's really working out just as it was planned, that this was the easiest way to make people feel immediately comfortable. All the inns are small--this is the largest category-- the smallest can hold about thirty; each was specifically designed and engineered to its site; no two are alike in form or relation to terrain, but all share the common esthetic derived from using indigenous materials, retaining the qualities of place. The inn owner/managers were encouraged by that diversity to impart their own particular magic, to transform the atmospheres away from the mediocrity of commercial stopovers.

Energy in each structure is derived from particularly local sources, whatever would work best and in conjunction: solar, wind, hydroelectric generation, methane collection and, of course, fireplaces. All share

the independence of being self-sufficient, linked up only through communication and transportation. It is a microcosm, a kind of working
model of what approaches absolute responsiveness to the needs of the
visitors, didn't I see?

I didn't.

Each of the inns has a small core group that operates it, and so
a community feeling based on the core--we like to call it the solar
family--has grown up. Each is of course so different and so individual that people have been known to travel from one to another sampling
the atmospheres ranging from luxury to hostel economy. Much of the
food is local, produce especially is grown in the greenhouses and the
surrounding gardens and arbors. Variety is attained through canning
and freezing, but the old-fashioned quality of the relationship between the land and the food you eat is maintained.

Edifying.

The inns' homeyness is in response to impersonal hotels with their
diminishing corridors of closed doors, extension-cord closets, he called them. You know, places where you begin sucking in your breath in
the elevator, compressing yourself unconsciously so that no part of
you touches anyone else. No, the atmosphere here is quite different,
quite open and liberating, human contact along with wilderness com-
mingling. With so much space outside, so much area to be in and be
alone in, we all seem a bit more able to take more of each other inside.

The smile on Charles' face was still good-humored as the door closed
leaving me in the simple room, almost spartan. But the light and view,
the colors and textures saved the small rectangle from being monastic
or antiseptic. It was merely minimal, a bed large enough for two, a
headboard of shelves. One simple chair, a small closet with suspended
hooks, a wide wall counter that would do nicely for the books and pads
and pencils I set out, tape recorder warming up, typewriter unzipped.
The room does have a kind of swift grace, it looks like me.

The subterranean steaminess was as expected, but the bath's proportions hewn out of the rocks were quite ingenious. I really couldn't
guess how large it was, yet every part of it had an intimacy that
was very pleasant and low-keyed. The hot tub, or series of hot tubs,
not until I was in did I realize there were separations of different
temperatures, was quite inviting, and not scalding--after you were in.

I find having my clothes off in public is only embarrassing
when anyone else is dressed. As well as the thought of it beforehand,
but that's only because I'm still dressed then. The heat and humidity,
the infusion of rest, the congeniality of the well-behaved, un-
aggressive crowd relaxed me. What strange plants they nourished
down here: varieties of fungus and other strange-textured growths--
lichen, algae, puffballs, even mushrooms. Interesting. I'd never
seen many of them before.

I've read so many of your books and articles. We were so thrill-
ed to hear you were here. And then to see you down here just like
everyone else.

Not like <u>every</u>one else, I hope.

Are you writing about this place?

No, I am not. I'm here because I go places... like everyone else. Besides, what would I write about here?

The crowd thinned and those remaining took on a Bonnard glow, steamed flesh reflecting the delicate hues of the underworld. I would be late for dinner but I settled in another, shallower nook and dozed some more. It didn't really matter, I addressed a Calvatia gigantea.

Dinner was set up in the greenhouse. Not the tropical, moisture-drenched variety beloved by botanical gardens and municipal conservatories, but rather a waist-high display of a highly motivated kitchen garden, Sissinghurst gone California. Tables were arranged in a single line down the two aisles. Charles continued to be solicitous. I guessed David was in the kitchen.

Did I have any objections about sitting near the onion family?

Only olfactory.

But did I really like reading at dinner or would I prefer company? Which would be more comfortable? I winced at the word, but found I had to think about what he was suggesting. Face-saving won out, of course, and I dined in splendid isolation among the scallions and shallots and swamp onions. I began to have a peculiar feeling, what with the things I usually eat so heedlessly growing at my eye level. The more I thought about this interesting new feeling, the more the possibilities grew into perverse analogies: mouth-watering steakhouses clustered around the Chicago stockyards, a frozen-foods store at Donner Pass, a barbecue stand in front of the Colosseum. I didn't feel revulsion when my salad was served before the entree, as they always do in California, but I do remember eating the croutons staring down the buckwheat growing in the corner.

The Michelin guide could recommend a detour for their food alone. The trout--golden, keep it secret that this variety is superior to the rainbow--was fresh and done to a succulent turn. The rest of the meal was simple, unfrilled by glossy gimmicks or the never-ending tendency to turn everything into the French bourgeoise cuisine. Casual, painstaking, the elegance of thought and preparation. I wondered what the lobby cafe was like as I sipped coffee and tried to overhear the neighboring conversations, my book open in front of me.

But then David emerged from the kitchen and involved me in conversation. Actually it was quite a pleasure even though I must be
honest, I felt I was a subject to be worked on for some purpose.
It was the insistence that I didn't quite understand, as if I were
some great catch they had to hook, almost like the hybrid trout. It
wasn't as if anything were stressed beyond the normal regard for a
guest's welfare, but what was it? The intensity underlining the surface innocuousness of the conversation? The tone behind the sentiments?
And admitting my own paranoia like this, isn't that a sign of ration-
ality on the subject?

I wandered about later looking at the sparse pickings, no real
nightlife, no bar--they served only beer and wine I remember David, or
was it Charles, say. Guests were in bed or out in the icy moonlight.
I didn't think I would like to be out there in the wilderness at
night. Too alien.

So in solitary parade, I retreated to a nook near the south side
recommended by Charles, and with a sollight supplementing what the
moon was sending down in teasespoons, I wrote a reverie I think of as
"Still," the first instance of the Muse's spontaneous company in more
time than I care to admit.

I got up to the accompaniment of violent, short-lived thunder-
showers and got in two hours of serious writing. Downstairs I watched the other eaters and then a shuttle train down from Fish Camp:
only one passenger and her entrance was neither confused nor awkward.
I decided to explore, but not before David was considerately marking
out the best route for my purpose--maddeningly they assume they know
more than I about what I'm doing--and packed a lunch knapsack, map,
an annotated Chang (CHinquapin Area Nature Guide) and still left me
room for pad, pencils, sharpener, recorder and compass. I was off in
the general direction of the snow on Glacier Point about four hours
away and really too far for a comfortable day's walk and back. I
thanked David for his observations and started off through the crunch
of the morning's robustly striding newcomers.

A steep climb along Indian Creek trail paralleling the cascading
white course, stopping to examine the peculiar upshoot of magenta
thumb-sized plants punctuating the forest floor. They suggested blood
beneath the pine needles.

I stopped on the peak of Henness Ridge where I could barely make
out the notch that was Chinquapin. Between the pines the distant, lower
peaks rose blue and purple in mists left by the morning rains. Hundreds
of ridges trailing down to the intersection of the Merced's middle and
south forks. North, one white cloud hanging motionless over a tremendous gap pointed out the valley. Cool contrast to the snow-covered icy
peaks beyond. I couldn't see Half Dome or El Capitan or the others,
but there was a distinct feeling as if walking within proximity of a
massive cathedral, the feeling that a presence was near.

*This place. It speaks for itself. Don't they
know that? Why are they speaking for it?*

This place. It speaks for itself. Don't they know that? Why are
they speaking for it?

I stopped on my trek back down Henness Ridge, taking a moment to
look over Chinquapin in the fading, brilliant, dry Sierra light. The
inn's three-pronged star shape was a functional wye intersecting the
line from El Portal and Fish Camp with a lightweight branch to Glacier
and down the valley. The solarskin roofs reflected intricacies of incense cedar, yellow pine and a single old red fir; the steep pitch
showed green below, white, gold, copper above: the lowering sun.
The longest wing looked lost, dropping down the steep ridge and pointing
toward the coast range. Do the panels reflect that pure light back
across half the state of California?

The building fitted the contour of the site like a triped insect
radiating webs out of three sides. That may also be unfair, but that's
what it looked like. The heavily vegetated area perimetered the inn,
its domestic order made me realize I was leaving wilderness. I was
tired but mellow when not four or five meters from me, three shuttlecars swooshed through, an essentially plastic noise for so solid an
assault. The Doppler effect gone psychephonic. Then it is gone,
leaving you in an empty space. I had to veer off to examine its
silvery wake less than a few centimeters above the ground. When you're
upon it, there's no mistaking it. But just the littlest bit away and
the track doesn't exist. How strange it is, silently lying there, not
raised on its own bed like old-fashioned rail or shouldered and tarred
like highways. Just there pillared on the ground in the midst of
plants and weeds growing all around and in between it like some in-
explicable ruin that has come to terms with nature.

I wonder what the animals make of it.

The warmest spot inside Chinquapin's shell was a sort of sunken
section warmed by a well-constructed fire. I deposited my burden and
crossed the floor for something to drink thinking about refusing
David's offer of his private stock of brandy last night.

Well, a half liter of mulled wine would do just fine until I take
another hot tub. The area's so fresh, clean trails and markers, no
litter, no signs of human indifference, bright people hopping back and
forth, obviously enjoying. Everyone talks to one another on trails,
yet back in human habitation they're afraid to. Maybe human-designed
environments are basically harmful to our appreciation of one another.

And yet this strange rail depot was designed by man. It doesn't
have that proud separation from nature designers delude each other into
producing. There's something intensely intriguing about airports and
bus depots and train stations. Maybe it's the numbers traveling together
that raises these places above the chaos of even the busiest parking
lot. To build a station apart and have no other activity there is to
lose another level of life's complexity and vitality.

And what do you think of this place?

What do I think of this place? A whole lot less for all the people asking me what I think about this place. But she looked too interesting for my attitude hovering between gut truth and rudeness. Care for some wine? It's quite good. I'll get another glass.

I'm interested to know what a man of your background, your experience would make of all this. You know your presence here hasn't gone unnoticed. David and Charles are very proud you're here.

No, I'm a visitor like you. Oh, of course. I'm sorry. I saw you at breakfast this morning. You were drinking chocolate. Tell me, do you really care about what I think of this place or were you... being polite?

Now you're being polite. I came up here because I wanted to see the last of winter as well as what's happened here. I really have no ulterior motive, although I keep finding myself having to deny I do.

Are you really surprised people assume you've come to write about this place? And maybe misunderstand it or rather judge too quickly, make it come out looking like a ladies' tearoom or some kind of simple-minded mountain spa.

Is that what you think then?

No, of course not. I just hope you understand. I've been coming here often, once in the autumn when the trees reminded me of Vermont, but not quite dazzling enough, an ironic comment for exotic California. I love what's happened here. I came up on the inaugural ride, and the special quality for me is that it hasn't diminished. Every place else seems decaying and deteriorating. And I wanted to find out what you think and mostly, to be honest, what you're going to do about it.

Do about it? What are you talking about? I don't even know what I think, much less whether I have any intentions whatever. And why should it be so important what I feel about it? Frankly I feel un-comfortable here. When everyone else is talking about comfort, I feel ill-at-ease.

It is different here, a separate pace and style.

I know; it's a case of new energy, a new way of looking at things and I haven't got my glasses on straight despite all the cheering and encouragement for me to look sharp. I may be stating it too strongly, but I don't make the connections about this place that everyone else seems to. I can see where it's pleasant and, yes, even comfortable; but that's hardly relevant. Any break from the usual modes of living acquires a feeling that's very seductive, very liberating. You can say the same things about places as harsh as Las Vegas and Miami Beach!

Any break from the usual modes of living acquires a feeling that's very seductive, very liberating.

And you believe that's true here?

It has a never-never-land quality that's just the sort of thing that people with the best of motives tend to overreact to. They exaggerate the positive virtues and denigrate everything else to raise it above criticism, more and more an answer to a question that's never posed. And there are many positive values here, I'm not insensitive to them. I just feel familiar enough with that pattern to warn someone like you--and David and Charles too, but they seem to be beyond warning-- to enjoy yourself and bask in the comfort that's so essential to your equilibrium, but don't delude yourself that it's anything more than that. It's just another way.

We both stared into the fire. A train from El Portal pulled in to our space almost without noise. Was I beginning to differentiate between driving styles? I arrived yesterday at this time. One day? What is time really? I watched people get on and off, some determined, some confused, some without any visible clues at all. And as she watched, I watched her. Only one person got off on our side and he, as soon as the train had glided out, moved across the tracks, over the platform, past the cafe and through the doors. We were the only ones left outside in front of the fire I had to feed once again before staring at the empty carafe.

You know we all have real feelings of self-determination. That we can in various ways perform actions and move the universe. That we are the doers. America is the living example of what we have achieved. It is the model of civilization. Other countries imitate our power, our technology, even in our style.

In how many generations did we take essentially raw wilderness and domesticate it, mold it into our image of what we wanted collectively? And only when that reached the level of sterility we have now arrived at, are we able to see that what we created was not at all flattering. Here, I understand perfectly well, what is being tried is the relaxation of our hold on our environment.

Ambrose Cappela

WRITERS FORUM
Spring 85

*Excerpts of the History of the CCT
as presented at Community Views Conference
Atlantic City 1985*

At first there was the negative reaction there usually is when anything new appears: how come this relatively small group, the few hundred who were working Yosemite, were now using television in a way never tried before?

It became apparent that what had been the exclusive dream of sci-fi writers was emerging — weirdly perhaps, but then what isn't? — as a tangible reality. Electronic democracy, on a limited scale, evolving not out of deep philosophical reflection, but ironically out of another consumer toy.

Citizen Channel Television follows the social principles of CB radios, that is, multichanneled, two-way communication using screens that receive and transmit. However, unlike CB radios the CCT's signal is not transmitted chaotically through the atmosphere. That was found to be both confusing to living beings within the signal area and too static-ridden for precise transmission. Instead, CCT signals are transmitted on laser beams through fiber optics which also carry telephone, datalink and conventional radio transmission. The one centimeter diameter transmission lighttubes roughly parallel and are often integrated with YR track.

The network is composed of around 2000 regular contributors who each have a locally modified version of the nationally available Trion wall-screen set, in either the 60 x 90 x 3 cm regular or the more portable 30 x 45 model. Modification of the sets is handled by a group of electronics wizards calling themselves Goldline Inc. who're located on the grounds of an old gold mine near Chinese Camp. They devised an ingenious device that allows images and sounds to be channeled and programmed by users; there is no central station. Called a Holintegrator, it's little more than a typical pocket computer; the secret is in the makeup of components and organization of the self-modifying program keyed to individual communities.

The Holintegrator keeps track of the telephonelike codes that plug the user into the network, dial a friend or friends, a team, community or even the whole network. It modulates image and volume automatically based on a series of logic memories; a typical one is geographic sensing where the volume of the various images adjusts to the sequence of distance from the viewer. The most important function of the Holintegrator is integration of the 72 channels and the range of viewer-modulated size and sound changes; you can also manually make any image larger or smaller, louder or softer. And data recorded in an optional bank can be retrieved if the viewer requests it.

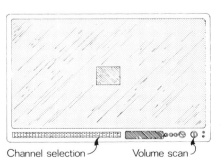

Channel selection   Volume scan

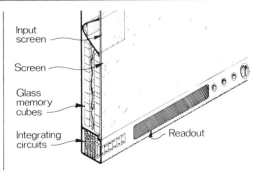

Input screen

Screen

Glass memory cubes

Integrating circuits

Readout

The 72 channels are confusing at first, since the screen can radiate one to 72 images at any one time, with a conceivable total of four or five hundred people talking and acting at once. The multiple images can be ordered as simply as a checkerboard or as randomly as a kaleidoscope. After a while you begin to focus in this psychedelic dimension. Looking at all those images is like seeing at once a cross-section of this region.

You're liable to run across everything from technical discussions to arguments over chipmunk species to reviews of the latest events like the visit of a dance company or an archaeological digs. Or it could be a visiting kayaker describing his white water, a biologist demonstrating technical species cloning, a home movie trip to Mexico, an El Portal town meeting or a discussion of a problem relating to everyone in the Park. You could even see the meeting splinter into five submeetings only to coalesce minutes or hours later into the original forum. Everyone talking, interrupting, dozing and even some listening as they would in any live meeting. It can show people arguing bitterly, even flipping fingers over that innocent screen; but it adds up to a community that seems to know itself, even thinking together, if not alike. The common reference point is this land. The communication inevitably comes back to how it's working "out there."

DOINGS

Unlike the anonymity of the old radio fad that just smoked out too many hams, the sight dimension of CCT acts as a kind of ballast, lending gravity to these spontaneous ad lib encounters. The use of the medium is, of course, open ended, coming up with excitingly real as well as a lot of tedious viewing. Contributors include the residents of the region between Merced and Lee Vining and Mariposa and Groveland — the greater Yosemite Park community — as well as visitors kibitzing and contributing. We've even involved people as far north as Angels Camp. They don't participate often in our decisions, but they're sure interested in our way of doing things. Seems there's a real native response to our updated version of community sovereignty.

Not that there wasn't hostility from some surrounding communities. Particularly towns like Oakdale where money had been made from the tourists driving to Yosemite. Even though they included themselves in the regional economic reorganization that preceded the railway's operation, they still felt resentment towards the "elitists" and "washed-up hippies" who had cut off their business. When CCT started it only aggravated the hostility by showing off the Park's workings and begging the obvious comparison with the nonworkings of surrounding communities. The implications of the project became frightening to a lot of those people. Here was a community among them that was truly governing itself; a community that no longer needed an outside THEM.

El Portal's got a CCT in practically every house. They're in bars from Mammoth Mountain — where the LA ski bums must look in disbelief at our activities — to sleazy saloons in Atwater, Merced and Sonora. When the residents of Sonora couldn't get the signal from their own cable company, they paid for a special cable connection. The royalties provide part of our outside income, but more importantly, point out the growing curiosity about what's going on here.

All the inns have at least one CCT and the innkeepers have been encouraging visitors to voice criticism — and praise — and questions and ideas and reactions. People involved in a project like Yosemite Park begin to get a little rarefied in their ivory tower. So much of it is so different from anything else going on around this country, they tend to forget that the whole thing is open to the view of the three million who come here. And they're the ones ultimately whom this whole thing is for. The overwhelming response revealed just how well the CCTs have worked. Many visitors encouraged by the CCT's accessibility have constructively criticized or contributed to the community. And among the locals, contributions have come not just from the loudmouths you'd expect, but also from the people whose opinions would never be overheard or found in the Letters to the Editor.

TYPICAL IMAGE ARRANGEMENTS

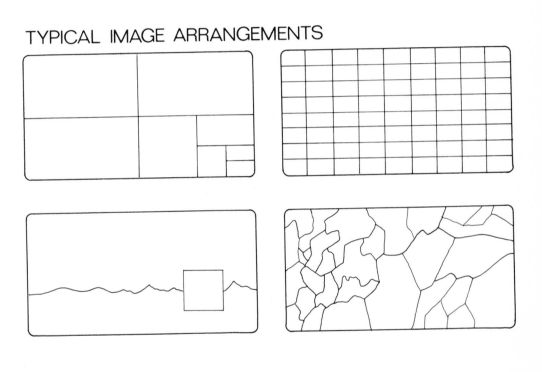

That's what it is, a kind of moving, anonymous, inquiring photographer directed by the desires of a whole community eliciting real, immediate, unedited responses and gut reactions. People telling everyone how well they like what's here, how beautiful and clean it all is, the encounter they had yesterday with a hungry black bear, visitors carrying on real communication with workers about various ways of approaching a specific task, and dozens of fleeting exchanges about the day-to-day trivialities we all love to share.

The general lack of interest up here in the four national networks' programming — despite how concerned the networks seem to be by their increasing number of documentaries about the planet's pressing problems — has caused some protest from network leaders who see the CCT's success as a threat. They want television to remain a spectator medium, a visual drug.

SHOWINGS

The CCTs began to evolve a feeling of their own at once. People got caught up communicating to one another in the weirdest ways — ski masks had a revival that year — but there wasn't the fear usually associated with commercial television in untrained hands. Perhaps because it was so local, people felt they could play with it. For months there were line parties, local comedians trying out material and all kinds of general clowning. In time everyone but the adolescents got over that phase and learned how to use the new tool in the process.

The play still went on, still does, but more and more there were things like Joel DeLucca down in Merced Falls explaining how the wheels on certain shuttle cars were wearing out too fast — and he showed them and explained the wear and fatigue factors. Simultaneously someone somehow contributed a video tape of squealing shuttle cars rounding Foresta curves. He narrowed the discussion down to the drivers he knew were taking corners too fast, at least two of whom were watching and immediately plugged in, one defensive, one curious. Joel verbally collared them, accompanied by the applause of some viewers, and went into a tirade about precisely how much it will cost in spare parts and labor should they accept responsibility, and if they didn't how much it would cost everyone — some booing accompanied that one. The drivers argued with his evidence. People not directly involved kidded and questioned them and finally they all convinced Joel to do a little more investigating and report back in a week or so. In the meantime the two drivers along with the three others implicated went down to Joel's and checked the evidence first hand. Joel's update included comments by the five drivers who all had agreed to be responsible for the excess wear on their wheels and — with a road racer's gleam in a few eyes — agreed to curb their speed.

The Ticket Accounting team preferred a regularly scheduled time to air their reports and problems. But even they learned how to make figures interesting. They use a computer databoard illustrating how money was coming in and going out — and even staying around, but it rarely does that. They are able to use their computers to make projections about every last little figure. Lately they've been making month-by-month projections detailing the money flow to the point where many people have become fascinated with the patterns and what they all too accurately reflect. Generally they've succeeded in teaching how money is a very precise indicator of value; in that sense it's one of our most honest forms of communication.

All the teams in Yosemite report on the CCTs what they're doing or not doing about every four to six weeks. Most of them don't take five minutes, but it sure is nice to follow the ones you get interested in and you'd be surprised how many of them you begin to listen to and keep abreast of not only on CCT, but out in the Park itself. Sometimes the driest report can evolve into the most fascinating dramas.

Recently there was a debate about whether to build another inn on the Crane Flat line. The other inns in the area were consistently overflowing with guests. The original estimate of demand on that area was wrong. But there was the basic question of growth. Could we let another structure be erected in such a potentially sensitive environment? Would this be a replay of the same scenario that went on in the valley and began this whole thing?

Nobody was sure, not even the people who raised the question. The inn teams in the area got together — I think there were six of them — and did an incredible job compiling information and generally commenting on a situation they see every day. They explained how if the new inn were built the two immediately down the line towards the valley would lose business, that it might overload the Crane Trail — a people-traffic maximum was defined to maintain deer migration across the trail and down to Big Meadow — and they expressed concern about whether this would be an exceptional addition or the continuation of the old growth habit. All other CCT communication faded out and this question became the meeting of the night with questions directed at the inn teams for hours. It turned into a real marathon — spontaneously and in response to a real problem.

The idea was too complicated to decide at once. It was resolved to shelve the issue for about a month. One of our famous tabling decisions.

This gave everyone a cooling-off period, and since it was June the opportunity of watching the Crane Flat line and the inns at their peak time. The CCTs buzzed the whole time with what people were seeing and saying, people panning their tiny CCTs over paths around Crane Flat and showing visitor density compared, for example, to areas around White Wolf or Chinquapin or the valley. Even a regular visitor got involved. Nancy Hawxhurst did an impromptu study of the deer situation by spending two weeks crisscrossing the area studying scat, hoofprints and actually following deer. She concluded that as long as the inn was located in a certain old highway cut, it wouldn't disrupt the deer. And everyone else seemed to agree there was need of more accommodations up there, and it didn't look as if the load could be shifted someplace else nor did it appear that a new inn would seriously damage the land. But did we have the money?

The accounting team was happy to work on that one. Everyone tuned back the CCTs for their summary. They constructed nine projections and explained each one down to the last decimal. Based on the previous and current performance of the other Crane Flat line inns, a loan for a new one could be had with the lowest interest rates. The next step, as spelled out in the Game Book, was calling in Overview to work out the potential advantages and disadvantages of a new inn relative to the railway, gardens and long-term wilderness health. Within a week they were on the CCT and reported that even with the necessary trade-offs — slight increase in shuttle traffic, two backpack camps becoming inn camps — the project was acceptable. They recommended a small inn, holding about thirty and acting as an overflow for the others down the line.

For reasons of expediency and because the new inn was being constructed out of phase with the others, a local architect/contractor group was contacted directly rather than using the competitive bidding style of the main construction work. They'd built two inns that bridged the railway, allowing animals to cross the gap on sod-covered roofs. The new inn would fill a third old highway cut just up the line from the other two.

Two weeks later — can you believe it? — the preliminary plans were shown over CCT. As usual there was great involvement with details, many using light pens to draw variations on their screens' images of plans, elevations and perspectives laid over full color images of the place. After earlier, similar work on structures in El Portal devotees were so practiced at this technique it only took a few hours to integrate the dozen or so changes, and get the majority compromise needed. The vote took place two days later; in turn, the jurisdiction shifted to the Yosemite Inns company.

Less than two months had passed and the proposed inn had gone from a hazy solution of a common problem to the beginning of working drawings. And those involved, that is anyone interested in being involved, in the discussions and the decision-making felt they had completed the process. The game was working.

One of the funny things that's happened is that the town meetings that used to be so popular and well-attended became less and less so in direct proportion to CCT use. That proved to be a little discouraging when the CCTs transmitted images of dwindling audiences. Then, spontaneously, people discovered that the town meeting regulars were watching on the CCT as well as a number of folks who had never come. Even visitors tuned in. So it was agreed that the town meetings needn't be in the Visitor Center's meeting hall every Thursday night, they could be held around the Park depending on season or a particular regional problem on the agenda. The meetings have become less tense and boring than the meeting hall events and there isn't the logistics hassle of everyone trying to be at a certain place at a certain time. Rarely is there the feeling that we'd better get the business over because it's getting late. People contribute to the meetings with the assumption that if it's important enough we'll simply schedule another meeting or carry it to the next scheduled one. This lack of urgency and false importance that used to characterize the town meetings has had the effect of diffusing the "issues" and allowing people to get to know one another.

MUSINGS

Not that the CCT works well all the time. There's a lot of meaningless communication going on, a lot of stuff over channels that could be put to better use. And there are a lot of people — tube boobs — who use the CCT to air their petty grievances and frustration, over and over again. But they defeat their own purpose quickly. People get to know who and what they are quickly enough and their credibility — if you'll excuse so nostalgic a word — evaporates: they're turned off. And then there are those who feel they have to expend a lot of listening and watching energy to keep up with all the things going on. We do try to schedule the formal voting and discussion parts of it around dinner time, when most people tend to be at home. But to those who still gripe, we do have an unbeatable answer, as true today as when it was spoken during the setting up of another game: "the price of liberty is eternal vigilance."

Our fluency with a tool so long around but only now helping us reach our potential has spawned awareness of the earlier, more tedious games. CCT is fast, clean of confusing bureaucratic roadblocks, immediately a part of practically everyone's life and — frighteningly at times — factually cold-blooded.

Lately the Game Book revisions have occupied the more organization-minded among us for four evenings in a row. Seeing that discussion on a few channels has reminded many of us of our past groping for some way we'd all think alike and avoid conflict. The Game Book grew from that time and it still represents most of our agreements. But now it's a living document being constantly changed — never final.

CCT has undoubtedly helped us function above community or geographical differences as one large animal might. Now everyone wonders if one day we won't need any electronic tool, we'll just know.

the interest in LOCAL CAPITALISM

This caught our eye from the pages of the *Foothills Fancier*, one of the most respected practitioners of grass roots journalism:

"Five years ago when the project began in earnest, there were only twenty people working down near Coulterville. As little as a year later, that number had tripled. Another year and it reached one hundred. What with the nearly one thousand people working on the railway, the inns and the other Yosemite services, this becomes a lot of folks for this region to absorb without losing its identity or integrity. But that's precisely what it's done."

So we started looking for other examples of this resurgence in local industry and community commerce near the area of Yosemite Park. What we discovered was that this boom — even though it can't be measured by that kind of dollar volume — consisted of innovative businesses that have taken advantage of new ways and products as well as established business services. We've been so encouraged by what we discovered over the past few weeks about this rialto renaissance in the Sierra that we thought we'd present what we culled in the words and ways the local media told it.

"This operation prevents damage to trees that were torn and bruised when felled, and also allows the whole tree to be transported to the mill. Branches and needles and other previously lost components have increasing value as organic fertilizing agents. The whole operation is thus practical and profitable."

The ship, constructed by the Phoenix Balloon Works of Phoenix, Arizona, is the prototype model for a number of other dirigibles being considered by lumber companies in Canada, the eastern United States and parts of Asia. The Wawona Wilderness Labs was instrumental in the research and development phases of this lumber management operation, pointing out, Armstrong concluded, "that the purpose of the environment study group is not limited to idealistic philanthropies in National Parks, but the rugged, down-to-earth problems of people making a living in the living world."

FRESNO FREE FARMER
Midpines, California, February 22, 1985

HELIUM LOGGING TREES IN THE AIR

The Yosemite Sugar Pine Lumber Company announced the successful testing of its prototype logging dirigible.

The lighter-than-air craft is capable of removing timber trees without the damage and waste of conventional logging and hauling methods.

Captain and company spokesman, George C. Armstrong, described the operation in these words: "The dirigible is constructed to hover over a section of target trees, allowing individual selection to be made. A cable is lowered from the balloon to the 'topper,' the man in the tree, who attaches it securely to the tree. The moment the base is cut through, the cable is tautened, pulling the tree up. The dirigible is capable of towing from one to ten full-size trees to the lumber mill economically and safely.

MARIPOSA MEDIATOR
Mariposa, California, March 2, 1985

SIERRA STREAM BEER BUST

The Sierra Stream Beer Company of Mariposa celebrated its third year of operation by holding a picnic/barbecue and beer drinking contest yesterday for employees, friends, town residents and employees of Yosemite Park.

"Well, you have to do something to show your appreciation," bubbled Mike Hennessey, president of the West's newest and fastest growing local lager producer. "You see when the railway was built, why Mariposa was just cut out of all the local car through traffic. But that didn't mean that the railway folks just said, 'Too bad.'

"We had this idea about beer. What with our water here, grain and malt from Fresno, hops from Healdsburg, why it was a natural for a revival of local capitalism. It just never had happened, see?

"The railway was under construction and they needed all the time and money they could get, but they took the trouble to help us organize, get us loans and such and a lot of technological knowledge and leads from some of the people now in the Wawona Wilderness Labs. Take the gelatin containers, why we couldn't have firmed up the technology for that one without their help. It was just a gimmick of course, but look what it has led to!

"Then they were the first to offer our beer — at their inns, on the trains. So we had two million customers coming to us! When these people began asking for it at home, we were able to get off the ground in distribution quickly, while maintaining our original quality. So that other company in Mendocino County had better watch its hops. I tell you it's been so good for us, we could float a few loans back to Yosemite — if they needed it — right on a barrel of our beer!"

Mrs. Herman J Scyleran, who runs a gas station in Mariposa, won the beer drinking event by consuming 27 cans in the hour-long event. "Even if I didn't win," Sudsie, as she likes to be called, later said after a short nap, "I could melt down the containers and use them in aspic. Herman doesn't drink, but he sure likes the containers."

THE NEW CALIFORNIA MAGAZINE
March 13, 1985

Talk Of The State

Yesterday we put on our hiking boots to visit Fred Murchison's tool maintenance shop in Fish Camp, near the southern entrance into Yosemite Park. Originally this repair shop was a rail/machine maintenance depot for the Yosemite Railway, but now it simply shares some of its facilities with a light service shop run by the YR.

Not until we stepped up to the madrone-railed porch and were engulfed in Murchison's rough but hearty handshake did we hear any of the sounds we expected from such an operation.

Pointing to a collection of random objects looking more like preying mantises, half-size caterpillars and other mechanized insects than objects of utility and production, "we had a real problem with the garden tools to begin with. Most of the gardens and orchards approaching the Park began as hobbies or leisure exercises. And the inn gardens and greenhouses were designed originally as kitchen gardens to supply their own needs. Adequate equipment was rare and supplying all the inns with some kind of standardized equipment went beyond the budget, just wasn't in the original plans. And everyone it seemed wanted what tools we had all at the same time, and that's when they went bad, just when they were needed.

"Take hand tools. Nine times out of a dozen it's the handle that breaks. So instead of replacing it with another built by a machine that never held a human hand, we started carving new ones, when we had the time, out of maple and oak. And as soon as a few of those got out and around, danged if everybody with a loose trowel or a cracked clipper wasn't pounding on our door to get a custom handle that fit the human fist, could be held a couple of different ways and looked just fine besides. Just because a tool's meant to be worked in the soil doesn't mean it can't be a precision instrument you can be proud of!

"As a matter of fact, I've more or less got a brand-new hobby, the repair of in-stream hydroelectric generators that provide a portion of the electric power to a local area without disrupting the stream or its life. You may not know it, but I'm kind of a fishing buff myself. Got a call from BC about giving 'em some advice on a project. I guess I can make it in time for the salmon run.

"In the beginning we did the best we could. We weren't quite so inundated with volunteers like we are now. George Anderson came up with the idea of the tool inventory, a central index of everything that was in the Park and where it was. Then when something had to be fixed and we couldn't get to it

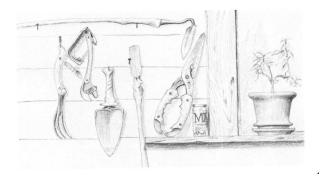

immediately, there was the distinct possibility that a replacement could be borrowed from somewhere else. The railway really cooperated on that one, becoming the best parcel post unit ever and always checking in with him to keep his clipboard and printout together. Not that George was reluctant to track down over-due tools himself using the CCT," he chuckled once more.

Fred Murchison who stands over two hundred centimeters and has twinkling brown eyes in a wrinkled, perpetually tanned face was born in Grand Rapids, Michigan on January 8, 1912 and started as a stoker for the Illinois Central Railroad in 1928 before becoming an apprentice machinist for the Reading Railroad and machinist with the Southern Pacific Railroad and International Harvester Company.

"After I retired — at the union's urging — I realized of course that they could subdivide my job so two men could be supported by the work; and there really was no denying I had achieved what they called security, but dang, that's what they were saying life was about and not what I say at all!

"Anyway an old crony of mine, Bill Jenkins, sort of a helper at one time, was going to organize and manage the Pohono Inn — you know even to design consulting and all the rest of the innovative things that were going on around here — so I just came out to take a gander, got to hanging around and tinkering just as I always do, and one thing leading to another, they began parking their iron elephants at my door, and before you knowed it the railway people asked if I could develop a grease stop at El Portal or some other place outside the Park. But I told 'em I had to be here where it was happening, right on the edge of the Park, and I guess they bought it because they let me design the shop here the way I thought it should be. And those others thought they had pensioned me

off to LeisureLand or some other death's waiting room!

"You can see what I did: how clean and light it is here even if what's scattered 'round here looks like every other reconverted Model T garage shop. And when we stopped working for the railway, they were real nice about letting us stay here; did some adding over to that side — there used to be a porch on that side too — and I help 'em a bit with light repair when things get a bit rough. Not as much as I'd like though. Must remember to tell Agnes about the Wawona shuttle grip.

"I'm kind of crazy I guess. I really look at machines and tools and see them as kind of special, individuals — things with rhythms and quirks and personalities," he continued walking us around showing us specimens like a chief gardener in a conservatory showing a ladies garden club what they weren't prepared to believe. "You have to put yourself inside to find out what the problem is. Like everything else, it's part experience, part intuition, but all involvement. Not that I'm exactly running a Mr Wizard shop where everything carried in will move out under its own steam. But you've got to face it, all machinery needs maintenance, which in some cases after being banged 'round and mangled awhile requires more contortions than ever creased the engineering head that designed it in the first place! Sometimes I can figure out shortcuts that bypass and get rid of those Rube-Goldberg-circuits believers in specialization insist on. And to think those guys get money for some of their deformities!

"But the best part of all this is that I'm able to teach this kind of madness to people who come up here because they're interested in the wilderness and some of the things that can keep it wilderness. Not to be high fallutin' about it or anything, but it really is to me like some kind of Renaissance workshop actually discovering connections between machines and land and people that haven't been plotted out before."

The skylights and airy, clean areas emphasized the noise and jocular activities of the dozen or so disciples, "the freight train of help" who are here to share Fred Murchison's art of poking, picking, prodding, probing, connecting, disengaging, testing, up-ending, clinking, rubbing and generally listening to the heartbeat — no matter how faint — of what they're repairing.

"Generally I start 'em off on what I call personal tools: crescent and socket wrenches, screwdrivers, even some of my old fishing reels, and then move 'em on to more elaborate examples, more detailed but still basic components of our tech. There really seems to develop a true craft feeling in most of the budding mechanics 'bout what they're doing. Not that I'm kidding myself or anything, this may not be a real craft workshop, but a tradition is being developed here and being handed down personally. And what better place for this kind of live passing down of what really makes up our culture than here?"

MANAGEMENT PROBLEMS

"How the hell did you people do all this in such a short time?" The emphasis was on "how," but the amazed expression on his face punctuated the whole question.

Debbie was working on the axle bearing of a railtruck, struggling with the damn thing, trying to get the rubber boot off. She looked up because he startled her, but after that she just kept looking. Why was something she took for granted--and that most people up here do too-- such a big deal to him? And to so many others as well?

And how can you explain something as simple as rhythm, the weaving of what you have to do with the way you are going to do it? You do the THING THAT DEMANDS THE MOST CONCENTRATION thing that demands the most concentration, and you get tired. Instead of continuing or doing something else equally as demanding, you shift to something simpler, something that doesn't require a lot of head time. While you're doing that, you can think about what you're doing and how it relates to the whole pattern as well as the next stitch. It's sort of rhythmic concentration.

"We follow our feelings up here. There's a certain amount of self-discipline involved, but mostly it's that we enjoy our work. And it's easy to slide from one job to another, keeping it all going like some fancy juggling act."

He asked her to be more explicit, and she told him it was a hard thing to explain. She decided telling him was worth her while and asked him what he did. He told her he was an account executive for a small computer firm.

139

"Still make contact with the machine?"

"The machine? The computer? Oh, yeah...once in a while."

"There's lots to be done around here, that's why lots gets done. Everyone can do a whole lot of different things, physical, mental, re-petitive, demanding. But there's no separation. Just progression. Un-derstand?"

"Well...I understand, but the amount and extent...."

"Stevenson, my boss--not that he doesn't do everything we do, but he's also in charge, for a time--well, last week he had this fit, he went psycho trying to figure out how to meet a deadline he had just found out about. And when Donald schizes, he doesn't care who knows about it. I mean by afternoon he was ready for the home. All of us were treading lightly when Eddie, he's my boyfriend and kind of a stand-up, started in kidding Donald. And when Don didn't even show teeth, why that's when we realized how much trouble he was in!

"Okay, so we all stopped what we were doing, because obviously _that_ was what we had to work on next. And we did. We talked--even if at first it was hard for him to listen--and we smoked and we drank and we went over to my sister Maxine's to eat, and finally, finally he got it. He jumped out of the frame, mentally shed his anxiety, saw how crazy he'd been acting and suddenly broke into laughter--too late for Eddie who'd already gone to his moonlight kayaking group. Stevenson wanted to go back to the shop then and there and start in. His whole problem had been that he didn't know what to do next when he was hit with that dead-line. So he couldn't do anything. As simple as that. Understand?"

"Well, sort of."

"Okay, even more than that, he had forgotten what to do when you don't know what to do!"

YR ANNUAL SURVEY
Employee Contributions
March, 1985

Conversation at Tenaya Lake

April 27, 1985

"But godammit I AM angry. Look at it, Royce, at all we've done up here, how we live well on a fraction of the energy and money they have to have down there and it doesn't make one damn bit of difference. They still think we're a bunch of freaks living in some Sierra Walden."

"But look at what's happened, Rick. Amtrak picked up the organization of our railway, modified the concept into a nationwide transportation system. Lake Tahoe project has returned a good part of the shoreline to wilderness. The San Francisco Bay fishery restoration and Los Angeles river projects grew out of what we did. Don't you think those were all direct results of work done here? An awful lot in four years."

"Tokens. This culture and its copiers are into a sleepwalking trip. They co-opt these little gestures, but ultimately they'll slide back into the old slumber."

Royce pulls his pipe and tobacco pouch out of the well-worn pocket of his wool coat. Looking over the lake, scanning the rippling dark blue water beyond the skin of ice a meter below his feet, he carefully packs a few fingers of tobacco into the meerschaum bowl. Rick watches the weathered hands manipulate the tobacco. Pulling his collar up to keep the cold lake breezes off his neck, he doesn't notice someone waving from a passing railbus. He is waiting for a response, a confirmation under the huge dead jeffrey pine.

"It's still going on. Goddamn rusty super-tanker went aground and covered the beaches of Monterey Bay with Alaskan oil only two weeks after that pipeline break that killed . . . ."

"I know about it." Royce says quietly out of one side of his mouth while he lights the pipe.

"When the hell is this going to stop? This kind of . . . ."

"It's stoppin'." Royce's words fade in the moist icy air.

"Shit, Royce, don't gimme that. It's not stopping and you know it! Same greed rolls on. All we've done is secure some national parks, a few wilderness areas. So what! They couldn't make money on parks, anyway." Rick kicks a small pebble. It skates across the thin ice, then plops into the water. "The only reason why Yosemite Park works is that it attracts people who work instead of spectators and opportunists who retreat into their shell anytime anyone asks them to be alive. I mean here we have a real working democracy and these idiots come up here looking for the star, our leader, or something. How many times do I have to explain that there ain't no leader, no chief, no shithead guru? I tell 'em to watch the CCT, to see how it works. But what do they do? They see who talks with the most authority and decide he's the leader. The next time they look it's someone or something else! They're looking to idolize the messenger and they're not listening to the message. Like singers or actors who mouth someone else's words and get the credit. People believe in shadows not substance."

"Rick, people are conditioned to look for authority. To that extent we're freaks up here 'cause we have no set way of doin' things. How many times have I explained how democracy is like our gardens. Intermix different plants and their health and productivity benefits. I even explained the trade-offs between certain plants — how one can repel insects or disease that harm others. Democracy is an exchange between different types, characters and ideas. Freedom exists in that exchange." Royce lights his pipe again.

"They attack that by implying that sameness and conformity is more efficient. It allows a better use of time and resources. What they're really saying is we can't afford the conflict that *is* freedom."

"People often don't see the connection between diversity and freedom. When things change rapidly as they have in the past twenty years, people want more order without realizing that real responsibility *and* freedom is in the clash between order and chaos, understanding and confusion."

"So is it too much to expect a little sanity in this world? To expect . . . ."

"Maybe your expectations are the real problem," Royce counters. "What are you really objectin' to?"

"I don't know. I guess I'm confused. Last night I watched the late skin movie on CBS and realized there still wasn't any choice among the four networks. They're throwing out the same crap they were when I was a kid. Some choice! So they've put on a few more documentaries to make the audience think they're socially concerned. Nothing changes! I guess what's bothering me is how we knock ourselves out trying to be real and productive and you switch back to them and they're still back there in the twilight zone as if Yosemite Park didn't exist."

"Why do you watch that stuff?" Royce laughs quietly. "You're just encouragin' it by watching it. You used to tell me that Yosemite Park focused energy in positive directions. When you get like this, you're ignoring that, you're demeaning what we've done." Royce closes with a long look at Rick.

Rick aims his next words down at the rock lapped by the ice. "Yeah, that's fine, but it's not stopping. Every day I read about some other catastrophe. More greed and stupidity. Where's the ethics? Does anyone care? Don't you see all that stuff?"

"'Course I hear about it. I remember when people thought of nature as their enemy. I felt pretty alone in the early 50s. I was learnin' how bad it was. I'd complain to anyone who'd listen that despite what people said no one really gave a shit. It was like being able to hear in a universe of the deaf. But I saw it change. I saw it go from a blind belief in Mammon to what I call a tenable balance. I'm surprised it happened at all!"

Rick scans the gathering cumulus clouds above the lake, wondering what balance has to do with his feelings at this moment. "You're talking about balance when half the planet's a festering sore? What're you, crazy?"

"'Course I'm crazy. I'm as crazy as those seagulls over there and as crazy as you. We have to be crazy to sit here in this weather and talk about this nonsense.

"If there is any advantage to age, it's perspective. I can see within my lifetime a tremendous change in values. What you're complainin' about used to be taken for granted. *Nobody* complained about any of it. The business of America was business and that was all there was to it. Now at least we have social and technological experimentation."

"Yeah, but what effect has it had? Aside from what you've mentioned, things haven't really changed."

"Relative to your life it hasn't changed much. But it's very different for me. I cheered when the first piece of asphalt was taken out of the Park because I grew up in a time when asphalt was everywhere. Yosemite Park represents a reevaluation of land. Look, right where we are. The road, I should say the highway was here. Now there's the trail and the train three times a day. It's made a real difference to this lake, this region. You didn't witness this change. You're coming along in the beginning of a brand new way."

"On one of my days off last summer, Royce, I watched a wildfire south of Wawona Village. There must've been a hundred tourists standing on that ridge watching its slow and quiet progression. Half of 'em were wondering why 'they' — meaning the Park Service I guess — didn't put it out while the rest were cheering every time the flames leaped. I mean that's the kind of idiots we're dealing with. Why haven't they woken up? We have. You'd think they'd make an effort to find out what wildfire is?"

"Give it time, give it time. I can remember the days when nobody, not even the people who lived in the mountains, rejoiced over any natural phenomenon like fire. Fires, floods, earthquakes and landslides were feared, the part of 'nature' that had to be controlled."

"But it's not just the wild and violent side of nature they're afraid of. They aren't comfortable in wilderness. They don't live here, they don't understand how natural a part of life it is. City is habitat naturalis for them. Just last Saturday I had to resort to threats to get any response from a group of teenagers who'd built a rock dam across a creek. I explained how their little dam would flood the campground, gave them all the reasons why what they were doing was destructive to the area. But the only thing they heard was the threats I had to resort to. Then just a bit later there was this bear intimidating a fisherman out of some granola bars. When I talked to the guy he said he had read the visitor's brochure and all the stuff on bears but it hadn't made any impression. The bear was bigger than he was! And what happens to all our carefully constructed switchbacks and trail routes? People break through them and go the shortest way because they all grew up on freeways. Or the people who want to climb Half Dome in an afternoon. Or the equipment freaks who use this place as a showroom for their stuff. People who don't know how to take a crap in the backcountry. And they all expect someone else to come in and clean out their garbage for them. They keep coming and they never learn and they never seem to want to really experience where they are, only parade their neuroses around in virgin territory. It just keeps happening and there doesn't seem to be anything to do about it."

"You remember the crazies that used to come up here when there were cars? They don't seem to be coming here anymore. We don't have the problems with petty crime like we used to." Royce paused and got up and stretched. "Let's walk. It's getting colder. You think being a ranger is a good profession? Think this Park can help people open their eyes to the ways of the natural "uncivilized" world? Think you can cope with the people that are comin' here?"

"I don't know. The problems seem endless."

"You're sittin' in this pile of self-pity. Do you think the whole world should just turn around and be what you want it to be? Isn't that what you're sayin'? Look at all this, the trees over there, the domes and mountains. Look at it! It exists. Have you ever thought about that? There were people who felt the way you did eighty years ago and they had the foresight to protect this place. Was that too much to do?"

"World was much simpler then. Look out for this boulder."

"They did what they felt was right and that's what you oughta be doin'. If you don't like what's happenin', if you can't take the reality of it then move on. There's no room here for self-pity."

"I know how bad it is out there!" Rick points off to the west, to the cities and the central valley beyond the ridges. "But, Royce, I'm so tired of the pain. I feel like we're being slowly suffocated by the shit they're piling up everywhere."

"But don't you see what I'm tryin' to tell you? If you focus on what's wrong, you'll never fight it. You must see that. We've become part of the effort here. It's just one step, but at least we've done that."

```
PROCESS

    We couldn't possibly see then when we were in the
midst of it how good it was to complete a project of
this breadth so quickly.  Only now looking back can we
grasp the importance of getting the trauma over quickly.
Get in, do it and get out: let the whole life system
grow back to normal living.
```

Royal Arches
Yosemite Valley
June 12, 1982

Dear Mother,

It's very hot and dry this afternoon. Steve's passed out on his sleeping bag and Jerry's off playing with a little boy from the next camp. I'm sitting on a boulder enjoying the solitude and using this time to bring you up to date.

I'm not going to say I told you so, but remember how you protested about us bringing Jerry on this trip? Well, she hasn't been any problem, in fact she spent the whole train ride looking out the window pointing at everything. Steve and I were just talking about all the

-2-

things we wouldn't have seen without her. They have these little red wagons for people who don't backpack — like us — and they're perfect for the little ones. Jerry loved riding on the top of our luggage, but Steve was exhausted pulling everything from the station to camp.

Steve's been sleeping for the past hour. He's tired from the drive and it's also the clinic. I don't think he's sure of what to do. Leave it alone or try to fight it out. He was, as you know, so hopeful when he began. Homeopathic medicine seemed so sensible when the clinic started and he

-3-

he had so many successes; but two weeks ago Ford closed the assembly plant. The local people got scared about their jobs and suddenly got conservative. I just wish these people would stop expecting someone to take care of them!! The directors of the clinic went back on their commitment to Steve, saying they can't afford the new medicine, no matter how good the results have been, they want to fall back on their drugs and ignore prevention.

So we'll probably have to leave Flagstaff and move to some other town. I can find another run-down house and fix it up. I'm getting

-4-

good at that.

We went for a walk earlier this afternoon. Jerry's growing so quickly. Did I grow that fast? At five she can keep up with Steve and me on the trails. She's curious about everything, particularly the birds. She watched an Acorn Woodpecker, with a red-topped head, for at least five minutes. The bird hopped right up to her and picked acorns around her feet. She didn't move. He just sat there with her big brown eyes glued to the bird's every movement. Children really are wonderful with wild things. They have no fear.

Jerry fell asleep with her head on my lap as we

- 5 -

sat on a pine needle covered rock by the river. Sitting there I remembered the four of us coming here by car. I was in the seventh grade. Must have been the summer of 1965. Anyway, that was the time Dad asked the lady in the restaurant to turn down the PA system. She wouldn't do it. We left that night with Dad saying he'd never come back. I remember being so embarrassed. Well the valley isn't like that anymore, even Dad would enjoy it now.

After only an afternoon I feel alive and refreshed. It may be just me but I think its quieter than ever before. Right now I see those big puffy cotton ball clouds all

- 6 -

edged with pink. The pink is reflecting off the granite walls casting this strange glow over the forest. There's a coyote walking by. Must remember to the tell Jenny and her friends that it's not a dog to pet.

I hope Jenny will have good memories of her first visit to Yosemite. I remember how Grandma use to say - poor love on - I feel like that's what people have done here.

I wish we could stay here and live and watch Jenny grow up with all that is beautiful. How I loathe going back to the city.

Steve just woke up, time to start dinner.

Love from all of us
Gail

EAGLE I

She floats on her large wings as she cruises above the meadow. Her head is moving in quick strokes from side to side searching for one moving thing down there in the grass. Or maybe just watching to watch.

Above the pines on a dead straight run toward a sequoia, she spots it. She drops and curls into a path above and behind. Increasing her speed with a few powerful strokes of her now tightening wings, her talons come forward from their rear-tucked position. Each claw is outstretched as if to grab the air.

Flying ten, then five then two lengths ahead, the robin suddenly drops as the pursuer takes up the wind above. A shadow envelops the red-chested bird and in a second, the talons reach and enclose the robin. With a sudden and loud beat, the wings pick up her weight and of the crunched, dying robin tucked back almost under her tailfeathers. She turns high above the sequoia and with a few broad strokes gains enough altitude to begin the long descent to the nest.

CHANGES IN WAWONA REGION

The other day some folks came up from Davis to teach a wildfire ecology summer class at the lab. While I was explaining how things are done around here, they asked just what had changed since the beginning of Yosemite Park. Halfway through the recitation I realized I had lost track of many of the details. Right then I decided to write down just what I myself have seen happen over the past years.

REMOVED:
- 66 km of asphalt highway: recycled to oil and gravel.
- 11 creeks freed by removal of highway fill and culverts.
- 22 km of dirt/gravel access roads: growing over.
- 19 buildings taken apart: recycled into usable lumber.
- 1 golf course: returning to wild meadow grass.
- 1 concrete highway bridge over South Fork Merced river: removed by two weeks of zealous high school kids wielding sledgehammers

BUILT or CHANGED:
- 94 km of mainline and shuttle railway track including a hair-raising, cliff-hanging section along the South Fork canyon and a 3 km tunnel through Pinoche Ridge.
- 67 cabins and homes around North and South Wawona have been disassembled, moved to North Wawona and rebuilt. One summer of chaos produced a pedestrian-oriented village with 90 percent more wildspace.
- 2 in-stream hydroelectric generators and 3 wind generators that, along with the solarskins, provide all the electricity for the area.
- 1 village plaza with a handmade ceramic fountain.
- 1 town meeting hall with stained glass walls that can be removed in good weather.
- 2 bird-watching platforms in wildspace surrounding Wawona Village Wawona Pioneer History Museum renovation. Present displays: wildlife as the pioneers saw it; the purpose behind eco-restoration.
- 1 stable rebuilt in a hillside.
- 1 National Park Service lab with a VTR electron microscope built in conjunction with Wawona Wilderness Labs. (Rangers insisted that lab facilities be accessible to them.)
- 1 railway station with a large-scale wall model of Wawona and two locally made stained and etched glass windows depicting wildlife in the Wawona region.
- 1 inn with dining facilities and lodging train tracks. Partially hidden building set back in hillside.
- 21 bridges constructed between Fish Camp and the valley: five covered bridge flagstops, eleven open-frame concrete and granite arch bridges, five log truss "invisible bridges."
- 14 inns between Fish Camp and the valley. All contain gardens, are connected by new trails paralleling the railway and all but two have nearby campgrounds. (Two of the inns were built almost entirely by handicapped persons.)
- 2 large vegetable gardens and several smaller ones growing within deer fences and buildings in Wawona Village. (Some have removable greenhouses during the winter.)
- 2 major new trails, one following the railline from Fish Camp to the valley, the other following the railline down to El Portal. Both have overlooks and unusual views discovered by the trail-building crews.
- 9 new campgrounds constructed along the Wawona trail (considered to be taking the load off the traffic in other backcountry camps).
- 6 campcircles constructed in the old South Wawona region.
- 2 trails blazed from Wawona down the South Fork Merced River. (One has a 15 m macrame netting suspension bridge over the river.)
- 2 minor trails cut from the Wawona line down the Merced River's gorge. (Both were built by students of local area schools as summer projects.)

Henry Bastoon
"Notes for an Article"
GRASSRAIL
July 9, 1985

EAGLE II

"I want you to know I just saw the first golden eagle nesting in Wawona!"

"Wha'? Where?"

"That really tall bent fir down by the covered bridge? She's built a nest near the top. And I think there are eaglets! I wouldn't have noticed at all except for the shadow of her wings: they must be at least two meters across."

"Do you realize what it means?"

"That they've come back?"

"Ten years ago I don't think there was even one south of Oregon. In '80 there was one sighted on the American river above Placerville. I never thought there'd be one down here, and so fast at that. It's more than two hundred kilometers!"

"If I hadn't seen her with my own eyes I wouldn't have believed it. They've actually returned here, and on their own. I never thought they would. Never!"

falls
by
gravity

Colin Pederson's trans-California Journal

5/6/85 El Portal 0935-0955

   A perfect spot to write: the roof of a rotary snowplow standing
on a siding. There's even a cupola to lean against while trying to
write in this little book. The morning sun's glare is too intense.
I should have bought darker paper.
   No matter how you avoid what horseback riders seem oblivious to,
it finally gets to you. I must've avoided at least two dozen piles
on the way from Clearinghouse, only to be had by two! And Vibram
soles! Do they hold horseshit forever?
   I used to pass El Portal on drives up here in my twenties. It
was such a tiny inconspicuous place, ugly in its maladapted motel
modern style. God, that would have been about 1966 or 67. A lot of
drugs in those days. Used to come to Yosemite weekends and eat mes-
caline or acid, then have to drive the MG back like a madman Sunday
night to make Monday's classes. What sticks in my mind is the great
cavalry charge of mounted park rangers tired of hippies taking drugs
in the valley meadows.
   In the morning sun all El Portal's roofs shine, reflecting the
excess light energy off solarskins. From here it looks like a small
Mediterranean fishing village out of the past. But I can smell fresh
bread being baked, bacon and eggs cooking on the same griddle with pan-
cakes and the slight tinge of ozone from the train that just passed.
   Despite its crisp and obviously new lines, the town's blaze of
varied color, the range of light and shadow tells more of a rich re-
discovered native heritage than the sterile future I grew up believing
was inevitable. It's filling just to look at this town; the almost
tactile sense that the town is a living organism. Electric carts,
bikes and cars make a fluctuating, barely audible hum. Horse clops
and foot traffic mingle with the punctuation of hammers and power saws.
And the continuous background, the bass sound of river rapids.
   What I can see are windows, trellises, orange brick and Tuscan
red tiles, chimneys, weathervanes, windmills, hundreds of oaks and
pine trees and roofs. I can see four people sunning on a deck, others
walking behind a low stone wall, the tanned backs of a man and woman
working on the rafters of a new structure and a scattered throng beyond the vine-laden trellis across the track from where I perch on my
snowplow.

"What're you building?"

"A new display--on El Portal. We're working for the Visitor's Center."

"El Portal? I thought the center was for geological displays, ecological information. What's El Portal got to do with that?"

"It's the Park Service. They decided to respond to the volume of visitors coming to see El Portal as well as Yosemite. It's contemporary anthropology, about how we live. Sort of a companion to, say, early nineteenth century indian life in the valley."

"What'll it show?"

"How the town grew. How the landform decided where buildings are placed and how they fit. West Coast structures and how they're adapted to particular terrain. Then over there, a model showing how our buildings live and dispose; where the solar power goes, how the system stores electricity, how the buildings heat and cool themselves automatically."

"What's that? That thing that looks like a flower?"

"Oh, that! It's the relationship of people to the land. It's a kind of abstract, but after we put the labels on it, people'll be able to figure it out. Shows how a group of people can evolve together, what the interactions between them and the supporting environment are. It's a model of human ecology --up here!"

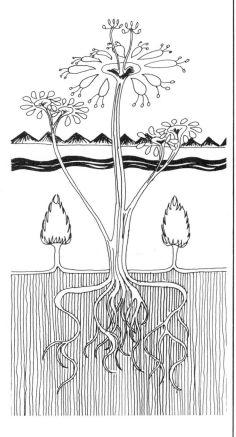

> Valley Station Visitor's Center
> May, 1985

A little way up the gorge   1030-1050

People here transiently are either tourists or visitors. The visitors were already halfway to the Visitor's Center, or the inns or the streets or the Del Portal Hotel. I walked through the station and the throngs hadn't moved much. Tourists hadn't figured out where they were yet.

Station: small compared to arch-roofed European depots, but it definitely had the feeling of station. The platform row of traders had practical goods to sell or trade: fruits and vegetables, local cheese, milk, new and used camping gear, mountain-climbing tools, guidebooks to all the nooks and crannies of Yosemite, photographs (those who think they can outdo Ansel Adams) and postcards and all kinds of clothes. I spoke with a bright woman selling oranges and

Linda,   June 20, 1986
You asked what I've been doing?
I've ridden one train, then a
lighter one, walked to a campground,
rode a shuttle car, hiked five hours,
floated back the river in a canoe,
rode back up river on a horse
and yesterday I pedaled
around the valley on a
bike. Tomorrow I'll ride the
train again and probably
hike another 15 kilometers!
      Exhausted, Love
            Bill

Linda Burton
21936 Goldyne Ave.
Encino, CA. 94124

wearing a blue cotton skirt, red silk blouse with engraved ironwood
buttons and pink roses embroidered around each buttonhole. She
loved making clothes in the winter and selling her fruit in the spring.
I bought her oranges--and her outfit.

So far the trail up the gorge has been as smooth as the one downstream. Walking the tamped earth and rock path has made me think of
the work crews' tan backs in the hot sun. The trail has held up well
despite the number of packers and horses that've used it in the past
two years. It has proved much more popular than expected, someone
on the trail near Clearinghouse told me.

I found a round rock in the river. Two small boulders led to it
like a stair. Upstream and down, white rocks looking like bleached
potatoes in the white watercourse bordered by dense dark green. The
river is a jump below, rapids up- and downstream. Water is uncannily
clear, azure, stained only around the edges with tannic colored leaves
and circling pine needles. Bubbly eddies fill niches between each boulder, carrying a spinning museum of spring's antiquities. Forms of fish
I don't know shimmer in the sunlight's refraction. There is no breeze,
not a soul in sight and the sun makes my sticky skin feel clean.

Orange: sucking the juice of each wedge by compression under the
tongue. Sunkissed, cooling acid purifying my throat as I look at the
few drops nestled in the fibers of white rind. The sun's reflection
in each drop. Watching them shrink into puddles on my pad, then evap-
orate.

My eye muscles, sore as from smiling, squint at all the sparkles
coming from everywhere: the rocks, water, trees, leaves and the windows and sides of one train sneaking down through the forest behind me.

Down from the rock, I kneeled, then crouched cupping clear icy water and smearing it through my sticky beard. The pleasing, cooling
liquid dripping onto rock around my shoes and shrinking like oil on a
hot griddle. Drinking like people have forever, seeing my reflection
marred only by a single dragonfly, I knew I had done something common
to every ancestor.

Getting ready to go before the sun pulls every drop of water out
of every pore. It's dangerous being white-skinned and feeling the burn
and knowing in time it could mean death. The purity of danger!

Valley View, Pohono Bridge   1405-1435

Another place I never noticed when I drove here. The road passed just north of the bridge. I think there was a turnout and direction signs. All that remains of that cluster is a pile of rocks where the signs to Wawona used to be and the bridge I'm sitting on at the moment that carries one lightweight track down the center. People walk alongside on stone-paved paths. Do they know what to make of a man with greasy brown dusty hair, a battered old Kelty pack whose zippers have been replaced by poorly sewn drawstrings and a dog-eared notebook? Looked up from the paper and this teenage guy had made a motion--he thought I wouldn't see--as if he were practicing to push me off the bridge. I intimidated him with a smile.

The Merced broils here. Balloons of current are accelerating into the gorge, distorting my reflection and the black shadow of the stone arch on the streaked sandy bottom worn smooth of large projections. It's hard to imagine this river azure and calm a few kilometers downstream.

Above this point the river meanders through the valley leaving silt for shoulder-high forests of shore life. Here its flood-cleaned banks support little but the most strongly rooted bushes. The river's clearly characterized by its racing middle, but the small side pools, peripheral currents and rivulets of contributing runoff display all its other attitudes.

All the way up the gorge and now at the valley's throat I've seen leaf shadows, dense tangled branches and mottled color over the rain of fallen boulders or those left by the glacier's long tongue. The valley is deceptively low in altitude. People assume it's higher, but it's little more than a thousand meters up. This allows great diversity in broad-leafed deciduous tree species mixed in with evergreen backgrounds. Like a large eddy in the river, the valley catches many plant species and mixes them, causing an unusual glow of wild colors.

SNOW PLANT

"There's something I want to show you!"

"What is it?"

"Better take along your pack: it'll be an overnighter. We have to go to Snow Lake!"

John and I got ready and went down to the station and caught the next inbound from Merced, got off at Valley Station and started walking.

"Actually it's in Snow Creek, up above, maybe northeast of Mirror Lake, less than a couple of kilometers."

"That's more than a little farther. It'd better be good! There are still snow patches up there!"

"Right. But that shouldn't bother you, Aquaria. This is kind of a belated gift. It starts then, around your birthday. But now's the time to see it."

Bridalveil Fall 1515-1545

On a low boulder close to the fall, so near the air is damp.

From the bridge I followed the Wawona lightrail. A crowded shuttle followed me before turning short of the abandoned highway route across Bridalveil Creek. I was tempted to board it on its way to Chinquapin and Wawona, to get off anywhere. But the valley holds a stronger pull.

The south side trail is between river and rails laid on old highway roadbed. It passes Fern and Moss springs, spongy soil regions where water seems to creep out of every crevice. The rails in this region are virtually invisible: rusting steel the same color except for its shiny top as the damp, moldy pine needles and leaves. A knee-high forest of seedlings cover and erode the embankment that once carried asphalt. They're mostly fir and incense cedar. Firs grow faster and for a time will dominate, but the cedars do better in this dampness and in the long haul will weave a sweet-smelling tunnel over the rails.

A single Anna's hummingbird hummed over me in its darting flight through the branches. I can't help but wonder about their incredibly good vision. Now like a Christmas ornament, the iridescent magenta head and throated bird hangs on the fir's neat comblike needles.

The steller's jays continue to hop and flutter. A whole flock are obviously hustling the loose crowd of people standing nearby, waiting for the tidbits. Deft sparrows, less than half the jays' size, flash into the scene; one steals a nut from right under a jay and flying off leaves the jays squawking in anger.

Bridalveil really does look like an old-fashioned wedding veil. A long arc of white spray around a core of solid white falling and expanding outward into a million silvery white showers. It makes, not a roar, but a steady whoosh. In Augusts past I can remember it silent and empty.

The base of Bridalveil seems to be a minor convention of valley life. Not just the twenty or so tourists, but squirrels, chipmunks, jays, sparrows, robins, swallows, a hawk, a purple finch, two lizards sunning themselves on rocks and a pair of coyotes nonchalantly sitting, one washing himself like a dog on the backporch, the other curling his tail around the base of a young fir. I wonder if the animals are here for a bath of spray.

After passing the barely recognizable sewage treatment plant ruins, I crossed a suspension footbridge, swaying cables and clinking slats. Walked along the main railline where it passes to the north of El Capitan Meadow. I've stopped at the junction with the light railline along the valley's north side, sitting on what's left of the old highway shoulder. There's a middle-aged buff taking a tripod held photograph of the footbridge with Cathedral Rocks in the background. The number of cameras I've seen already! People trying to capture their realities to carry them around later. At least the bridge looks good enough to photograph.

Tufts of fresh-smelling meadow grass growing in the crunchy beds of previous generations. Matted and decaying grasses and needles beneath that harbor, a tiny junglelike world of insects and larvae. The looming presence of El Capitan behind and 1100 meters above. What I've read about Yosemite is about the individual rocks, spires and cliffs, discussions of them as distinct personalities. As if El Cap up there stood by itself! It's a small portion of the granite block that rims the valley floor. The wall is composed of many varieties of granite ranging from hard and monolithic to crumbly and fractured, all the result of a single mammoth flow, hot millions of years before the icy glaciation carved it.

I'm really in the valley now, even feel its embrace. If its walls were devoid of softening trees and rock falls, would it appear a vast prison, frightening and confining? But it doesn't feel that at all, rather a cathedral with no roof, liberating in its spirit.

The sun is reaching its afternoon peak when the light is hot and the day's heat radiates back from the ground. Wish I had sunglasses. Looking down is no relief from the bright walls of El Cap, since white decomposed granite granules reflect the sun with a million more reflective surfaces than their parents.

People passing by, smiling and hesitating to say hello, to interrupt my writing. Their voices are reduced by the vastness of the space to a barely audible mumble. I wonder if the overwhelming presence of this place is muting the voices. Do people whisper in Notre Dame?

A big black ant has just found his way all the way up to my note pad. I can hear his bulging abdomen dragging across the paper. Now he's following the pen, or is it the word? Flick,off you go.

There's a story about some climbers scaling El Cap a number of years back. They used cotton ropes to suspend their sleeping sacks from the vertical wall. One of the sleeping climbers heard a rat nibbling on the cotton rope. He shooed the littlest climber off just in time. Sweet dreams!

SNOW PLANT   continued

It was a pine forest with mature trees, maybe five times my girth. The place was getting ready for spring.

"There, you can see it now, Aquaria. There's one and there. There's another!"

Brown, still wet from the thin snow ledge surrounding it, still covered with pine needles and looking like it was plastered with black fungus, with bits of half-rotted bark trimming it: bright red protuberances. Artichokes elongated like ears of corn, bright magenta red.

"What are they? I've never seen anything like them before!"

John pointed to the others. They reached various sizes, the smallest in snow, others, taller, in melting puddles, the tallest in moist dark soil. Twenty, fifty of them. Who knew how many there were in this pine grove.

"What are they? They look like they come from another planet. Are they poisonous?"

He only smiled at me, the rat!

"Wait, it's a root, a bulb, some kind of wild onion, an artichoke, maybe the mother of all artichokes?"

Scaly red petals nested on top of one another like a pine cone too shy to unfold. Whatever it was, it had literally broken through the ground. Small mounds of soil were piled all around its bed.

"Come," was all John said.

We went through the forest seeing more of the strange outgrowths. In a sheltered glen, getting the afternoon sun were more of them, taller ones, maturer ones looking as if they were about to burst. They grew to about 15 centimeters above the ground. At least none were higher. Then we went around the small rock sheltering another field. There, the petals had opened, each making a single brilliant crimson flower, maybe twenty or thirty petals to a stalk burned the crisp March air.

I gasped. They were incredible.

"Snow plant," John finally revealed. "By the time summer warms the Earth, these plants will long since have melted."

Visitor's Center, Valley Station 1730-1745

I'm still panting from the climb: 215 steps up. They get narrower as you get higher. From the top--stone parapet, a pipe railing around the stairway and a cedar lattice supporting four leaf-patterned cast bronze bells--I can see the entire heart of Yosemite Valley. The arched station covered with grass, restaurant beyond, Visitor Center below and a plaza full of new arrivals. There's practically no one here. Does the simple door and lack of sign deprive most people of this view?

Down below inside there's a model of the valley that includes the ranges and tributary canyons. So that now, standing up here above the treetops, I can see the valley's rim and understand the land beyond. I'm learning how to see the large from the small, like seeing the mountain range depicted in the crack of a rock.

Up here there's a family with two children and two couples. Points are being named as if names were important. One of the couples is standing motionless, facing Yosemite Falls, saying not a word as they gaze. When I was little I was awed by Yosemite. As I aged I didn't come here because it was too crowded. Now I've no more need of names and Yosemite is more wild and awesome than before.

Yosemite Falls Campground 1819-1850

At first I didn't see the campground, trusting the signs that
somewhere among these boulders there'd be one.

From my seat on my sleeping bag I can barely see down the narrow
notch between two boulders big as a house. The entrance is framed by
the biggest oak I've ever seen. Its curving trunk and curlicue limbs
embrace the boulders with shadows and accumulations of stain beneath
leaves brushing the white granite.

I'm glad I have a pack. There's something plebian about the wagon
camps: they remind me of car camping. Besides they're down on the flat
near the stations. Much more interesting to be here in the rocks. The
campcircle isn't really a circle; it's more a series of stepped levels
between boulders. Now I know why the valley seemed so empty of campgrounds. Half of them are up in these rocky niches.

I can hear Yosemite Falls.

Yosemite Falls 2010-2100

Back from the walk. Sollight's bright enough on its short
charge for a few minutes of writing. No one's in this campground so
there's no campfire to interrupt my moonlight view of the valley's
south rim.

Frozen spray on the bridge below the falls. Made my nose twitch
as it came down in waves. My cheeks are still tight. And I'm still
wiping the tears away.

The top of the falls: a niche in the granite, in the blue-black moonlit sky. Snow up there or the day's melt frozen into clefts and cracks. Couldn't tell. Cold roar coming out of that wall and bouncing off others until reaching my pink ears.

Water was alternately motionless--a silver satin column--then falling faster than fast, further than 780 meters down--interrupted by a cataract I couldn't see--before thundering into the shrunken ice cone only 50 meters from me. Below the bridge Yosemite Creek divides into dozens of white tongues pouring out of black mouths.

5/7/85   Dome with no name   1235-1310

Slept well, started early, walked up Tenaya Canyon and, with a well executed stride, went up the Snow Creek trail switchback. Now I'm sitting on top of a dome with no name, least not on my map.

My right palm is mottled white on pink depressions, the positive print of the stone it leaned on: granite's sandpapery surface with sparkling flecks of black mica. The chunk I'm lying on is about to separate from the larger mass beneath. It could happen in fifty years, next week or maybe today. The cracks all around are thicker than my outstretched hand. Tiny pine seedlings grab the meager soil and expose their roots like Barrymore's hand when he becomes Mr. Hyde.

My butt's in a salad bowl and my feet in a cat's dish. Granite pockmarked with rounded ice, water-formed depressions. Like a giant sitting on Greenland looking down at New England, I'm on the edge looking down at the valley. Maybe half my vision at the moment is over the edge. Another two, maybe three, meters forward and it would be so steep I'd slip off. The dome protrudes from Tenaya's steep canyon and is almost separated from the forested slope by the curve and fall of Snow Creek. Behind and left, by at least a kilometer, are small pinnacles, runts compared to Mt. Watkins of which they are a part. To the right big Basket Dome, its massive volume obscuring any view of the valley's northern rim.

Cobalt blue sky, high-altitude sunlight and searing granite reflection. I can only squint. I hold this notebook in the noon shadow of my head. Hot sun, yet my bare arm from rolled-up sleeve to the fingers holding this pen shows goosebumps and standing hair vibrating to a blur. The few nearby pines sing with breeze curling through their twisted trunks. Quiet intervals, hearing the roar of Snow Creek Falls and the scree, scree of a hawk out of the forest climbing effortless ramps of hot air.

Birds of prey are such unbelievably beautiful creatures, I cannot imagine why anyone--ever--shot one.

He soars out across the vast space between my perch and Half Dome which is straight across Tenaya Canyon: a gap one kilometer by three wide. Despite the large bird's scale I'm at a loss for size. Like El Cap yesterday, I have absolutely no idea of the size of Half Dome. It's too large to grasp.

Craaaaaaak! What? Came from over there! Was it rock? Ice? Eeerah! A whole side of granite. Big as a city block. That crack loosened a smooth rib of late-melting snow over ice probably frozen in the crack. There're small pieces of snow dropping down...CRAAAAACK!!! Gunshot--no--like a cannon--that did it--now it's moving--faster. Sliding down the slope--breaking up--cracks delayed by distance--spinning--slamming into ridges--puffs of dust--smaller pieces scattering--snow in chunks seeming to vaporize--slamming into another slab breaking its edge--nothing will slow....

Crash--muffled--staggering trees--one sheared with a snap--a razor at 60--chunks falling into a symphony of rippling and rattling--pieces scattered into talus--cloud of dust around fallen tree--wind dispersing it into trees--hawk fluttering quickly to nearest tree--silence.

Wawona Wilderness Lab
 June 7, 1985

Dear Richard:

I couldn't reach you at the hotel or at the conference so I'm resorting to traditional communication. Nothing ever seems fast enough for us! Yesterday, unexpectedly, a group of game managers from Kenya/Tanzania came to look at our wildlife restoration projects. They were particularly hot about our predator program and the relationship between wildfire and grazing area.

They expressed interest, particularly a Mr. Kobacan with an impeccable accent, in developing a railroad. They already have a highly developed rail network. They are considering extending these raillines--which use concrete ties--into the more scenic areas of their parks using the track system we developed for the flatland route of the YR. He wants to talk to you about this. Apparently they are having quite a problem there with people driving cars and trucks and jeeps all across grassland and ruining the surface ecosystem. And their dirt roads become rutted and hopelessly muddy during the rainy season.

They are also intrigued with the idea of building all the equipment--except for the electric components and such--in the neighboring villages and small towns. This method might offset the problem they're experiencing with people leaving the rural regions for the overcrowded cities. It would be far simpler and more sensible to bring the technology to the indigenous culture than having the natives continue to rush to the technology centers. This influx of rural villagers into the cities is destroying their culture.

He also wanted to know if elephants could crush the rails!

I'm sure you can help him,

Yosemite Railway Shops
Merced Falls, California

158

Bent Snowplow In June

Hot sun, pine cones like crunchy cornflakes and seething insects. Stepped through all of it towards a coveralled body lying half under a railway car. He must have heard me because he crawled out like a skittering crab out of a niche. He shielded his eyes with grease-stained twill.

"You wanna know what I'm doin'? I'm breaking my ass, that's what I'm doin' when I should be down at the river with my kids. Davis, that goddamn perfectionist! I bent this damn snowplow a couple a' days ago, and he wants it back in position tomorrow. He needs it, this particular one, tomorrow morning, Monday morning. I'm no mechanic. But when does he get round to tellin' me I have to fix it? Last night. After dark!"

"Whew, okay," I reeled, turning to look at the damage. It was definitely out of alignment, still curled would more accurately describe it.

"You just passin' through?" he asked with more than a touch of curiosity, like maybe he needed some help but didn't want to ask.

"Yeah, I was walking around, looking at Wawona: such a quiet place . . . and such a clear day."

"Sure is a scorcher! Got to get back under this thing, try and loosen the bracket so I can bend it straight. Oh, screw it. Wanna beer?"

"Sure. Sounds okay!" We walked the length of the car, one of those nose or head-end affairs. "Locomotive?"

"Chief: lead car, lounge, cab, nose, all in one."

The shop the chief was backed into was a barnlike building half into the side of the hill like so many of the service structures up here. From a cooler he pulled an eight-pack. Two burps, many gulps. Mountain beer was dark and shivery. We climbed the back platform and walked through, up to the cab.

"But why do *you* have to fix it? Aren't there any mechanics here?"

He smiled and sipped. "Yeah, but they do the normal maintenance things and the kind of stuff the rest of us don't know how to. When there's a' accident, they don't have to be responsible if it's something you yourself can do. There aren't supposed to be any accidents on this railway; we're supposed to be payin' attention. Mishaps, lapses of bein' conscious, so-called accidents aren't expected to happen. And they don't get excused when they do!"

"C'mon! Everybody makes mistakes; it's inhuman to figure it isn't going to happen."

"Well, we don't assume it *is* going to happen: that's the difference. If you do then it will — every time — and you'll end up havin' to pay some fat insurance company a mint to carry the risk. Here, we're responsible for all the little errors, the slips."

I must have looked at him quizzically, as if what he was saying didn't make sense.

"Look, I own part of the action, a working share of the stock. That means I take responsibility for what I do. See, anytime there's a' accident round here, we start lookin' round for who wasn't. We just don't have any cushions on this railway; nobody can go round breakin' things and gettin' off with a lame excuse. I know it's not done this way in some companies, and it may sound heavy, but it's one reason why we can keep our prices low. If we charged for it, we could cover up. But we don't, so we can't."

"It still seems a buster you have to spend this hot Sunday fixing that . . . that cowcatcher."

He had finished his beer and was eating the gelatin container. "Pretzel flavor; I thought it was a potato chip one."

"You can never tell for sure until you finish off the beer."

"Yeah. I'd sure like bein' down there with the kids right now. But I have to say that, eh . . . I concur with the arbiter's judgment. Was fair."

"Who?"

"The arbiter, one of us. We all get a crack at doin' it. You spend six weeks decidin' about all kinds of disputes, legal questions, differences of opinion; you even get to assigning responsibility. Last winter I was on the other side of this, so I kind of know what it's about. When somebody else screwed up and there was a question of liability, I had to decide against 'em. See, there's this clause in everybody's contract, the one you sign when you begin work here, that says . . . I've forgotten the words exactly, wait . . . ability to respond. It's the catch when it comes to accidents. Now I was pushing the throttle round the bend near Eleven-mile Creek and when I saw it, I tried to stop but couldn't make it fast enough. So we sort of skidded into the boulder, a thousand kilo monster, at least. Just fast enough to bend the snowplow down."

"That's crazy! You mean a boulder falls down there and you're responsible for that? That's bullshit! You didn't push the mother down!"

"True enough, but guess who gets to fix the plow?"

"But there are people who get paid to do work like that!"

"There are, but not in this case. Davis helped me with it before the lucky bastard went to Chilnualna Fall. He spent about an hour showing me how to do it.

"Look, there's a bottom line here: when I'm drivin' this train, I'm the captain, just like on a ship. It's my domain, so it's up to me to have the answer when anything happens. When you're carrying around as many as four hundred people with you, you don't take your eyes off that track ahead; you just don't allow yourself to make mistakes.

"Now the arbiter's coming from a strong awareness that when I'm drivin' the train, that's where the action is. Not a hundred kilometers away in some office somewhere, but right there where it happened. And they expect those who were there — and doin' it — to put it right."

He finished gulping down his second Sierra Stream. "Another pretzel! If the arbiter can arrive within minutes, then the thing, whatever it is, can be pieced out, put to right while it's still real in everybody's mind. Maybe they're still sore then, but it's quick enough to stop 'em from gettin' carried away with their imaginations.

"It's like driving a car. Suppose a bolt or something breaks at 85 kph and there's a' accident? Is it my fault cause I bought the clinker without examining all the parts? Do I sue the car company and they claim metal fatigue then or some other bullshit? Or they make their insurance pay? The point is, when there's human error, people shy away from dealing with it. Generally we really don't want to be accountable for our actions. We want to spread the responsibility.

"Let me explain it another way. You buy something made somewhere by somebody: there's no way to talk with the maker. Either you like it or you don't buy it. And the maker doesn't get your opinion either; no way to change it, adapt it, make it more personal for whoever's buying it. This dialogue about trade is what really is civilization. Life is what you learn and when there's no learning, what have you got?"

"Potato chip. Want it?" I handed him the container with a smile. "I was going to fink out and wait until you asked me to help fix that thing, but that's · bullshit! Let's get to that bracket. Maybe we'll be able to get you down to the river while the sun's still up."

June 11, 1985

To: Richard Farber

From: Cheryl Billanger

These are the abstracts I'm sending the Kenya/Tanzania delegates. Have I missed anything that you think would be valuable to them?

WILDFIRE and GRAZING LANDS
HUMAN IMPACT on RANGELAND
WILD ANIMAL BIRTH CYCLES and FEAR of HUMANS
GROUNDWATER: RELATIONSHIP TO INSECT/BIRD FOOD CHAINS
"HOLDING LIMITS" for HUMAN USE of WILD LAND
THE POLITICS of WILDERNESS

Thank God they all read English! Oh, yes, Kobacan told me that this kind of exchange of information among people is so much more of value to them than the government-sponsored stuff! Hip, hip, hooray for egalitarians!

WCBN-TV
Transcript *VideoSpeaks/Wawona*
date: *7/23/85*
broadcast: *Quarles/Doc*
file: *D-f723982.1*
section: *News/Public Affairs*

SOUND   "Wawona may be the number two town up here, but that's reverse snobbery for these residents of this backbone of the Park. This is Grace Quarles continuing with VideoSpeaks' 'Yosemite Project,' Part Four: 'Town Meeting of the Woods.'"

IMAGE   We see the turtlenecked, Levi'd, booted commentator out of her urban element standing on Wawona Dome. Just perceivable over her right shoulder is Wawona Village. Her smiling image slowly explodes like an opening time-lapsed rose into a long between-the-trees view of the village square. Maybe the size of four tennis courts served end to end but widened at the center, the plaza is surrounded, even infiltrated by mature pines. It looks like a clearing, almost but not quite natural. The camera distortion makes it look larger, more imposing than it is. But the half-visible pattern of houses and spare buildings tucked into the rich forest--the extent of the community in this place--is evident.

SOUND   "If true for anywhere up here, the charge of elitism would hit closest the mark in Wawona. To the casual visitor, much less than 30 percent of today's Park tourists, Wawona Village looks like the laziest, mellowist corner of Yosemite. The urbanity of El Portal, the ruggedness of the backcountry, the ever-increasing popularity of the valley, all this is definitely not the style of Wawona. Once little more than an access to the Park's southern flank, this hamlet of approximately four hundred permanent and another five hundred milder season vacationers has the definite feeling of neighborhood."

IMAGE   The camera has tracked around the irregularly oval square, picking out images of rustic vistas and the sparseness of the human traffic before turning to the porch of the town's living room, Albert's Saloon and Mealtime Cafe. Through the lens this establishment looks like an edge of the commons that's been temporarily taken over by an assortment of wood benches, tables and chairs. But as we near it, the interested viewer can make out behind it a ramshackle cabin-like structure that obviously evolved piece by room around a dozen trees.

SOUND   "And while El Portal's 2500 natives, as they like to call themselves, can service and accommodate three times their number at any time, Wawona Village in no way offers hospitality that indiscriminantly."

IMAGE   The camera moves away from Albert's, hiking through the trees in the square, passing houses and shops on the slope. The verticality of the three-story-high tiers of houses is accented by tree trunks and swooping branches. You can almost feel the breeze electronically. Beyond the village something stretches white and taut in the treetops. The twenty or so ropes that hold it become increasingly distinct, and curiosity is finally satisfied: a macrameed spider web--that's the form it imitates--a net supporting a shelter of light wood revealing its spiral regularity as we come closer to it. Suspended from sugar pines and white firs, it's about 30 meters from the forest floor, but appears higher on the screen.

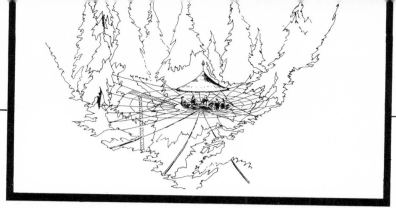

SOUND   "This live report brings you to this outgrowth of Albert's, where the wind rustles and the trees sway and your innards change places. Among the locals this aerie is known as the 'Teahouse of Mariposa Moons.'"

IMAGE   Out of a group of four, no five, people gently rocking and lolling, Grace Quarles turns and smiles down at the camera's swaying rope ladder perch. In the transportation from Wawona Dome she has changed into a cullotted spacesuit with hood and knee-length boots in a star-patterned aluminum mylar. Almost as if she were leaving on a shuttle flight to America-View satellite station, and not twenty kilometers from Sequoia Gate.

SOUND   "It's so comfortable and...spacious here, and my feeling is that the canopy is very strong and very secure. Reassuring to acrophobes like me. But you're not interested in my childhood. From here you can see..."

IMAGE   and the camera does...

SOUND   "across to the Wawona Hotel, that white clapboard building, and the low ridge covered with dark green trees, well despite its appearance, that's Wawona Point and the left--east--that cleft is the South Fork of the Merced River Canyon. And this is Albert, our smiling host."

IMAGE   Albert is a large man, even without camera distortion, and looks like Santa Claus but with dark, very dark hair and beard. He has to take his pipe out of his mouth to speak.

SOUND   "This place is not really...."
"Haven't you learned to bite on that thing and talk at the same time? My father could do that!"
"He must have snapped a gross of 'em!"
"No, but he did scatter a lot of tobacco. You're an old resident of Wawona, aren't you...I mean a former resident?"
"That's better. Yup, here before the rail!"
"Can you tell us about the differences then and now?"
"Well, I like to think about the parallels. Everybody makes out a case for all the stuff that's different and when you have to listen to it as much as I do.... So let's just say Wawona is more a village, less a summer camp."
"But even more than that I'm told. I myself can see how quiet and private it is around here, sort of safe from the tourist bombardment."
"What'a'ya mean? No gates up. Everything wide open. It's not restricted. I don't understand the things that folks come out with. No more than a coupl'a hundred houses clustered around here. Some pretty looking, utilitarian houses, very modern but sort of old-fashioned, definitely high Sierra, Wawona houses. This place has been summer home for a lot of people for five or six decades now, and those old styles have a nice way about 'em. Even a lot of the old wood was used in the newer ones, what'd they used to call that...recycling?"

IMAGE   Albert looks sincere but disgruntled, his speech slowing down,
          his gestures accelerating as he makes his points. Grace's
interrogations are ignored by the camera that focuses in on Albert who
has abandoned his pipe and is rolling up the sleeves of his shirt.

SOUND   "But just anyone, that is new people, can't move up here.
          Don't you consider that exclusive?"

     "No, just sane and sensible. Look at this place. How could we al-
low more to built without ruining the way it looks and feels? But even
that's not it. Water and visitor needs for wildspace are our limits.
The number of separate dwellings here already, the way the population
balloons out from spring to fall, all this adds up to...a limit! We simply can't afford more growth of anything except wilderness. If we extended the village, built out in every direction, followed the national,
irrational growing pattern, what would have happened to us? We'd have
become like every place else. So we expended our effort to move the
houses closer together, clustering them. And you can see the results
for yourself. Instead of removing the whole village, we tripled the
area and health of the surrounding wilderness. We can walk all around
now instead of having to ride. Let El Portal get into the building boom
business. They pioneered community sovereignty, they designed their town
with intelligence instead of growth and job possibilities. But now El
Portal can't come to grips with the growth it has encouraged. Here, we
simply said no!"

     "What about the allegations that the higher echelon of the whole pro-
ject have settled in here, grabbed it first, became the old timers... not
you, Albert; there's a pretty vocal group down in EP that feels there's
been some deals made, elitism and all that!"

     "I'll lay it on the line for you, if you like. Birds of a feather
do flock together. There's a common attitude among people up here, and
I don't think that's being special or exclusive. We group here because
there are a lot of the same interests here. People wanting to live nearby
one another isn't a conspiracy, it's simply a group of friends. When you
take part in life, you become connected. Otherwise, you're only a spectator with no responsibility, no rights either.

     "Those charges of exclusivity! We're no more exclusive than any small
town in New England. We encouraged our community's character. Uncontrolled growth would change that irrevocably. Community sovereignty is the
basic right of a group to prevent being swallowed into a larger one. I
think we'd all agree that it is as basic as the Bill of Rights."

     "But that isn't in the Bill of Rights."

     "Well, maybe it's time to add something there about air and water and
a healthy environment! Some testimony to quality of life."

     "And what quality would you say Wawona demonstrates?"

     "Look, before the changes around here, I spent most of my time inside
my saloon, only then it was a bar. I ignored the community outside and so
did most other folks. That's why Wawona was a blight in an otherwise
beautiful corner of the Park. The railway spirited change, allowed grass
roots strength to grow. I, and others up here, got involved. We built
the plaza where the parking lots used to be, we clustered the houses,
planted trees: we made a village that doesn't look out of place in the
majesty of Yosemite. I sit out front now, watching the world and living
in my community!"

IMAGE   The camera, or the director back in Los Angeles, switches to
         a new view. The on-camera is mounted in a helicopter circl-
ing lazily right over the village, observing the peace, the lack of activity, the everyday no nonsense; it rises higher looking for something besides the forest sprinkled with angled walls, steep pitched roofs, windows
that reflect back the forest, pine needle crusted sills. The whole pattern is a geometric puzzle overlaid with a matrix of vertical lines: shadows of treetrunks.

SOUND   "Rustle of Spring" fades as Grace observes, "Transportation
         in the area is two-footed, but bikes and horses are also pop-
ular. And you can see an occasional mule."

IMAGE   Dirt skateboards with high eccentric wheels seem to compete
         down the slope to the river with the riders' slalom shadows.
Trails lead everywhere; we notice, if we're into figures, five north,
three south, as many east and two west. The single primary railline
passes between the overgrowing, back-to-meadow former golf course and the
Wawona Hotel, then passes along the river to the station before paralleling the water on the other side and vanishing into the forest. And across
it, we hover above an absorbing cabin whose weathervane of rocks, shells,
gears and wheels hangs from a sparkling solar generator twice the size of
a basketball: the sign above the door proclaims the Small Appliance, Home
Tool Recuperation Sanitorium.

SOUND   "What's involved in the local animal restoration projects?"
         Grace finally gets around to asking.

IMAGE   Grace Quarles is near the river looking up toward the village
         with another man and woman, but she's smiling into the camera.
The man is thinner than Albert, and probably taller though it's difficult
to tell; he has more of an authoritative ring in his voice. But it's
pleasant like the voice of someone who gets things done. He doesn't
smoke, but all the time he's talking he's chewing on something.

SOUND   "It's a complicated problem," Martin admits as he earnestly
         tries to catch her attention. "Many factors," he pauses to
sum it up best, "are involved. Will the region benefit, and in precisely
what ways? Does greater diversity encourage all life? And what about our
ultimate aim, to achieve wilderness that lives without out tampering? How
will that be in balance?
    "Balance?"
    "The white man was like a typhoon causing death to some species and
massive imbalances in others. Time will heal we hope and another healthy
balance will reassert. We're like homeopathic doctors only removing blockages, encouraging new growth, stewarding the land back to balance."
    "Isn't it rather presumptuous, perhaps even a contradiction, this idea
of ecological restoration?"
    "Presumptuous? A lot less so than leveling mountains, filling up
valleys, changing the course of rivers, even blocking them up. We're growing less presumptuous as time goes on. I agree it would be a contradiction if we tried to make it like it was. I don't think we're trying to

do that. The life system can think for itself. Whatever happens will
always be different and new. We aren't predicting, just allowing."

    "Why do you think so many of the personnel for the restorations and
the other nonrecreation projects live in Wawona?"

    "You do keep coming back to that one! Could you be looking for an
issue where none exists? Many project people live in EP, Fish Camp, Foresta, even at White Wolf and there are two down at Mono Lake. Insinuating
that Wawona is a private club is nonsense. It's so small here any kind of
bond sticks out. In EP there are so many activities and groups that
people connected by similar interests don't stand out. And we have certain affiliations here, the colleagues and interests we have reflect an
international flavor, friends around the country, in LA and San Francisco.
We trade information with restoration projects all over the world. EP is
still responsive to the foothills--Mariposa, Coulterville, Groveland. But
why don't you get down to the real issues here, not pettiness and jealou-
sy?"

    "All right! If you want to duck that conflict, let's talk about
something more serious. The grizzlies, just for example. As I understand it, reintroduction was one of the issues that split...."

    "There was some...well, undue fear among certain groups in El
Portal."

    "Well, I can certainly understand their feelings. Don't you
think reintroduction of so dangerous an animal to the Park would be
risking the lives of millions of visitors?"

    "You know Yosemite means grizzly. The problem...Ellen, you tell
it, you were a major part of how it happened."

    IMAGE   The camera leaves the gray-haired, intense, pleasant-faced man
             and turns toward a mature woman, sensible-looking, efficient,
    capable. After a moment her head becomes silhouetted with footage taken
    by the Wawona Wilderness Laboratory team at Snake River: telephoto close-
    ups of the bears moving around, off, away, turning and going in every di-
    rection.

    SOUND   "Our hard-won consensus on the principles of animal restora-
             tion broke down when the practical questions began to emerge.
    People are terrified of grizzlies despite evidence that they're barely
    more dangerous than black bears. We've gotten lots of corroborative in-
    formation from the Snake River reintroduction. We based most of our pro-
    jections on that study, how they coexisted right alongside of range cattle
    and all the rest of it. Anyway, a lot of resistence coalesced...now that
    I remember it, largely based in EP. Maybe there's a correlation there,
    Martin, with how the bad feelings began? Anyway they held up appropria-
    tions, made us go out of our way to prove that we could handle really bi-
    zarre emergencies...but you don't want to hear all about this backbiting.
    We got results though, but we're all still keeping our fingers crossed.
    Next fall we get our first immigrants: five from Glacier and probably
    seven from the Yukon. Autumn's the best time for it: they'll be able to
    look around before going into their winter low energy cycle. There's less
    chance for people interruption then, they can get comfortable. And by a
    year from now, they'll be loose in their own territory just as they were
    in the past."

"Where are they going to be!"

"They're going to the Stubblefield Canyon area; it's similar to what they're accustomed to and not many people get there. But if successful, they'll spread out."

"But what if you met one? There're going to move around, be in the backcountry. Can you seriously tell me that there's no danger?"

"There's always risk, but there have been only three recorded incidents in the past twenty years of death due to grizzly bears. And those were due to human stupidity, ignorance of the animal and its behavior. When you enter wilderness, you have to accept the responsibility of knowing how to treat its denizens. If you don't know what you're doing, Yosemite will tell you soon enough."

IMAGE   The camera has been examining overgrown foundations of old summer houses behind Wawona, the only area in the Park that's on public lease hold. When it shifts, Grace wearing yet another costume is at the top of the plaza holding her hand under the dripping fountain and squinting her eyes against the lowering sun. Isolated windows gleam gold behind her. She's talking to an intense young man who speaks very quickly and decisively, but quietly.

SOUND   "Somebody's turned it on even though it's been broken since winter when it froze. It only dribbles now. But the bats use it."

"Bats?"

"Saw one before dawn just a day or two ago, right out of the shadow of the trees, darting forward as if going to crash in the water; but within milliseconds of disaster it pulled back, wings fluttering on an axis 45 degrees to the water, holding its body near vertical, mouth down and open. Flying in a tight spiral over the circular pool looking for bugs and stuff."

"I think our viewers by now might be getting the impression that this place is a refuge for all kinds of wayward beasts!"

"We can't judge animals by human standards."

"What are you talking about? Oh, look at that now, isn't she cute? Got a peanut?"

"Why do you assume that that chipmunk's female?"

"By the smartness of her coat, of course. How about a cracker?"

"We try not to feed the animals around here, no matter how cute they are. It's better for them, doesn't foist dependence."

"Oh, I see. Yes I do. I can begin to understand why people feel the way they do about the people who live in Wawona!"

sequoia gate

May Day 1985

Jonathan Magista
Department of Architecture
Columbia University
New York City

Dear Jonathan:

You accused me of dropping out, the only one of your
personal students who considered himself "too good" for
the years of lavatory details before the "honor" of practicing architecture. You were right, I haven't pushed the
pencil and don't intend to: I've been learning how to let
it flow.

You viciously attacked the "woodsy style" of the Yosemite project, "a denigration of the professional community,"
you wrote and a "neo-Romantic turd plopped on the unsuspect-
ing landscape." And you were here what? Exactly once!
Yes, you are right. It is not clean, crisp or minimal.
But this is a park, not Park Avenue.

I'm communicating with you again after so long out of
rage, yes, but mostly because I still can hear your voice,
my personal testament to your power as a teacher and your
dedication to architecture as an art and a craft and a
discipline. I write to point out to you that you've lost
sight of how real learning occurs. And how really great
architecture evolves. And you've forgotten that you once
described the Parthenon as the ultimate statement of the
Greek way of relating the universe.

You've been blinded by your own absorption into contemporary urban American architecture. No longer can you see
that it's packaging, it's flash, only fit for corporation
climbers with fantasies about thousand dollar desks in
 corner offices. Its injection-molded esthetic isn't in
touch with the life of the city, the aspirations of real
human beings. It's designed for architectural glossies where
the thickness of the page is the measure of its dimension.

It's capitalism gone mad, the profit motivating all:
the same pattern as Gothic churches in which salvation is
preached but whose shapes structurally express the strain
of pushing a culture to the pinnacles of guilt.

Point is we don't need architecture that expresses fear with sterility. We don't need more buildings that mirror emptiness. We need to be in places warm and open, buildings that allow--no, encourage--life to grow and evolve openly. Not enclosures for rats in the maze.

What you also seem to have forgotten is that learning doesn't start with--nor is it--a product. It is a process. From the simplest toy to the most intricate complex, it is an evolution of thought.

Somehow you're looking backward. Along with the whole professional world--not just building designers. Practically everyone stuck in professionalism still labors under the assumption that you make it be, not let it be. There's a massive illusion that you can learn all there is to learn-- in your field, of course--and then you can stop. Once you have the knowledge then you can live off it forever, like dividends, like your shingle, like your interest. The master builder who "knows" it all!

When I came up here I was one of your best disciples in spite of myself. I was filled with that haughty, egotistical holier-than-thou--but never more than you--attitude. As if all the people living and working here were ignorant, and I was going to show them how to live, how to build, how to understand what a building was.

What a shock! I had been taught working with people meant lowering my standards. At all costs avoid compromising with the client; get the solution you designed built exactly the way you designed it. Flatten out the land: it's merely the pedestal for your sculpture. Never mind the ideas that e- volve in the process. Ignore the people who are going to use the building. Close your eyes to the spirit of the place, pinch your nose against the breath.

I had carefully incorporated a drip rail above a window to prevent rainwater from running into the top seal. The carpenter made it larger than I had drawn it. I told him to change it. He told me to change it myself. Later I asked him, politely, if he'd changed it. He said no. I asked why. He said if I cared about it so much I could change it! It wasn't my job--I'm an architect, not a carpenter. He said he was a human being, not a carpenter. He said he was put off because I hadn't even asked him why he had changed it in the first place. It seemed I forgot about icicles. That they curve in under drip rails and that if the drip rail had been built the way I designed it, the ice would have seeped into the window seal and broken the glass.

I thanked him for the lesson--two days later.

That's the point!

The primary need here is not to create a space designed to advance the architect's professional standing, to
be another finished work in his portfolio, but to create a
space for those who are going to use it. Not to make something resembling the standards of something else somewhere
else, but to accomplish what is needed right here, right now.

We don't come to sites here with prepared notions of
what we're going to put there--and in what style. The
attempt--regardless of profession or place--is to see what
Yosemite needs, what each individual site needs, and how
our purposes fit with this ongoing evolution of wilderness.
We come together, work out the basic design and begin
elaborating Like a family decorating a Christmas tree. I
may at times be the conductor, but I need the orchestra as
much as it needs me. Always, the thrust is to solve the
problem impeccably in process and product.

Richard Magnem
Sequoia Gate Inn
Yosemite Park

VideoSpeaks II

"CCT channel 19. That you Greg? Got a haircut or something?"
"Yeah, Bruce."
"What'ya think?"
"Not a thinking matter. Bad as that documentary on the CCTs last year!"
"Worse and they keep coming back. Why?"
"Cause we let 'em. They have this perverse curiosity about this project, yet don't seem to notice similar efforts in their own LA backyard. By the way, who the hell okay'd the helicopter? They're supposed to be for emergencies only!"
"Must have been Trout on Overview. Rest assured it'll be on the agenda next maintenance session!"
"At least Martin brought it out about her making problems where there aren't any. I hope that got across. But Albert should've told her the teahouse wasn't built as an extension of his saloon. Our bird sighting would be nowhere without such platforms. No mention of that!"
"Well, maybe the program will make a few people understand what we're doing here, though I can't help but get the feeling that they want us to be an exhibition, a sideshow in a National Park."
"Maybe, but I don't think most people are going to understand that what we're doing here is our own way of doing things. The way of a small community that has more than two million visitors every year. It's like that eco-restoration question. They think that term either means returning to some romanticized past or our work is frivolous and somehow...."
"Useless? Of course it looks useless to the media. It doesn't fit their expectation of one solution, one answer, a single panacea for a thousand problems. How can you possibly explain the subtleties of living with wilderness to people who see like that? They can't see out of their either/or frame. To them it's either cavemen or cosmopolitan living. Nothing in-between. They can't help but miss what's happening here. An on-going search for healthy evolution is simply not audience-attracting material."
"I guess you're right, but it's all so frustrating. Here we are with so much to learn, facing so much that's exciting, and they want simplistic causes and effects!"
"Don't take it so personally. Just remember the visitors and the looks on their faces. That's the real response, not the sensationalism the national media's looking for."
"I suppose so. You don't think there's really anything at all to that elitism business, do you?"
"Well...do _you_ live in Wawona?"

CONVERSATION: Evelyn Ventar

The solarskin invented in 81, turned out to be the revolutionary device that simultaneously collected solar heat and generated electricity. Ventar was born in Southern California in 1948 after his parent immigrated from England. He now lives in a simple wood house in Wawona Village with his wife of two years, Ali Leiberman. He stands about 180 cm, his lean body carrying little excess weight. His hands and face are weathered and wrinkled and he looks as comfortable outdoors as in. This interview was conducted on a sunny afternoon on a deck he shares with neighbors and was interrupted by a feisty ring-tailed cat who tried to steal a sponge from the kitchen windowsill.

ST: . . . and so solar energy was chosen here?

V: Not that there weren't other alternatives. Much of the interest in solar heating and electrical generation wasn't predicated on energy shortages but rather dissatisfaction with previous energy techs. For example, even by 80 they were thinking up here of a small diesel generating station to power the trains with a steam turbine and boiler system operating off oil, even wood. Although either of those systems would've worked, they were discarded because they depended on large centralized plants.

ST: Was purchasing power from local utilities considered? Or hydroelectric power? Or wind?

V: At first they'd assumed power, at least for the buildings, must be purchased from the local utilities. It was also considered for the train, but there was the same objection: it would further the use of large plants, in this case oil-burning steam-generating stations. Hydroelectric was considered a clean source, but after the drought in the late 70s it was no longer considered a dependable source on a large scale. Plus what hydro power there is around Yosemite was pretty much spoken for already. And wind power except for small-scale applications simply wasn't constant or dependable enough.

ST: What was the specific objection to centralized plants?

V: They're just inefficient, particularly big steam generating stations. For example, they must remain operating throughout the evening, when use is down, simply to maintain full power potential for peak periods like morning and dinnertime. Small-scale, locally based power keyed to a particular use seemed the best approach. It wasn't solely a matter of cold engineering logic, rather an intuition not to become dependent on outside oil or high tech.

ST: That's the reasoning behind the development of the solar stations and the solarskins?

V: Yeah, the solar stations grew as a synthesis of many people's thoughts — both here and in labs all over the world. Some components, notably the heat transfer system, are very sophisticated and require a high technical proficiency to build. But the idea was that it was a sound trade-off here: in time we'll be able to simplify the device.
But even now it answers our major objective. It'll generate electricity for decades, quietly, efficiently, cleanly, and with very little maintenance.

ST: We've heard all kinds of stories about the invention of the solarskin. How did it come about?

V: I was lying in the hot spring outside Tecopa — near Death Valley — and suddenly it came to me. Feeling the sun, the water, the electricity in the air. I realized that all those high tech people I'd been working for had been

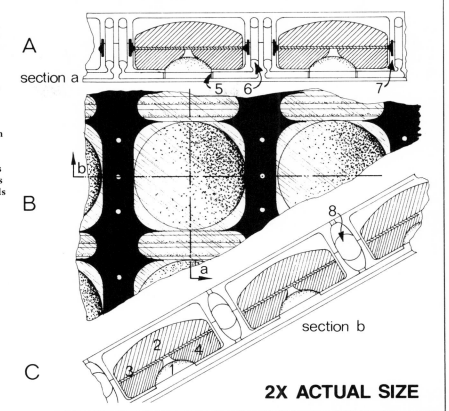

Section a: Solarskin cross section showing gas tubes

Rainwater enters through holes (center of B) and graywater (pumped up from storage tanks) flows down from roofpeak. Both travel down to (C1) where water is cracked into hydrogen and oxygen by electrolysis. Sunlight is converted into electricity in solar cell (2). Glass circuit chip (3) distributes electricity to copper bands (7) for direct electric use or for energizing the cracking chip (4). Hydrogen and oxygen pass out of separate membranes (A5) at either side of the chamber. Suction draws gas into tubes (A6) and eventually into the building's storage tanks. Uncracked water can be sun-heated on the black surface above the water tubes (8).

section a

section b

2X ACTUAL SIZE

separating the generation of electricity from the collection of heat. They aren't dissimilar objectives, so I began to synthesize a method of doing both within one flexible covering material so that each house could heat itself — which is a low order of energy — and light and power itself — which is a high order — at the same time.

ST: It came to you in the proverbial flash?

V: It was really a matter of letting go. Letting your perception of the universe go, seeing it the way it is, seeing that very clearly. Then it comes.

ST: But then it had to be developed?

V: Of course. After that, leaving the hot springs, I drove up to spend time in the high Sierra. I knew about Yosemite Park — but I wasn't too hopeful what with Ford collapsing and the Pakistan war. I met the people at Ellery Lake who'd been enthusiastic about my earlier work on solar furnaces and we went to their workshop in Mariposa and I saw the extent of their commitment and realized Yosemite Park wasn't a flash in the pan. I've been here ever since.

ST: And have no intention of leaving?

V: Of course not, who knows? But I feel invigorated here. You know, people who come here, those who don't have solar power at home, swear there's a difference. The water, the heat feels different to them somehow when it's solar.

ST: How has your work with Yosemite Park changed you?

V: I feel my work is related to something fine, it's going somewhere. It has to do with people learning how to live better rather than just keeping their balance on the industrial treadmill. More and more I'm beginning to look beyond the questions and conflicts of daily life. Beginning to look into the universe not at it.

SunTech Magazine, March, 1986

27 May 1985

Jonathan Magista
Department of Architecture
Columbia University
New York City

Dear Jonathan:

Sorry I unleashed such a torrent. I'd just read your article and I fumed all afternoon. It was a release and I'm glad you responded, and the way you did.

I want you to know that there's no freak of humanity up here. We haven't suddenly become egalitarians cooperatingly creating heavenly gates.

Those I work with and most of the people of this project have simply seen how their own self-interest is served by clearly perceiving a course that all can share instead of trying to outdo one another.

We've learned--not without pain and joy--that the only intention we can agree on is our need of acknowledgment. That above all else, we need to feel others aware that we live, that we exist, that we work.

This need for reassurance used to take the form of excessive accomplishment. We'd create endlessly, a circuitous, even tortuous, way of gaining notice. Instead of asking for attention by smile or word, we'd build things in the hope that someone would say it was good. And by extension that we were worthwhile.

And perhaps more than all this, I've begun to learn that love is not romance, it is not simple sharing, nor generous giving: it is not a fixed thing, not even a thing. It is the flight of truth: quick, fleeting, spontaneous. It is communion with all life at once. And that is, exactly, what this project is.

Come up again, soon

Robard

P.S. ENCLOSED ARE ROOF AND FLOOR PLANS OF THE
SEQOUIA GATE BATHHOUSE WE JUST COMPLETED.

174

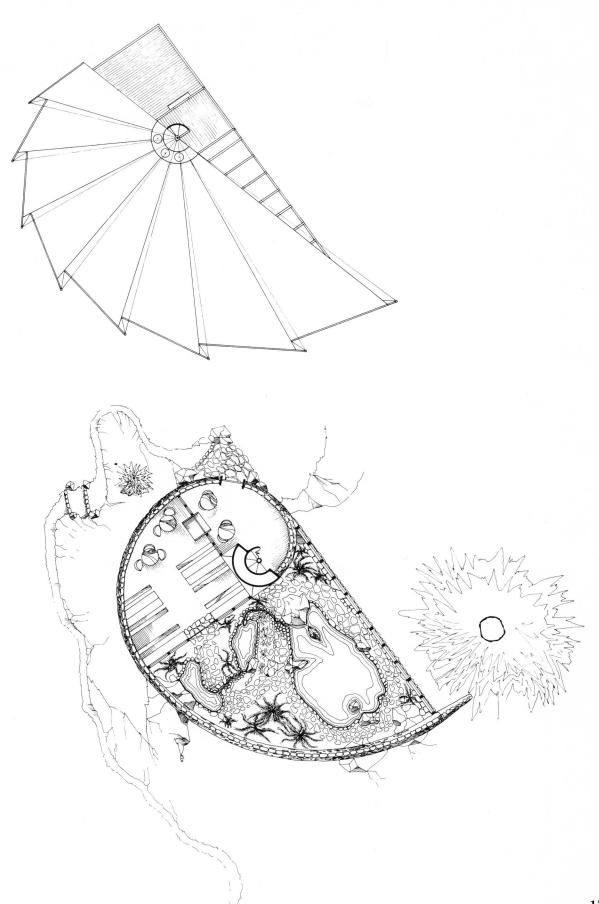

Ski Magazine: excerpt from "Yosemite's Slope,"
March 1986

"But the best thing about Badger now is that the
little valley doesn't have parked cars or garish permanent buildings. You can ski down the runs right out
into the flat valley floor. And if you're really adven-
turous, you can continue right down along the railline
to Chinquapin.

Shuttle cars, small electric railcars, provide transport from anywhere along the old Wawona road (now
a railline) back up the slopes above Badger; this provides excellent service for cross-country as well as
downhill enthusiasts. It encourages longer runs with
the pleasant assurance of quiet, frequent transport
back up the mountain.

The chairlifts at Badger have been replaced by
eight modified shuttles (each carrying 25) traveling
up through the trees to all the ski runs. Down skiers
are thus free of former visual obstructions.

During the season lodging trains — five-to-ten-car
parked trains with small compartments, restaurant
and service spaces — are moved into the vicinity when
they are needed so the visitor isn't confronted with
a collection of half-used resort buildings in the off-
season.

Special ski trains inaugurated this season allow
visitors to board cars in Merced, travel up to Badger
in the comfort of their own rooms which they may
keep when the train parks on a siding to function
as a lodge during their stay in Yosemite."

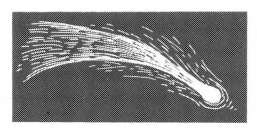

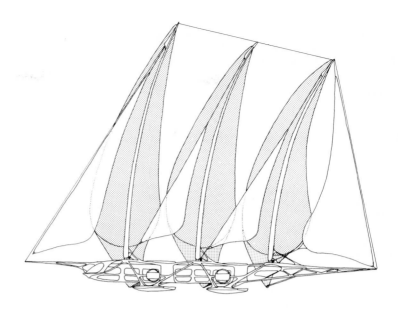

WINDSHIP

I. BAND 1007 CCT: 1745, 13 April 1986

"Now--the windships."

"I don't even understand why we're discussing it. I can't see how those things floating over the valley would interfere or even...."

"Fred, play around with your focus: you're wobbling. That's better. The question, if you and Craig remember the protest, was not noise, but visual intrusion. Like jet vapor trails. Craig, you lived near Boston's Logan...."

"No, Jack. The problem there was the birds living near the runways. They got sucked into the planes."

"Oh, then that isn't relevant. The problem here, the objection exactly was, let me see...."

"I think it's on that pile of stuff to your...right, Jack."

"Thanks, Fred. Yes...'denigration of the wilderness experience.'"

"Experience? I ran into this smiling skier near Lembert Dome. She was cross-countrying, had pulled a buckle, and I just ambled right over--no mean feat in all that snow...."

"Bleep it, Craig. Stop wasting our time and anyone else's who's watching. I want to get finished! This looks like another hang glider number. We're not the ones to decide what's the appropriate way of seeing or being in the wilderness."

"Right, the only decision that made any difference was getting the cars and roads out."

"So we're back to where we started. Do we allow the windships to cruise over the Park twice every day--when the wind's right? I don't want to get into the ethical word games or disputed rights: that's bullshit, and a kettle of worms, and I don't think a real issue. So do we draft a polite we-decided-not-to-act-on-it or pass it along to this month's community vote?

"What else is on the ballot?"

"The eastern Sierra water rights dispute and the approval--that is, money--for the consulting team to go to the Willamette valley initiative."

"Well, why not add a throwaway?"

"I vote 'vote.'"

"That makes two."

"Okay, put it to them!"

GARDEN PEACE

"Well, now tell me, just how did you come to this project? It's Mrs Prisk, is it not?"

"It's Adele, dear, that means . . . do you know? Noble, it means noble. Gives me a goal to live up to.

"Let's see. I came up here five years ago. Yes, it was right after my husband died. But we don't have to go into that. I was ready for the retirement home. The study hall for aged teachers. I couldn't bear the thought of it. So I came up here thinking I could contribute something to this place. Always loved it here, the air, the scents and the mountains. It's so wonderful here, don't you think? So up I came and found the most remarkable people. All full of excitement about building a new world. Just what I needed. They never questioned my age, just whether I really cared for this place. What was wanted were people who really cared. So I never even asked about money or where I'd live or anything, just started right in talking and pretty soon we had it all going."

"You mean the gardens? Why gardens up here? It would seem like there's more space to grow food down in the San Joaquin? And besides, my son said the purpose of all this was to restore the environment of Yosemite. Gardens seem . . . well, they seem inconsistent."

"Heavens, that's really a huge question. It's about quality of life and the ways in which we can determine that quality. You see, one of the main ideas up here is not only to restore — actually that's not the right word because we could never really restore this place — it'll never be what it was. Really we're curing this place of a malady brought on by too much of our carelessness."

"My son always calls Yosemite California's church and I always felt it was a shame to install a hamburger stand in Notre Dame."

"Yes, exactly. Now what was I saying? Oh yes, one thing was that we viewed land in a peculiar, categorized set: like campers only camping where it's supposed to be done; it isn't done on flat agricultural land, it's only done in the mountains. Isn't that odd? It is, isn't it? Monoculture is like that: it's an insane way of growing things. Reminds me of wheat stalks growing out of stainless steel soil, a painting I saw once. Monoculture is a moneyman's way of growing things. They spend half their energy trying to erase all traces of wilderness, making the Earth look like the face of the moon, and then they try and grow things in the dead soil.

"Large centralized farms with fields devoted to single crops like tomatoes just don't work. Their efficiency is deadly, destroying the social and ecological fabric of life. People living apart from their food source develop very foolish — and dangerous — illusions about life. They seem to forget they're interdependent.

"It all comes down to some simple ideas. The relation of as many people as possible to the process of growing food and scattering the food-growing activities throughout a wild system."

178

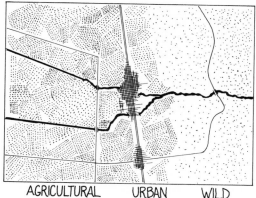 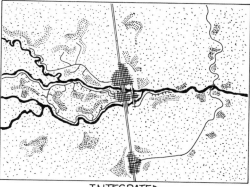

AGRICULTURAL   URBAN   WILD   INTEGRATED

"I read an article about how we've been so overwhelmed by our own creations, machines that is, that we've gone and forced life into patterns . . . . "

"Into patterns like machines. It's quite true. We've tried to make the Earth work like a battleship. Continental Remodeling, indeed!

"Would you like some more tea? No trouble; I'll get the water going . . . yes, now where were we? Gardens. Our gardens are wonderful little jungles of life — have you ever been in the Amazon? That's where you can learn about Nature. Stand in that soil too long and you begin to grow. Anyway, our gardens produce three to twenty times what one of those big factory farms produces. That's per acre, of course. And we do it with a much greater and tastier variety of crops. Would you like anything in your tea? Good, good, I hate putting honey or milk in my tea: just doesn't taste like Yosemite then. "Yosemite Garden Tea," isn't that sweet?"

"Just fine. The way I like it."

"We don't have much waste up here, our gardens are so totally organic. This expert — UCLA, I think — said we use 20 percent less energy than comparable mechanized farms. I think he meant both human and mechanical or something.

"Then there's all the space between gardens, the forests and so on. So the gardens are like islands in a wilderness. Any species of insect or microbe that might harm one garden has little chance of making it to another.

"You see, dear, there's a point to all this: we wanted to show how it is possible for a small number of people to live up here without having to import all their necessities. And without totally altering the land and the life. We step lightly here, but with great care."

"My, you have so much to say about all this!"

"Yes, I never tire of my gardens. I get my hands in the soil. You know, I feel sometimes like my gardens are my children. I know them better than I ever knew my own children."

"I am curious about one thing. Don't the gardens — I came up on last night's train and I couldn't see a thing — don't they take up a lot of space? I should think . . . "

"The gardens are quite small. Half are within the inns' greenhouses, the rest are serenely integrated with the buildings and surrounding environment. I doubt if any of them could be spotted from a windship.

"Each garden has beds of thick — up to 75 centimeters — aerated soil full of organic matter. The containers' wooden sides are perforated so that air can pass through the soil and reach the roots. The crumbly soil encourages roots to grow down, not out, so everything can be planted extremely close together. We group them to take advantage of their natural symbiotic relationships — you know, like green beans, strawberries, bibb lettuce and spinach — and irrigate through small drip tubes placed over the beds. The leaf-mulch cover we've devel-

Twenty inns within Yosemite Park are surrounded by exterior gardens totaling 37,160 square meters: less than .00048 percent of the Park's total acreage. This inn-border area produced 367,253 kilograms of food during 1984's six to eight month growing season: the equivalent of feeding 2500 to 3000 people for a year. The inn greenhouses within the Park produced another 170,000 kilograms of fruit and vegetables, enough food for another 1500 more people a year.

oped practically eliminates evaporation so we need about one-tenth the water conveyor-belt agriculture needs. Of course all our water is collected rainwater so that we don't have to tap any stream or creek or river here."

"Is it hard work?"

"Yes, but not much of it. After the first few years — building up the soil, developing the techniques, refining our relationship to the gardens — it's come to where people spend only a few hours a week gardening. It's come to be a pleasurable avocation for people tired of dealing with the millions of visitors.

"By the way, I wanted to tell you, the next time you go to the store, just think about who handled and how far they carried that artichoke or whatever. Think about what that costs. We have virtually no complicated transportation, no middlemen. Walk out and pick it, or buy it from the produce train that carries the surplus."

"Are the gardens worth it? They must be a tremendous amount of work. I can understand all you say about big agriculture, but don't you think, well, that you might have gone overboard in the opposite direction?"

"If I thought that I wouldn't be here. My life is these gardens. I detest those chemical tomatoes, everything grown with that stuff. It's possible to grow a tremendous amount of food in a small space, without oil and wasted energy and tractors. And we're doing it, simply. We grow over a quarter of what is eaten within the Yosemite region and almost 80 percent of what we, those who live and work here, need in fruit and vegetables. And the gardens take up less than half of one percent of the region's land area. Come for dinner, I'll show you quality!"

"You love Yosemite, don't you? It's really wonderful to see people love where they are. I wish I could feel that!"

"You can, my dear. We can all, for example, share the sense of the life here. Every year millions come up here and we hear them say they can't believe what we've done here. Well, we can hardly believe it ourselves. They come for their few days and they tell us how much they love the place and they think they've felt something. Lord, if they only knew what it's like to live here year round! What I'm saying is, why don't you join us, dear? You'd love it here and it's much better that sitting in a tiny room waiting for the mailman. You listen to me. I know, I was there once!"

" . . . . "

"If you want love for a lifetime, work in a garden."

"Adele . . . really now, what are you telling me? It's rugged and requires tremendous effort. Act your age. We're mature women, much too old to be engaged in such work!"

"That's ridiculous. I may be well past sixty, but there isn't much I can't do. I went down to one of our new gardens the other day. It's right down near Merced Falls in the middle of the railway storage yards. Trains parked under the fig trees and the blackberry vines. I walked the top of a rail. I just stepped up there like a child and started walking with my arms stretched out just like this!"

"Well, I don't think I could do that. I'm just not able to do things like that anymore."

"That's a shame. You know there're people working down there in the railway yards that are older than you and I. There was one wonderful gentleman who's been working as a mechanic all his life. He'd grown tight over the years and was starting to have heart trouble — once that happens you live in fear — well, he came to work here and after his other work he gardened. He said he loosened up in no time. He's 72 and last year he kayaked down the Merced."

"You don't take care of the railroad gardens, do you?"

"Of course not, the railway people do. It gives them all a break from working with hard mechanical things. Working with those things will make you hard inside. We shouldn't spend so much time with machines.

"Walk around the greenhouses. There's one in every inn and many of the stations. Smell the scents mixing with the forest; feel how it all fits. Talk with the people here. Plants are interesting but people are unbelievable, and I wouldn't have said that five years ago. We may have created some beautiful gardens, but the best one is the one around us. And it's the spirit that links us. That and our form of organization. We call it participatory democracy. Sounds a little odd, but . . . . "

"Politics too. My, Adele, I think that you . . . . "

"It's just like a garden. If you know what to put in and what not to, then you can be pretty sure of getting what you want. We're all one big garden really, a bunch of weeds growing in the forest."

"I can't believe that people can really take part in decisions. Adele, you can't be serious. Politics is a play of power, of fear, it just doesn't work any other way."

"Participatory democracy doesn't work by guilt or fear: it works by pure self-interest. You know that people are basically selfish. Really, you know that, I know that and I should think everyone with half a mind would also."

"Well, I think it's good to feel for others."

"Of course it is. But, dear, you must see this one thing. I make the garden grow and the life I give helps my life. It's just a circle like all the rest. You receive the love you give."

"Well, I don't know. I suppose . . . . "

"Dear, please . . . don't judge until after your eyes have seen."

April 1986
Wawona Village

First food I ate in Los Angeles, I had a lettuce and tomato salad. I'm used to eating fresh vegetables as you know, daily, and getting a lift within about an hour. Even two hours later, I noticed no increase in energy.

The next three days there I continued experimenting. Ate vegetables wherever I went. They tasted okay and seemed fresh and nutritious, but I never got that lift. I felt tired, as if I hadn't eaten anything.

Didn't think all that much about it until I ran into Adele Prisk on my way home. I told her about it in front of Fignon's Hardware on Foresta Street. She said she wasn't surprised. Said that practically all commercially grown tomatoes produced with chemical techniques, for example, are inferior to organically grown ones. And not only do they have less nutritive value, but their taste is flat. Now maybe I understand why Alice and Ted in LA are so tired!

Back home I devoured a huge salad with every imaginable vegetable. The tomatoes were so flavorful I thought I'd eaten the pick of the patch. But they were the ordinary El Portal tomatoes I'd been eating for the last three years. Felt like I could lift Half Dome almost as soon as I'd finished.

May 18, 1986

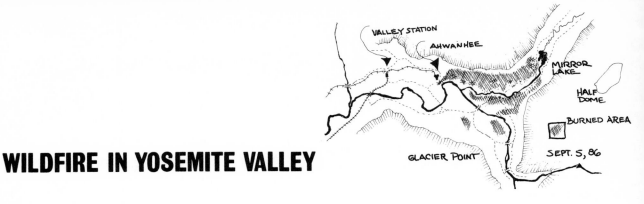

WILDFIRE IN YOSEMITE VALLEY

Joanne Searls reporting to the Overview Safety team on CTT about the valley's first uncontrolled wildfire, Saturday, September 5, 1986. She showed tapes, films and candids of the event.

A loud crack followed by flashes of lightning and rolling thunder wakened Stuart Cobb at dawn. Scanning the forest around Mirror Lake campcircle, he saw the brush at the base of a rotting cedar 100 meters from the camp was burning. Pulling on his jeans and leaving his tent, he ran out in the light rain to the camp phone. Valley Station Ranger Office asked him to begin evacuating the campers at Mirror Lake. Ranger Dan G. Foster while alerting the CCT network calculated the fire's potential. The forest was dry, the rain was too light to dampen the underbrush. Foster conferred with Aileen Jasperson and Ed Kanlowitz who had just come to work. They decided this might be the one to let burn. Aileen alerted the fire teams in El Portal and Crane Flat. Foster climbed the bell tower: four soft deep notes as he took a long careful survey of the widening streaks of white smoke. Aileen and Ed called the campcircles in the fire's path.

The "wildfire game" had been played practically everywhere in Yosemite but the valley until now. Aileen and Ed decided Dan had enough experience to lead the important action. And they knew this because they knew him. Aileen called back El Portal and asked them to bring the fire train up code two, "because we're not sure what will happen." Ed called Wawona Wilderness Labs and within a few seconds the CCT screen in Valley Station Ranger Office was full image with scientists conferring about how to tape the fire, fire crews in other sections debating about equipment. The question that unified the rapid talk was whether to allow spectators. The Merced dispatcher picked up the dialogue and delayed the morning train pending the decision.

Mason J. Overberry on Valley Station Operation team took it upon himself to check the station's sprinkler systems. He reported over CCT that his "buildings were ready for anything "

Fire, Ranger Overview and Valley Biome Study teams agreed within thirteen minutes of the first call that once the fire train with its helicopter was in Valley Station, visitors would be okay.

Within thirty minutes all five campcircles in proximity of the expanding fire were evacuated; one ranger checked for stragglers. Low flames arced to 800 meters west of Mirror Lake, and the billowing white smoke had replaced the stormclouds in an otherwise bright sunrise. Three rangers at Valley Station, three from El Cap and Sentinel stations and eight up from El Portal in a railtruck fanned out like sentries along each trail into the fire area.

"People are often terrified
of natural catastrophes like
earthquakes, wildfires, tor-
nadoes and storms far out
of proportion to the harm
these phenomena bring about.
At the same time we have
invented artificial and controlled violence to make
up for the reality we have
suppressed. These are called spectator sports."

From Max Bauer's
impromptu after-
dinner speech
following the
fire team's dis-
cussion of the
wildfire in the
valley, Sept. 5,
1986.

They informed everyone they met to stay out of the smoke,
away from the fire, watch out for rattlesnakes and what to do
if they were accidentally caught in the fire. They cautioned
people to be especially careful of children and that getting
close to a fire "is your own risk."

By noon regular trains, a special hastily assembled for
El Portal residents and twelve shuttlecars full of scientists,
their equipment as well as campers and inn visitors from the
Crane and Wawona lines--six to seven hundred people--swelled
the thousand or so valley campers. They clustered in knots
from the Ahwahnee all the way across to Stoneman Meadow. Acrid
white smoke and occasional flare-ups as white firs "crowned-out"
was all they could see. But that didn't matter, they had plenty
to talk about anyway.

By midafternoon flames neared the Ahwahnee. The helicopter
with a full waterload was hovering just in case. A cluster of
firs went up and spectators who couldn't see the building
thought the shooting flames was the Ahwahnee. But soaked by
its own sprinklers, the building suffered only a few scorched
shingles. Four scientists who'd been studying wildfire video-
taped the scene from a window on the second floor. The fire
burned on.

A peculiar orange-pink light in the smoky forest was sunset. Most of the spectators had long since gone back to their
camps or homes or inns to wash the ashes off. The fire died
down along with the winds and a twilight thundershower provided
a spectacular show of lightning illuminating fog mixed with smoke.
The fire was out.

There were only three injuries: one ranger was bitten by
a rattler, a backpacker was slightly burned after taking up a
dare to run through the flames and Mason J. Overberry, checking
Valley Station's unused water sprinklers for the fourth time,
slipped off the roof breaking his collarbone. A few thousand
insects were probably incinerated; the injury to birds is estimated
to be light and there's no evidence of any large mammals being
killed.

The following December, after a few fall rains, the fire
zone was alive with new grass and the seedlings of new trees.
Many trees with blackened trunks measured a spurt in growth and
fungus infections are unusually light. More deer and other
animals are reported in that area of the valley. There has
already been a rush on spring tour reservations from flower clubs
and other groups interested in witnessing the expected wild-
flower explosion.

WINDSHIP

II. 4000 m asl: 1333, 2 Dec 86

One white rope shivering in the icy wind, its gray shadow flickers on the billowing conch shell. The edges of the sail curl with ice. Shards peel off and drop on the steel-ribbed glass roof; they hover undecidedly before sliding off the curve and disappearing. A paperweight snowstorm, only outside.

Inside Tina Spencemuller removes her metal frames after distinctly feeling they were about to freeze to her nose. The captain repeats his encouragements from the front of the ship. As cheerleader he'd make second string. "We're doing okay. We got the trouble isolated. We know what's wrong at least. As soon as we can couple the thermoclip back to the solarskin, we'll have heat again."

"I don't believe it," a shivering man up front mutters loud enough for all but the very last rows of passengers to hear. "I always knew solar energy was bullshit."

Listing, tilting, unsteady in the changing current of the wind, the craft waddles over Tioga Pass — a thousand meters over — like a white poodle.

Tina tries to plot the vectors, but gives up as the windship shudders, tacking on the Pacific's air ocean. They were definitely encountering another weather pattern. The storm's freezing wetness was now behind evaporating before it could even mist the sage of the Nevada high desert. No one in the windship could touch the ice or snow either. But they could feel it through the cold glass.

After two hours, the storm and the loss of heat, the excursion passengers were not interested in recreation. "They've lost it," Tina gloats. "The older you get, the less able you are to flush things like this Even I'm cornering, but what a story it'll make. There's only one way you can go with it, cradle your fear in the motion," she looks up beyond the sail to the lenticular clouds backdropping the entire scene. "Resist and you'll get so airsick no bag will hold you." She lets her giggle ease out into a lullaby, humming softly her father's reassurance: "If it bends in the breeze, it'll build in the wind."

"I know that rope is going to break," a woman finally erupts. Separated from the captain by no more than the back of his seat, she hurls her accusation at him. He turns around and then advances a few feet into the aisle, the only opaque surface in the ship. "There's no need to be upset: the worst is over. Our windship is under control." Then more softly because of safer ground, "and the heat's coming back on. Can you feel it? Just relax and get warm. We'll be in Monterey in about 41 minutes." Adults hiding from the sharpness of experience."

The unthawed woman almost shouts across the aisle at a woman whose orange and purple scarf has slipped to the floor, "Now he thinks he can control the wind. How does he know when we'll get there?" Getting no response she turns back to the man beside her. "Why did I ever let you take me on this thing? Joy ride? We're going to be killed."

Some laugh, some frown, but most turn away. At least the noise of humanity is heard again in the gondola. The returning warm air visibly defrosts white and green and pinched faces.

"That other woman has lost more than her scarf. She's been to the john about four times. Drunk and not on this! And the rest of them! They're scared! Not one of them is sitting back in the seats' enveloping pillows. They've all popped out of them. That guy in front of me hasn't looked outside at all that I can remember. And in the face of all California! What is it that makes them so wrapped up in their own fears?
Tina opens her notebook. "Glad I didn't bring a recorder. I think they'd weird out if they heard what I'm thinking."

"Keeping the log?" The man next to her has a reassuring smile.

"I wish I were, but no one's asked me to. I'm taking notes for a science project. I want to go to Bennington in the fall and I have to do an independent research project."

"You look too young for college."

"I've skipped a few grades. I really want to go east. I've never been. Are you scared?"

"Why no, not particularly. I'm not steady, but I'm not anxious. Yes, I'm enjoying it. So . . . you're taking notes for a research study?"

"I want to get an overview of the Park, the whole area around here. I want to see if I can see anything. I wanted to do it by chopper but around here *they're used only for emergencies. My father said the windship would be better for a first look, and if I found anything interesting, then he'd see about the helicopter."*

"Commendable reason. I came along just for the ride. Or rather went to it: Owens Valley isn't exactly my cup of tea. Especially since the aqueduct dynamitings have started in again. But this is quite a ride, isn't it? Even the sun's coming out for it."

"What slams me looking at it from here is that the snow isn't covering up what's down there. It shows patterns you can't see from the ground. Look at those shadows on the domes and the icy blue lakes. The forests have a sharp, knife-edge look. But bristly. The canopy pattern is sculpted in white."

Heads turn left, then there's a rush: ski runs at Badger Pass.

"After the snow comes the slide," he laughs and turns back to Tina who's looking right below her at wisps of blue smoke climbing in the cold air until something — temperature, moisture, altitude — flatten them. "People exhaust," Tina points.

"That's funny! I'd like to see what you've written."

"Here," she tosses him her notebook and peers down below her hiking boots resting on the clear glass. "It's really strange to watch things right below you. Like glass-bottom boats. Only the minnows are human."

He reads: "From halfway to the moon, Earth's storm clouds look wispy, transparent. The atmosphere looks like a filmy membrane. Even above the Earth's aura, the satellites picture tan blotches, green squares, dots of clouds. From out in space it's all wilderness — you can't see the cities. What do I see? the sharpness of experience."

"That's good."

"Don't be polite. You don't have to encourage me, or treat me like a child."

"I'm not. Don't get offended. What I meant to say," he hands back the book to her, "was that it's like something that's been reported to you or that you've seen reproduced. Not yet using your own eyes. Where do you go to school?"

"Carmel: RRJ and SHS. Ronald Reagan Junior and Senior High Schools. I live in Pebble Beach. What do you do for a living?"

"I'm a bacteriologist, I work for Conglomerate Products."

"I could have called it! What do you do specifically?"

"Oh, it's kind of specialized. Let's just say I search through microscopes for relationships. But I'm interested in what you're doing. What's your project about?"

"Water patterns in land forms, I think."

"That sounds ambitious."

"Depends. Look at those trees. I've never been able to see this from airplanes. They fly too high or too fast. You can tell the types of trees down there from the snow. From how much is left and the direction it fell in. Look straight down, to the right: those are sugar pines: they're more green than white. The wind in the canyon sort of vacuumed the needles. And those below. See how the snow piles in the tight clusters, the leaflike needles? They're cedars."

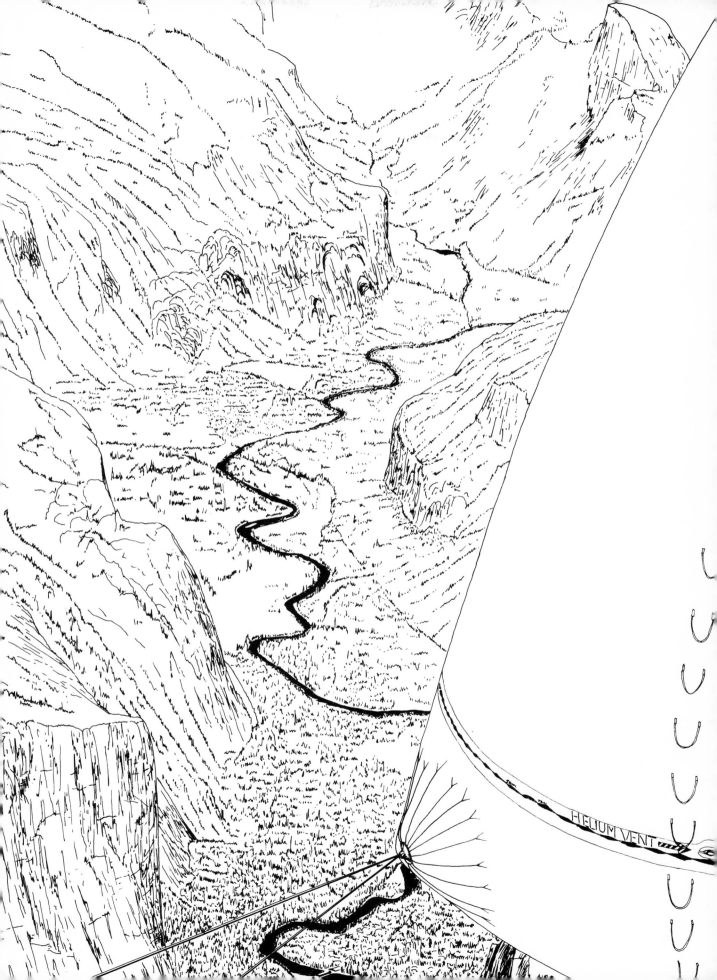

HELIUM VENT only

"I take it back. You do have good eyes."

"Would you know, really, if I were wrong?"

"I think so. You're a strange child."

"They keep telling me my trouble is that I've never been a child," she smiles and then looks away. He felt suddenly bruised inside. So he looks across the aisle and quickly gaps the silence. "That's odd, those big patches of bare granite. Look, you can see the gray sides of those domes."

"The sides are so smooth that the weight of the snow, curtains of snow, pushes it all down: it slides and piles up, buckles really, near the base. It's like an imitation of the foliating of granite. It's a solid representation. Water usually seeps into the cracks in those rocks. Then it freezes and expands and breaks off slabs of strata like onion peels.

"The white snow makes me think of the glacier. Water frozen into rivers of ice. I can almost see them: hundreds of ice floes pouring down all those canyons. What if we could see — like with X-ray eyes — where all the water is right now? If I could visualize it all flowing at this instant, that'd be incredible! Maybe I could? Then I'd be seeing holistically, like Mrs. Campbell said. Grasping the whole, not focusing on the parts."

A strong wind tilts the windship hard to the north bringing Tina's eyes into direct line with triangular, square, peaked, but all snow-laden roofs of the inns along the Crane Flat line.

"People irrigating with water, even on such a small scale, have altered the way it was. It looks like there's new growth below those inns. From the runoff from the gardens. Look, see the way it merges: the wild foliage, so diverse, the more regular fruit-and nut-bearing trees and the clipped growth around the trellises and snow-covered rails."

"You're really bursting with energy. It's exciting to listen to you. I can't believe you're only in high school!"

"You can thank my father for that. When we passed over those fields north of Bishop, remember? The river entered the valley, breaking down into irrigation channels, branching out into the neat square fields. It's easy to explain fields. Everybody knows what they look like: you can see mental images of the pattern. But mountains! Their water and life systems are so much more complicated; very few people have a whole picture of it. We have no language for what's wild, only for the tame."

"What's your name?"

"Tina Spencemuller."

"I'll be damned. George Spencemuller's little girl? Tell your father you sat next to Wally Ferguson."

But Tina was feverishly writing.

"What are you getting down?"

"That area north, see above Hetch Hetchy? Look how diverse it looks. But it doesn't look chaotic; there's a coevolutionary pattern behind the composition of rocks, snowfall, the species of tree, the mountain forms. It seems intact. Looks 'eco-logical.' It looks right. But over there, to the west: see where the powerlines march through the forest there? Those straight lines look crazy if you perceive what the pattern of the land is. The land, our Earth, has been a foreign language to us. Until we can think in it, we don't understand it."

"And you know when it — the land — is right?"

"I think I do. What do you think?"

"We're beyond the valley. Look up ahead; there's the Central Valley."

"The storm didn't even touch it. Look how parched it looks."

"Parched? What do you mean? Doesn't look parched to me."

"Look at that green; it's almost gray; it's not bright or alive."

"Look, Tina, not to pull your pins, but I think maybe you've been influenced by those accounts of the death of the San Joaquin fields."

Tina ignores this, turns back to her writing: "There is definitely a strong — no, a marked — change from the mountains and their foothills to the valley below. The grassland is dry and sick-looking. Even the areas around the normally wet deltas are looking that way: the disturbance seems to be spreading, like a fungus. Virtually nothing follows the pattern of the land. Trees are planted in orderly rows despite the meandering of the delta. Crops are planted evenly despite the curves of the land. The rivers have been altered, their bottoms scoured for gold, the dredging remnants look like stone dunes. It's all soilless there."

"Come to any other conclusions?"

"It's different here. The land is different, it isn't as diverse; the relationship between growing things and water isn't natural."

"What do you mean? Agriculture is as natural as us."

"Doesn't it look sick to you?"

"How else could it be?"

"I don't know. It just doesn't look right. There isn't any pattern, there's only a rigid grid imposed on it."

"What?"

"Well, back there you could see the trees, water and land all working together in harmony. But down here it's like we don't consider things. We don't follow water flow on flatland because it's flat. Streams aren't visible raging torrents; they're lazy and calm. The slopes are so gradual they're ignored."

"So?"

"All this land down here. Well, it was wilderness too once, wasn't it?"

"I guess so."

"And it's been broken, domesticated, bred for our purposes, used, its way ignored?"

"If you want to put it that way."

"Like domestic animals. Something has been taken away from them too: native intelligence, freedom, independence, a response to themselves?"

"Yes."

"With land, clearing and using it, making it work for us, has lessened its diversity and lowered its strength, its health. Our crops are intruders rather than partners. Because of us the land cannot function on its own. It needs our management."

"What do you mean function on its own?"

"To support itself and the things that live on it in a healthy way. If we withdrew right this instant we would leave a decaying life system in no way as rich and varied and wholesome as it was before we came. In thousands of years it may revitalize itself, but that's if we leave it alone."

"Surely you're just exaggerating to make a point. We have used and lived off the land on Earth for ten thousand years like other animals."

"Okay. That's society's excuse. But what do we give back to the Earth? I can't think of anything except our own dead bodies."

LIVING HISTORY

What has the Living History team been doing? Trying to incorporate natural and human and cultural history pertaining to this region into an available, meaningful form! Keeping a living record as well as a repository of all the ramifications of what's happening here. That means tapes, film, records, writing, oral tradition, observations — all the myriad forms of memory we can collect and preserve so that this project may be understood in detail as well as in breadth. Our other primary endeavor is to provide a foundation for initiating Past History research and retrieval.

Our publications started with our quarterly *Natural Yosemite Notes*, and we are now at the point where we will be publishing other contemporarily relevant information. Among the first series of books we plan to publish is a history of the Curry family by Francine Armitage tentatively titled *Yosemite Curry* and the working diary of the railway's route engineer, George Spencemuller, *Plumb Survey*. Let me just whet your taste with some excerpts from his diary:

March 22, 1979

The energy crisis has become the basis of our thinking. It's comparatively easy to change personal habits, not to use as much energy, to drive less, walk more, to take care of your own body more and prevent rather than react to sickness and so attain individual responsibility. But the civilization is structured with technology that's inappropriate, unhealthy and increasingly dangerous. The institutions that develop, support and operate the technology are imbued with a style of centralization that's paralyzing.

June 19, 1979

We realized that the technology to help people get to Yosemite had to be minimal enough to avoid altering the place. Our problem is to enhance the wilderness experience by the lack of technology.

May 15, 1980

Just spent the afternoon with the survey crew up at Pinoche Tunnel. Had lunch on a rock cluster above where the southeast portal is to be. Someone said something about the view from the train as it popped out of the tunnel. I looked up at the midday sun and realized the potential. I just faded out of the conversation and let my imagination leap into the dark claustrophobic tunnel and settle in the vantage point of the nose of the train. The light at the end got lighter and lighter. Suddenly, we shoot out of the darkness with a slap of air. If the portal were positioned carefully, we'd come out without being able to see where the track goes. It would look as if we were about to launch out into the canyon. For a breathless second or two until the curve would grab us and shift the whole view back over a small creek before the dark forest. We'll have to make sure Brady would work out the effect carefully. He and his crazy crew are sure to get behind the effort but may not be visionary enough to see it beforehand. We have to touch them with a bit of Zen; they've been doing highways so long they may have forgotten the drama of a train.

REPORTS

Fall/Winter 1986, Volume III, Number 3

Natural Yosemite Notes is a quarterly compendium of things we find interesting up here day-to-day and year-to-year. Sort of a continuation of the long defunct *Yosemite Nature Notes*, it has some of the charm of that magazine, funky and down-home we would say in place of their "homey." Here is one excerpt:

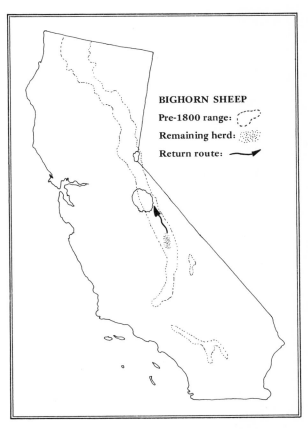

BIGHORN SHEEP
Pre-1800 range:
Remaining herd:
Return route:

the return of Bighorn

The dream of seeing these sheep return to the areas of the Park where they once grazed may yet be realized. One neighboring herd, scattered east of Sequoia National Park and west of Mt. Whitney, numbers between 275 and 325. Five years ago the largest estimate of the hard-to-count herd was around 250. Owens Valley residents who have been following developments credit the increase to the Department of Forestry's wildlife management: discouraging the use of certain high-country trails, eliminating others and generally alerting those who pack into that area about how not to ruin the bighorn's delicate habitat.

Before the white man, it is estimated that the bighorn sheep, who normally live between one and two thousand meters, numbered between five and ten thousands in herds stretching from the San Bernadino and Tehachapi Mountains north across the entire Sierra Nevada and into the Cascades. Hunting was the main destroyer and the animals have developed a not-unreasonable fear of man. Any proposal of introducing a small herd back into the Yosemite has to take this factor into account.

Michael and Linn Alder, members of the Bighorn Reintroduction Team, proposed a method they presented to the Overview Team for approval. First, they rule out tranquillizing the animals to transport them to their new home site. That, we have already learned with wolves, is a traumatic experience, one that the more delicate bighorns may not recover from.

Instead, the Alders propose camping with the herd, following it and familiarizing themselves with it for an indefinite period. They've come to trust the intelligence of these ruminants and feel that with time the bighorn will trust them. When the animals' patterns and movements are sufficiently well-known to them, they believe they can cull a suitable group from the main herd and begin moving them north.

The undertaking is very delicate: the two animal biologists don't know whether they can move the group far or just a short distance and then wait for it to reach a stable size before culling another group out of it and continuing the trek. Obviously this could take many years.

The primary objective is to get even a small group to cross the San Joaquin Canyon into the Yosemite area. The only break in a continuous chain of north-south high peaks is a comparative lowland — usually avoided by the sheep — and near the Mammoth ski area and highly popular with backpackers. Once that crossing is accomplished, it's a relatively simple matter for the sheep to climb up into the Ritter range and on to the high peaks of Yosemite and farther north.

As yet no one knows more about this *Ovis* species than the Alders, and even they can't guarantee that the test herd can be coaxed north, a distance of 150 kilometers, even over three or four years.

...We have known over the past 150 years a rate of technological creation unprecedented in the planet's histroy. In the last twenty years this rate of development has become increasingly difficult to sustain. Greater and greater investment in research and development has become necessary to refine invention, even to the point of diminishing returns.

It is like constructing a tall building: beyond 120 stories conventional construction reaches a point where support for upper stories becomes a dense forest of structure on lower ones, unfeasible technologically and economically.

While we have been concentrating on increased "progress," we have been ignoring the social and ecological implications at the foundation. Pollution and socio-economic confusion are just two symptoms of this oversight.

What seems apparent for us to do is concentrate our efforts not on building but on refining the process of how things are built, the reasons for building it and how it is used. We must learn how to integrate our technology with our lives and the life of our planet.

Gavin Collins
FUTURIST MAGAZINE seminar
Del Portal Hotel
El Portal, December 14, 1986

---

mimeo notice: please place on bulletin board
Wawona Village, El Portal stations

Catalina Project representatives are inspecting work done here at Yosemite, concentrating on the still incomplete sections of rail near Wawona. They are also interested in recruiting people who have worked here for their project and would be pleased to talk to interested people and take applications at the Wawona hotel this week. Ask for Wendy.

For those of you who need more filler, the Catalina Project, still in preliminary research, has a long-term goal of demonstrating the island's self-sufficiency. Solar heating and energy generation is the first target, to be followed by a light rail transportation system like ours combined with small sun-charged electric cars. The arid Mediterranean-climated island's substantial wilderness areas will be analyzed to determine:
 1. how restoration can be achieved after decades of haphazard and confused attempts to introduce domestic grazing animals,
 2. how wild animals and domestic gardens can supply the island's people with a sizable percentage of their food, and
 3. how reef fishing, once a large part of the island's economy, can be restored both as a source of local food and as a surplus cash crop.
California's recent legalized gambling laws--allowing counties to license gambling operations based on statewide criteria--has revitalized Catalina's once-active casino. Its owners, in the interest of preserving the island's character and wildness, are providing much of the funding for the project.

PETS UNLIMITED

Wawona Village was the first community to give in. Then Crane Flat followed, as it frequently does. Even mighty El Portal is gradually capitulating. Giving them up is a painful thing to do.

But the realization has taken hold that one of the major barriers keeping wild animals at a distance was the presence, often the superabundance, of domestic pets.

However, there are advantages to this sacrifice. People in Wawona have begun to share with their wild neighbors. At least one household is regularly visited by a raccoon, another by a gray fox. A burrowing owl has located itself in a corner of a garden right off Wawona's main plaza. And pigmy owls regularly perch in favored houses. Coyotes have been discovered to be very friendly, though a little guarded. But the most popular wild pet species is the ring-tailed cat. There are at least five homes I know of that have been adopted by these relatively docile creatures. They are nocturnal and weren't very visible until the household dogs and cats left, but interestingly enough the gold miners used to keep them around to catch rats and mice.

April 22, 1986

Allen:

Moving east into the Sierra the train passed numerous small inns, one example after another of careful siting: some on cliffs, others on flatland, even a few as bridges over the Merced River. I must say I saw some sloppy construction, amateur work. But there _is_ soul in them thar hills and I'll forgive a great deal for that commodity too often missing from contemporary construction. I'm writing this from a bay window in an inn overlooking El Portal; it's like sitting in a tree house!

Andrew

P.S.: I'll be back in NYC on the 3rd

Yosemite Railway, 3rd Anniversary Party
Excerpt, Speech of Clive Henderson, Yosemite Inn Company Team Captain

"....And many of us here today came from other places to focus our attention on this place for a time. We care about Yosemite not only because Yosemite is a beautiful place, but because Earth is our home and more beautiful, we trust, for what we have nurtured and for the folks who have worked the dream into reality. But ultimately many, if not all, of us will leave for other places. We are the seed, planting, tending for a while, then leaving it all in the care of those who replace us, those who will maintain the garden we have started.

"It is only proper that this should happen. Nothing is permanent. We take care of what is here, make it more fruitful by adding our own touches, and then we move on."

THREE DEAD MYSTERIOUS 1st WINDSHIP ACCIDENT

(Copperopolis, Ca., Dec. 3, 1986) A windship carrying 28 passengers and three crew members mysteriously crashed en route from Owens Valley to Monterey over this eastern San Joaquin Valley town about 1400 this afternoon.

Reported dead were Tina Spencemuller, age 16, daughter of George Spencemuller of Pebble Beach, Mabel Clegg of Tonapah Nev., and Robert Austin of Santa Cruz.

Preliminary investigation suggests a mid-air collision but no other aircraft was in the area at the time.

By Gravity from Glacier Point March 21,1987

shuttle rounding
Turtleback Dome -
gravity car route

Nineteen thirty, almost dark and quiet in El Portal. Down from dinner Larry, Ellie and I, walking, looking at white rocks and moonlit Merced rapids. "How would the granite faces around the valley be lit by this light?"

"Take the gravity car to Glacier Point and see?"

Station light and platform already disappearing. Headlight's bright reach keeps our attention — roaring Merced River near — V-shaped narrow floor canyon — cold black water, silvery blue rapids — moonlight silhouettes limbs, needles, cones and bats zapping insects in blackness — quivering moths stinging our cold red cheeks. Up the Wawona line — wet grasses sparkling in headlight — cold Bridalveil spray — coyote tail behind a lit boulder — squealing sound, squelched with a muffled bark — black damp tunnel — tiny incandescent marker lights — glowing blue icicles — ears stinging, parka hoods up, drawstrings taut.

Turtleback Dome — ice on granite black like stove steel — trees battle alone with searing, whistling up-canyon wind — screeching owl, flapping wings — then, blending into black too quickly to identify. Pohono Inn, Longview Inn, Avalanche Inn — diamonds on silver string of rail — Chinquapin Junction — quiet transition — side wheels click through guides — sleeping building, island of glow — dark forest, a thousand paths of moonlight going everywhere at once.

GRAVITY CAR

A small, open shuttle car accommodating 25 persons on the Crane
Flat and Wawona raillines. The cars are powered by conventional electric motors upgrade. Downgrade, they acknowledge gravity to a top
speed of 80.

The service is provided on Monday afternoons and on clear full
moonlight evenings throughout the year. It is an ideal way to witness
the life in Yosemite without disturbance. The car coasts through meadows and down vistas without a murmur.

Yosemite Railway Brochure

Cresting Badger Pass — purring motors, rails lost in meadow grass — luxuriant green, wet blades where we pass, edged with frost like dust in the light — mouse leaping from rail — a still badger — beady, black eyes in my afterimage — music of water — echo under bridge — Bridalve . . . Cre . . . — another afterimage — blinking eyes, tears wiped into gloves. Around a point — a snow patch, pools of blue sparkling off pearl white — fluttering wildflowers poking color in snow, dim yellow, orange. Climbing — a dark, forested wall — "Sssshh, don't make a sound" — two deer to the right — left, a coyote — we, a rolling interruption — by and away — we, as Mr. Toad's wild ride, over a hill again, down into forest again — I sense a large depression nearby.

Loops of silver in snow — quiet — ice on rail — gliding under shivering canopy, ridge-edge pines — six pyramids etched in light in the snow — lodge, almost underground.

Owl outside, too cold to take the while to see him. Inside: floppy knitted colored caps stuck on curled ski tips, healthy, sweatered people, hands around warm glasses, butts to the fire — six skylight pyramids in pine beam roof: moon windows.

To the Point, thinking of fear — stumbling and looking: Half Dome's round backside varnished — crisp, glowing edge of white light extending up Clouds Rest — North Dome, Basket Dome's shining response — Little Yosemite over there — all the cliffs, domes, points, arrows, edges, ridges, blocks and moun-tains shaded and lit to the Cathedral Range — everything folded, treed and snowed in between. Nevada Fall draining the vision of white.

On the Point: Larry, Ellie and I crisp in ripstop parkas — plastic skins on icy rock — wiggling hips seeking fit — up, way over on boulder tip out over Yosemite Valley, glacier's trail — we, sparrows branched over the river.

Beyond the Point: steel gray, phosphorescent white-topped clouds, little cluffs of stuff standing, waiting — yet they move — we move — waves of aware-ness, intensifying as I look, as I fly without wings or movement, vision expand-ing over huge chasms, over chilling, grinding ice-blue river — the vastness of a grand canyon — the inexorable wondrous onward-moving universe — sssssssseething reality — edges of reality seeing it ALL.

Perception clear of concept blinders — water falling up or down? — I can fall in any direction? Shadows dancing — hearing sighs and cries and strings torn by the wind — eyes darting, following eddies of energy I cannot see — flicking attention into each story: bobcat stalking a noise — a click, a twig depressed — a breath — throaty snarl — cry — red on snow. Tiny pecking sound — scratching — crack — crack — soft chirping — pecking — crack — cheeping — new bird?

"Warm?" "Ready?" "Comfortable?" "ALL ABOARD!"

Up slowly through loops of rail, brushes of pine and wind. First crest: icy wind spreads my hair, pulling jacket tight — are we descending now? "Not yet, a little grade first." Anticipation, a headless horseman out there? A figure among those rocks — a tree's bent elbow — owl's sudden flight down, maybe a surprised quarry. Twisted tree roots, grabbing black hands, indistinct, freaky forms, no soft summer place this night: cold living Yosemite. Accelerating to 45 kph down, down, first time down by gravity — ehhhhhhh! — rolling faster — coasting across meadow — coyote gone, deer gone. "What's that?" "No, over there!" A mountain lion, no, King Kong? Driver: "You see what you want to see!"

Far-off flickering campfire flames, bodies passing by the flames. A sign: Lost Bear Meadow, another Bridalveil Cre . . . — sounds of water rushing on its night fall into the valley — motors pulling — climbing Badger Pass again — falling into pine needle canyon — occasional slots of moonlight, white snow flickering through trees — 40, 60, 70 — down fast through broad-banked curves, around grabbing shadows, branches as hands, could they touch me? They did! Next curve — hard against the seat — fingernail picking upholstery — clawing anticipation — as speed bright headlight illuminating crescent — disappearing track — racing into its gradual appearance. CRACK, broken branch — my seat leaves the seat — sudden rush of air — wind? — or us? Over bridge like bowling ball on loose planks — tight moonlit railroad canyon, waving pines to both sides — pine-needle rain stinging my forehead — another curve — looking straight ahead, quickly — spin out in my mind.

Red light ahead. Jesus what does that mean? — brakes, squealing, stopped — still air — blood rushing to cheeks, earlobes — silence — brushing sound in trees above — flying squirrel across the stars from tree to tree — hissing, "242, 242, Chinquapin clear in 2, clear in 2, please hold" — radio voice echoing in pressured ears — still for a time — wash of wind in trees like a sea way back in the woods.

Brakes unleashed, wheels roll — wind whistling by cold lobes — another curve, another — headlight picking out sign, blue letters sparkling, CHINQUAPIN — brakes for a switch — frail form on platform — head, gold-rimmed glasses, old man following our pass. Now down the curves of the Merced's canyon, down faster than before — ahhhhhhh — tantalizing sight of ribbonlike curves ahead — rails up to right, down on level, then up to left — a stretched, twisting "S" in front — shoot through it — around, over falling roars of white water — glancing back in taillight glow — ghostly form of latticelike bridge, barely there in the night — out to points of ridges, around, then back into a creek's noise — another bridge — Avalanche Creek — shadowed tree drops a chunk of snow — bat darts across headlight — a pair of eyes see me, I them — out to a point — slow to 10, to see California — asparagus-tipped forest below — foothills beyond like arteries standing out on my arm — distant sparkling city lights before the silhouetted coast range — open up to 40, through curves, then 50 — ghosting passage — quiet rolling through gentle curves — relax — watch the trees standing tip to the stars above — 60 — rails tightly bent again, curling around ridges, cuts of boulders, clinging bushes — raccoon's banded face in the black — another curve, would we fly off? We would, we'd come down like a toy wooden airplane — impaled on a forest of standing arrows, points of shadow, tingling points of cold air — rails always fling us back around the ridge — panning light on a new tangent ahead, around the next — a crescent of incandescent — Pohono Inn — flash of a body walking by a window — down a curve — I hold on — right hand to the cold aluminum handrail — rock — boulder right there on the rails — oh shit, this is it, we're gonna go off this damn mountain, we're gonna get shafted by a sugar pine! — rails appear in the light — likewise my fear — rails to the right of the rock — past it — up on my left — leaping, vanishing ring-tailed cat stepping up the broken granite.

Down around Turtleback Dome — open track across balding forehead — El Capitan, Half Dome and the whole valley in the distance — dim but immense space we're all falling into — looking left, down the forehead to the nose, beard, wind-gnarled hair of pines low in up-the-gorge air — 60 into forest again — moon behind the ridge, black gorge below — pieces of river music heard in the dark forest — a cracking sound, something breaks out there — ahead, two red lanterns — brakes on. Workmen: still passing faces over tight parka collars, standing blue coveralls — late show tableau — who were they? Speed again — black tunnel portal — black — no exit — one track going in — light ahead on rails — blinding to my gaping lenses — clickety-clack, clickety-clack, click, click — switch — light ahead — closer, closer — wheels loud — reverberating wheel roll under jagged granite arch, dirty icicles with broken tips — up-shuttle passes — faces seen in glowing interior to our left — what were we to them?

Out of tunnel into a view — sudden image of Yosemite Valley — distance-less vista — immediately back in the forest — wetness — up-blowing spray, Bridalveil Fall — squeaky windshield wiper, crusty, ice-coating glass, fingernails on blackboard. Slow, bottom of grade — green switch signals a line clear to El Portal — cold boiling black water, Merced River, right there — we cross stone bridge — bats swerving and curving, darting against wavering white dogwood blossoms — headlight sparkling on thin chrome bicycle spokes — leather seat dull with frost — who'd left it there? where were they? Night fantasies born of the black river — leaning head back, up to Fireplace Bluffs — stained granite glimpsed between trees, faces staring through forest — April's river wind with us — down the gorge — down with cascades to our left — white waterfalls out of cracks on our right — flick, an airborne spider — off my shoulder — through Arch Rock — ohhhhhhh! — inn quiet and dark — man walking hurriedly into the forest — a cluster of cottonwoods, their leaves flapping like hands clapping — no sound — falling into curves, tight, fast and banked — the smoother main line — wheel flanges slapping rails — huge white boulders marking our way. Yellow caution light burning in the headlight's crescent of illuminated weeds — slowing — lights of El Portal — crawling — squeak — stop.

SPEECH delivered by Leroy G. Edindour
                    Public Opinion Officer
                    Mammoth Mountain Minute Men

              at the Ahwanhee Research Center
                    Autumn Equinox, 1987

              to Members of the Three Companies
              and carried on 25 CCT channels

     And so what have you people really done? Changed the concept of
the Park? Rewritten the definition of recreation? Acted as guardian
to the wilderness? Performed a much-needed public service? Conducted
a mini-experiment in Yosemite for the rest of the country to take as a
model?
     Let me, ladies and gentlemen, go over the record with you, in case
you've forgotten or aren't aware of the specifics.
     The roads and cars came out, the train went in. The buildings in
the valley were taken out, new campgrounds and trails went in. As well
as inns, shuttle lines and all the rest of it. Haven't you put as much
back as you've taken out?
     Do people see the entrance corridors to the Park as places of in-
terest? Have they really left the trains to walk and hike and horseback ride and bicycle and canoe and kayak?
     Per capita not one bit more than they did before!
     Have they been using the many areas previously unvisited instead
of concentrating in the valley and the meadows?
     The visitor influx in the valley is even more than it was before.
People now feel stranded in the Park and tend to stay in one place, one
convenient place--the valley--more than before. Admittedly Tuolumne
Meadows has less visitor concentration than before, but that's because
of the general feeling that it's too difficult or inconvenient to get
to, and when people do they are stranded there; there are no easy ac-
cesses except by using the railway. So what do you think you have accomplished?
     The plan was to reduce the number of visitors congregating in the
summer and spread the amount through the year. Yet even with year-
round facilities, staggered school and business vacation schedules, the
main thrust of visitors still falls on the same four summer months.
Your estimate was wrong, you had no grasp on what was happening or the
means to prepare for it adequately.
     The new trails built in the area that people neglected before--most
conspicuously around Foresta and Wawona--still tally the least number
of hikers, campers and travelers.
     The Fish Camp entrance to the Park is a disgrace. Its use was to
be discouraged, the main thrust taken by El Portal. What has ensued?
It's regularly the biggest bottleneck in the Park; the trains from
there are constantly jammed well beyond the 10-percent-below-capacity
limit agreed on. The Fish Camp station is a virtual garage of abandoned
cars throughout the summer. The campgrounds there are always filled.
The northern Crane Flat access hasn't reached this nadir, but how long
until it does?
     The question has to be raised whether the Park is even a pleasant
place to visit anymore. For example the "restoration" projects undertaken by the Park community have grown out of proportion to the Park's
function as a National Park and recreation area. In 1985 and '86 Happy
Isles campground--the major one in the southeast corner of the valley--
was closed to visitors in order to study bluejay's habits in the ab-
sense of visitors!
     And that's not an isolated example. The wildlife research under-
takings were originally conceived to be funded by profits from visitor
services and fees. They were labeled as ecologically designed efforts
to explore the holistic interaction between land, animals, plants and
atmosphere. Praiseworthy objectives even if the means turned out not
to be up to the same standards. The estimates of money, energy and interest were wholly out of line with the work's cost. For example, to

round out the wildfire preparation program, land outside the Park had to be added to the managed fire preparatory work. National Park funds could not be used for this, neither would National Forest people assume financial responsibility. So this expensive undertaking had to be absorbed by Yosemite Park in midstream as it were.

The controversy over using government money in combination with the poor showing of Wawona Wilderness Labs data has already led to personnel cutbacks in other projects. At this time one five-person team is monitoring both the grizzly and wolf reintroductions. Maybe the ambitious Labs has overextended itself. Certainly the publication of the now famous Tuolumne river, Central Valley report, "California Dry," brought howls of protest not just from the scientific community but from prominent federal, state and local representatives. The already shaky autonomy of Yosemite Park--tolerated as a kind of experimental project extraordinary--has been all but completely upset by this latest toe-stepping.

Then there are the inns, those supposed marvels of architectural planning able to accommodate all the visitors to the Park, those 42 inns (I am including those on the access routes) designed to be decentralized, not to intrude upon the Park's wilderness, retain an intimate, relaxed quality, be economical but not cheap, conducive to a happy vacation and able to hold emergency overflows without trouble or effort!

Another pipe dream. The whole reservation system had to be abandoned. Quite irreverently, the promoters of this latest deregulation insist there's no need here in Yosemite to acquiesce to the outside world's preoccupation with schedules, days off, seasonal fluctuations, weekend orientation and other forms of rigid structuring. What an attitude!

People come to the Park and have to pray to be lucky enough to get accommodations. And what happens if they don't? The CCTs are used to find out what inns still have vacancies and people are shuttled all around the Park, to areas they have no interest in, like moving tokens on a checkerboard; there is no respect for human desires, just expediency. The inns are used as base camps, rooms kept unoccupied for days at a time. The problem of the inns may be the single most serious failure of the Yosemite project: certainly the number of letters of complaint stress this sore spot more than any other. And what does it do to the shuttle cars having people traveling all over the Park like a bunch of immigrants in search of a protected, indoor place to stay? And the innkeepers, do they care? They tell the overflow, use the dormitory space or go camping. Just no consideration for the visitors.

Because of increased use of the trails immediately surrounding the inns--to the point of requiring separate, extra maintenance--the inns came into direct conflict with the National Park Service. The inns insisted they couldn't afford this trail upkeep and maintain reasonable prices. The Service refused to pay for damage caused by the unexpected popularity of what's been called the inns' corridor trail. Consequently, the Avalanche and Coyote inns have been closed as an economy measure in off-seasons to meet these unexpected costs. The same Avalanche inn, I may add, that suffered severe external damage in last year's wildfire.

Then there's El Portal, created as a service center, a consolidation of visitor functions so that the Park itself could be free of these awful intrusions of civilization. Ivory tower, indeed. And even if the goal of limited growth could have been achieved, what would that cutoff, inaccessible town be like? We'll never know since it's grown at a staggering rate. Originally restricted to a small piece of annexed National Park Service land, what has happened to the limited growth concept? The western boundaries near Rancheria Flat have been taken over and built as if a new gold rush boomed in this section of the Sierra. Growth is at crisis level. The place is like a casino in the wilderness, an oddity therefore a tourist attraction of unlikely proportions. More cafes and bars and nightlife amusement in El Portal even than by that once pristine lake on the Nevada border. And then there are the internecine squabbles with Wawona Village. The prestige feuds. What sort of reactions to that do our visitors leave with?

But these are just the problems that have to do with simple organization, everyday life and activities. What about the more far-reaching endeavors undertaken by this idealistic, environmentalists' heaven? The camping in the valley, wasn't it supposed to be organized outside of and away from the animal routes and the regions of dense population? Wasn't the first criterion to be the needs of the indigenous creatures of the area rather than the selfish interests of the holiday seekers? Have people stopped camping where they might interfere with the animals? Have they stopped feeding them and foisting bad habits and practices on the animals? Do they give up swimming just because a riverbank is downgrading and becoming a potential problem for all the plants and animals?

And the reintroduction of species! Besides the obvious hazards of trying to turn back the ecological clock, even the attempts have been unsuccessful. What happened to the two groups of wolves introduced near Lake Eleanor? Have they mated, have they reproduced? But that's only the beginning. Now you're starting to reintroduce the grizzlies. Do you want to turn the whole area back into a wilderness, yes a wilderness of fear and a refuge for wild animals who are animal-killers? Have you already divvied up the safari concession?

And the wildfire incendiaries! Being quite complacent about burning down the place so that the budding Neros can fiddle. Burn up the dominant tree species and let the weaker ones succeed. Kill people, destroy a whole area, run the risk of uncontrolled catastrophes. Who cares, do they? No, just so long as they can spray their precious inn buildings, their Neo-Regionalistic monuments, with water, then everything is fine with them. Do I have to remind you of the Wolfback inn disaster where 16 people suffered smoke inhalation and serious burns? And all because safety precautions weren't considered important enough while they were building a new wing and so they shut down the water system during construction!

All of this, for what? So that the visitors can be educated about what wilderness is? Well, there are enough real wildernesses left in this country and if anybody is in fit enough condition, has enough experience and expertise to deal with the kinds of experiences that test human survival, they are quite welcome to go to those refuges and wander around them testing their machismo.

This is a place of human recreation, a place for people out in the wilds, one of the most popular vacation areas in the country. And what has it been turned into? A wilds that is out of control, about to turn into a chaos of misguided principles and mismanagement. A return-to-nature scheme that violates all the principles of human decency and intelligence.

And this is what you have done here! This is your great project, the way into the future! You've become so self-satisfied and complacent with what you have achieved you can't see the harm you have done along with it. The project was funded with the understanding that it was an experiment in a world in crisis. And now when the crisis is deepening you're too concerned with regional problems to return the favor and help out as you should.

You've become an entrenched elite, rigid in your superiority. You act as if the visitors here are a nuisance you have to put up with, ungraciously at that. Don't you understand that your responsibility is to the visitors to this place as much as to this place? What picture are they bringing back from here? I can assure you it is not a very flattering one.

You are committing the act of hubris, taking so much pride in your own achievements that you ignore criticism even when it is constructive. You're beginning to think you can do no wrong and this valley is becoming a monument to your narrowness.

I believe the time may have come for you to be relieved of your stewardship. The experiment has failed. The Park must be returned to the sole supervision of the National Park Service once more before you destroy it completely. So far we've collected nearly 20,000 names on a petition to do precisely that. And I challenge you to tell me why this should not be done!

WALLA WALLA TO HETCH HETCHY

1 Pendleton, Oregon to Nolin, Oregon
Amos looked ten meters ahead at Bill's brand new railvan. "Glad I didn't wait. None of that new crap or gimmicks makes up for this 82 Homemade. Even if he can get better mileage both on the road and the freerail. This is a classic already, the prototype of an entire trend."

"I'm convinced, you incorrigible car fanatic."

"General Motors' Custom Standard! Dumb tradenames. They're going to have to do better than that model of Bill's to compete with the Homemades."

"Amos, you sound like one of those crazy guys building 'em from the ground up — coachbuilders, is that what they're called? Did you get a chance to look at the freezer before we started?"

"Sorry. I was so anxious to get . . . . There's the 80 interchange. Are we still on linked channels?" He plays with the CB in front of him, looking at the overhead rail dashboard. "Bilcor, Bilcor? This is Double A. We're almost at the changeover. How're ya' doing, Bill? Or is Coral driving?"

"Double A, we're doing fine, just fine. This is the first time you know!" Bill's van in front of Amos waddles — a fighter pilot's salutation.

"I'm picking you up as 88.42 kph. Express?"

"What should it be?"

"When you get on the accelrail, try to stay on 90 close as you can, Bilcor — I'll catch up to you and couple before you deflate. Smoother that way!"

"Okay, I think I can get it. Never done this before."

"Well, enjoy! You too, Coral. See you in five. Aura's fixing dinner. We can leave this channel open."

After dinner westbound traffic on Oregon 80 is light on August Friday evenings. The smaller and newer of the two railvans moves from the freeway's right entrance lane to the next and when the second van has followed, it continues one lane more.

"That's fine, Bill. Any second now."

Ahead of their convoy and coming up fast, an overpass with a sign almost obscured by trees: "Accelrail to THE DALLES, Freerail to PORTLAND." The sign is duplicated on the databoard to the left of Amos' wheel. Vans get into the lane, vans get off the lane: none come between the two from Walla Walla. Amos touches the transition switch. The board above his head comes alive. Green and red lines and dials, eerie and iridescent. The most striking, the parallax rangefinder: the outlines of two interconnected eyes glow red.

Outside, rails set in concrete begin to rush under the wheels of the van. Tires don't even squeal as they go over the steel. Above the driver the red lines move together, lunge apart, move together again. Amos accelerates and the eyes' circles come together. They burst neon green. There's only a few meters of blurred steel and concrete between the two vans. Amos looks up at the speedometers: the numbers are only a few hundredths off. He looks down to the narrow space between the back of Bilcor's van and his own wooden bumper. He flips the connect button and to his right, from a bulge surrounding the windshield's middle panel, a clear plastic diaphragm begins to inflate, vibrating in the buffeting wind.

"Bilcor, connect button."

Instantaneously a similar diaphragm pops out of its O-shaped container on the back of the forward van. Closer and closer the two vinyl ducts maneuver. A soft hissing sound, a slight sucking noise as the two appendages find each other. Thrump! Suction cups meeting head-on. Glass doors immediately open, air pressure in everyone's ears immediately changes. Another green light bursts above Amos' head.

"Damn, Amos, that was sloppy. I spilled the marinade. Could you have been driving this thing too long?"

"Sorry, hon. I'll help you clean it in a minute."

Amos checks his speed again, keeping an eye on the wobbling fifty-centimeter tube connecting the two vans. He flips off the radio, leans down and calls through the tube. "Okay, Bill? When I count three, hit the deflate button. Watch the parallax finder. One . . . two . . . THREE!"

Both vans sink about six centimeters. A slight wobbling ripples through the vinyl connection. The steel wheels inside the tires — also the brake drums — going the same rate as the rubber tires, hit the flush rails with a slight jerk: the technological moment of truth! Another second of hesitation and then it's over. Amos pushes his steering wheel out of the way, rises half out of his seat and presses the transition switch that turns green. In less than four seconds, both vehicles, one after another, begin their long diagonal swoop onto the freerail. The sudden quiet pinpoints the wind noise around the windshield, the wheels' soft whirring sound and the hum of the turbine.

Office of the Governor
Sacramento, California

```
To:       Garry
From:     Fred Weynkins
Topic:    "Mono Lake as National Monument"
          Lee Vining, California
          April 2-3, 1987
```

Governor, you asked me for a detailed personal rundown of last week's conference.

Two days? Because they needed the time to make the lake and its peculiarities understood. They took us around the lake and showed its alkaline problem--stagnant inland sea; interconnection with the ecology of the eastern Sierra; effect on climate, population, land, animals; disaster history of the past decades; and the reasons and assumptions, in detail. Then we struggled into five rowboats where the problems of the increasingly wide shoreline--and its fragility--were made only too evident. Then a row around the lake and a look sea (pardon me) at the Mono brine shrimp that you will remember (and you will, Governor, because the environmentalists will never let you forget) live *only here!*

We explored the string of volcanos (active a mere five hundred years ago. All volcanos are potentially active even if every geologist licensed by the University of California swears the contrary!) in the southern part of the surprisingly extensive lake. Then a general tour around the cinder cones fortified with a picnic lunch on the one cone that's still an island before continuing an even more thorough examination of the peripheral sage-grown sedge. Then they let us rest a bit (there is, are you surprised, little else to do there?) fed us another good home-cooked meal, and, you guessed it, a moonlight cruise back on old salty, this time to watch birds land or not land, and see the moonlight possibilities of the sage and marsh. Very classy PR indeed!

The next morning they got down to business: the principal runoff to the lake, the Dana plateau watershed, has long since been diverted to Southern California Edison and other interests--dropping the lake's level by about one meter a year--has finally been curtailed.(What else could they do after the Owens Valley blowups? Even their own moviemakers are against them!) Eventually (within three years) it will stop altogether. But the conference was called so that it could be pointed out--dramatically-- that the damage has been done and what is required is major rehabilitation, like giving it monument status, to reestablish it. (I don't think they like that solution any more than we, but imagine Ricky Ferguson looking me straight in the eye and saying, "Have you or the Governor any other solution?")

Of course it would be simplest to declare the whole state a monument and the problem of protecting the environment could be considered in toto. But to be practical, they showed that bizarre and exotic landforms--salt flats, marshes, volcanic flows and all the rest of that marginalia--like Honey Lake, Monument Valley, Death Valley--are increasingly popular and are going to be more so with the people who spend their time looking at such things. Popular appeal of conventionally beautiful tourist spots seems to have leveled off. So in the light of our desire to accommodate populist fads and in view of their irrefutable statistics, the Mono monument people have us there too.

Next, and most important: the lake is a unique occurrence (more unique, if you will pardon me again, than most); the fragile shore and the lake harbor is a precarious if limited life system. As a bird habitat and migration stop (the Pacific on the way to Pyramid Lake and the Great Salt Lake) it is invaluable; already many predators previously restrained by the lake from seeking out the island bird stations (where California gulls, avocets, Wilson's phalaropes and other species congregate) are finding their way out there.

The obligation to return the lake to its former flourishing state requires:

    a. restoring the lake's former natural watershed function
    b. encouraging regrowth over the shore's trails, jeep tracks, etcetera, so
    c. the shore can return to its former state as an integral part of the lake and
    d. developing means of allowing people to visit and appreciate the area without damage or impairment to its natural function.

A national monument! It is interesting to observe that, generally, this was a similar situation that faced Yosemite before the railway, even though the details and aspects of their problem were entirely different!

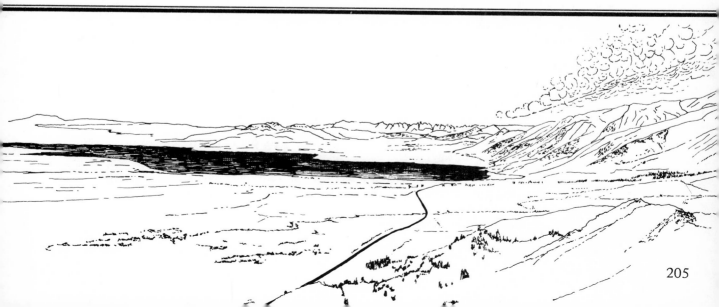

BIGHORN: Home Free!

Fifty-eight healthy, wooly bighorn sheep are alive and well in the Ritter range near Yosemite Park's southern boundary. They have been grazing in their new home since spring of last year and all indications, especially the phenomenal growth in numbers from the original 45 that made the trek, indicate that the transfer is permanent.

The migration of these animals planned and supervised by the Bighorn Reintroduction team had to be accelerated when the only other extant herd in California — located in the San Bernardino mountains east of Los Angeles — was decimated in the summer and fall of 1985 by a still unexplained disease suspected to be a microbe present only in the chemical mixture of fog and smog blown east from Los Angeles. When more than twenty of that herd of around one hundred died, the team took emergency measures to protect the Sequoia range sheep. Top priority was allocated to driving some of them north into the precincts near Yosemite to encourage the birth rate and ensure the species' survival in the event of any more manmade or natural plagues.

For a year and a half, Michael and Linn Alder, animal biologists on the Reintroduction team, lived with the herd, accustoming the animals to their human presence and searching for ways to encourage migration. Finally, after more than a year, the first ewe allowed Linn to approach, even to touch her. With tears in her eyes, Mrs Alder vividly remembers that moment when she "knew for the first time that the planned undertaking would be possible."

The move of the selected 45 sheep took place in the late winter and spring of 86 and covered a distance of approximately 150 kilometers. Besides enduring all sorts of criticism and alarmist advice from conservationists, scientists and other interested onlookers who felt that the separation of so many of the sheep was risky and would weaken the main herd, the Alders faced all sorts of problems along the way. Would the herd keep moving? Would there be enough forage in unfamiliar areas? But most important, would other human beings keep out of the San Joaquin headwater region during the migration, or at least away from the herd? Sheep are frightened of human contact, and the area near Mammoth was an especial hazard in this respect. But the Alders and the sheep made it after five harrowing months of moving and grazing and moving and grazing.

Their success has been so encouraging, the Alders are planning to move a small portion of their herd farther north into the Cathedral range, probably within the next two years, and so reintroduce bighorns into Yosemite Park.

The Alders are in contact with two other groups working for the Tahoe Region Restoration Project about the possibility of continuing the northward migration by training new people in their methods and so eventually bring the bighorns to the Cascades, an undertaking that might take as long as twenty years.

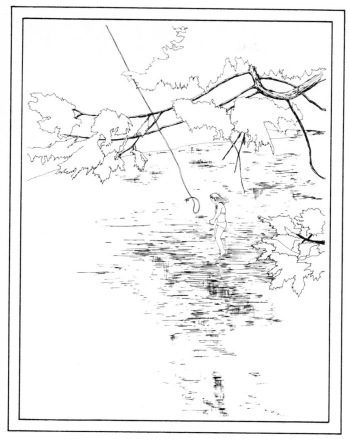

You wouldn't think anything good could come out of a drought, but guess again. Curiously it was the remembered experience of camping in the very watershed where it was stored that triggered water conservation practices. Remembered ways of washing dishes, sponge baths, waterless teeth brushing, making a carried amount of water last until the next refill, these and other practices were what people returned to, remembered with a chuckle when the western drought simply never really left off.

Of course we've come a long way since then in our thinking about water: composting toilets, in-house water recycling and roof rainwater collection, industrial solar-powered water reuse and all the other ways we've come to respect water rather than take it for granted. But it was those wilderness experiences that pointed the way!

UNIVERSITY OF NORTHERN CALIFORNIA
El Portal Extension
Spring Quarter 1986

Small-scale intensive mountain farming   Agriculture 10.7
                                            California Regional
M, Th 1800-1930; field work   Resources 22.7
3 units

   Designed to introduce and involve all aspects of intensive mountain farming, including opening up inhospitable regions. Site choosing
and preparation, terracing, mulch chemistry, soil testing and classifi-
cation, acidity balancing, water sources and relationships.
   Vegetable, fruit and grain crops; relationships, vagaries and dependence on the environment; selection, rotation and diversification.
   Introduction of new wild hybrids including fruit like apples,
pears and berries; and natural grains. Regional economics of small-
scale farming for maintenance and surplus production. Intensive methods, approaches and characteristics.

No prerequisites; enrollment limited to 15.

Lecturer: Charles K. Lamont, owner/manager Chinquapin Inn; author of
Eat Feat: An Exhaustive Guide to Intensive Farming and *Wild Peach,
Hybrid Extraordinaire.*

Badger Pass

On impulse--it was a balmy spring day--Merrie Swinson decided to stop the train at Badger Pass. Stepping off, what she saw was spring grass not quite covering a passing track, a couple of switches and a single pair of rails vanishing south beyond a peculiar notch which was what she headed towards.

The notch opened up all at once into the bowl-shaped valley. A strange geological phenomenon, Badger is a valley almost completely self-contained, a half-hidden enclave. Another of Yosemite's unexpected surprises. Ranging up the sides of the curving slopes like so many brushes were tall, thick cedar and sugar, lodgepole and ponderosa pine, all neatly separated from the main ski runs--Turtle, Beaver, Chipmunk. All, Merrie thought, cutely named before the railway and still barking the brochure sound of resorts. Is that a snob reaction? Who knows, she continued to think, in how many years that style will be selling again and ours--whatever that is--will be colder than Tioga in the winter.

The ski runs she was looking at were certainly not wide white swaths of Sierra powder. Not exactly garden paths either. The soft stubby grass tolerated tiny clusters of wildflowers and dark green water-seeped patches, but apparently not people. Oh, I'm wrong, there's someone; no, it's a couple ambling along a piney ridge. You can see everything there is to see from here, and when you see only two other people, I guess that's seeing yourself in perspective. Even looking to the glass-fronted inn and the ranger station back in the mountainside as if waiting in the valley's wings, Merrie had to search several minutes before she spied two rangers emerging from their billet. And there, Merrie scored again; people on the middle level of the terrace. No, it's actually one waiter, clearing and straightening.

She walked along the railline that traveled up the slopes through the forest, a path that looked like a tree-shaded avenue this month. In winter skiers are carried to the top of each of those animal-named slopes on it. There are no lifts, so the green ribbons up the sides of the bowl look, Merrie fantasized, like raw material for some watercolor illustration out of children's books: maybe outsized cups and tipsy saucers filled with laughing children billowing, cascading down the flowery, grassy paths. That's much more fitting than the biting imprint of skis, the punctuation of poles.

How strange it all is out of season. Unreal, inappropriate. Don't be ridiculous! This isn't out of season for this valley. It's growing. It's flowering beautifully. It's alive! But there is that other thing! I really get the feeling here that this is not its time. Too much social propaganda? Just my human perception imposing on reality? Thank God I can see that. I wonder if they...?

She increased her stride, pleased with her purpose and walked directly up to the front, waiting for her turn as three women passed out through the inn's glass. The shimmering front revealed nothing. Only inside did the enormous room backed with stone walls scooped with fireplaces suggest a ski resort. Two wide diagonal freestanding stairways, ascending on lodgepole logs, connected the lower space to the upper sleeping areas. Underneath, to the side and to the back, almost unnoticed among the folded chairs and piled tables, three slicker-yellow elec-

Out of Season

tric snowmobiles parked on their sides, guts open and batteries
humming. Merrie got closer to inspect the green National Park
Service emblems pointing straight up, the orange Emergency sign
looking meek. As she continued, the space built for crowds
echoed her footsteps. Two pine doors closed since the last
snow in February opened into a dining room even bigger than the
lobby. All the empty space suggesting to Merrie a waiting room
for pregnant elephants.

Merrie stopped. All of this unused. All of this abandoned,
unused, and not ten kilometers from here the valley's getting
its spring influx. The first of the season's multitudes!

We still haven't gotten the message! There's no understanding even yet. Always the easy way: no deposit, no return
rather than the inconvenience of the handling. Still cities
of buildings empty two thirds of the time. Monuments to waste!
They light up the emptiness at night and we still can't see it!

So sublimated, the waste isn't recognized even in the accounting. Now, give me 75 good reasons why this pretty valley
shouldn't be used between now and the next snow! I knew there was
some reason why I got off that train at the flagstop. I think
it's time I had another go at the land use team. I've been
put off before about philosophical questions not practical
enough to take up our time. What do they think this place is
for if not to be grappling with questions like this? Glacier
Point? I've been there at least a hundred times!

The average visitor to Yosemite might encounter
around ten different animal species. Unseen are over
seventy other mammals, maybe fifty or so bird varieties, a couple of dozen kinds of reptiles and insect
families by the hundreds.

> Martin Schmidt
> Wawona Wilderness Labs
> "The Five-Year Plan Didn't
> Turn Out Like We Thought"
> Yosemite Natural Notes,
> Winter 87/88

The natural environment, the wilderness isn't what's wrong
or at fault. It's the economy.

How long can we continue to twist our Earth to conform
with an artificial, anachronistic, selfishly inefficient system?
Since we formed our economy to meet specific goals, we can
certainly reform it so that it yields to natural conditions.

> Evelyn Ventar
> Northwest Solar Seminar
> Vancouver, November 7-9, 1987

To: Lee Vining Gazette
P.O. Box A 111
Lee Vining, California
April 20, 1987

Dear Editor:

I don't often write to papers even though I have opinions that differ from what's appeared in your newspaper. But the proposed Mono National Monument is too important an issue — for those of us who live around here to just let go without a fight.

I have a fair-sized cattle spread, the Walking W, near Yerington, Nevada, but I've also been experimenting with a small herd of pronghorn antelope. That's neither here nor there, and may not say much, but what it does imply is that I'm not entrenched in old ways or stuck to a rigid interpretation of the life going on around me.

The life I've lived in this area has been a good one, but a hard one. Turning this area into a stepping stone to Yosemite, making it a national monument to protect the habitat really means our giving up control, saying that we can't do what we always have done ourselves. Having to deal with endless boards and commissions to get any-thing done is not my idea of upgrading the quality of this place. I've got eyes, I can see the deterioration of the lake and its edges. But it'll come back. If anyone thinks flooding the area with a lot of gawkers from L.A. hot off their rail buses, or establishing resorts and inns and all that egalitarian nonsense that has turned Yosemite into a museum instead of a park an hour's drive away, they're just fooling themselves and trying to kid me.

Sure it sounds nice and progressive: nationwide publicity so when you tell someone the name of your place they'll know what you're talking about. But what are the real advantages of the proposal? I'll tell you, there aren't any. We've been here when they didn't think it was beautiful and when it wasn't popular. And I'll be damned if I'm going to sit back and let them — now that they've discovered this place — dump a whole lot of rules and edicts and dictums around here simply so a bunch of tourists can learn how they should wipe their asses. That kind of bureaucratic management will destroy whatever qualities there are here and bring a lot of new-comers who don't know what they're seeing, but sure as hell will be telling us what to do with our own lake!

Respectfully indignant,
Wesley R. Hagendorff
Chairman,
Free Mono Committee

WW TO HH

2 Echo, Oregon to El Portal , California

"Bill, are we switching off in Portland?"

"What's that? Oh, the connection light! That panel looks like a jet's. We transfer to Interstate 5 in Portland."

"All those lights and switches and dials," Coral sighs. "You know they remind me of space disaster movies. I don't think I could handle this freerail business. And what's more, I don't know if I want to!"

"Nonsense, course you could," Bill snaps his wheel forward and swivels his seat 180 degrees. "There's nothing to it. See how we're approaching the freerail? In about five seconds we'll clear the switch."

"And we're getting faster, Bill! We're doing 150 kilometers! We were just doing 90!"

"Ahhh, Coral, relax. That's the speed in this section. Ours automatically adjusts to the van ahead and the one behind!"

"But we're connected to the one behind!"

"Doesn't matter." Bill scans the instruments, then looks up at the path of purple wildflowers broken by the two silver rails gleaming in the orange sun. A glance at the driver of an old station wagon in the right lane and then he begins to crawl through the fifty centimeter opening of the vibrating tube at the rear of the van. "It's like an air mattress," he shouts back at Coral. She looks at him and thinks, "Mock turtle."

Ahead to her right, another van on the accelrail hurtles diagonally through the transition track as the shadow of an overpass cuts through her space. "But it's slower," she gasps and sucks in more air as that van sprints onto the freerail less than ten meters in front of her driverless vehicle. She pulls back and presses into the leather, bracing her hand within millimeters of the air bag switch. She's too terrified to move, to look at anything but that van. It accelerates to maintain freerail separation, pulling away through a grove of trees overhanging a broad-banked left turn.

"Am I disappointed?" She looks out at the right short distance lanes. She passes car after car, almost as if they weren't moving at all. Nearly every one she passes shows some interest in her progress. "This is very different from watching the vans pass me!" She begins thinking of all those parallel lives the way she has since childhood's peering glances out of car windows.

The forest is thickening, closing in almost in time with night. The last shafts of sunlight deep in the woods. "Where are we now?" She reaches over across Bill's empty seat and picks out the program disks from their slot. She watches the tiny red dot trace their route on the databoard from Walla Walla until it glows brightly near a place called Coldsprings Wildlife Refuge.

Coral slides through the transparent duct remembering how it felt when she tried it in Marguerite Weil's van factory in Spokane. "This is definitely tighter or I've gotten, umph, larger."

". . . steam turbine uses gas or kerosene, while your newer ones burn diesel or alcohol. Generator provides electricity to the wheelmotors — quiet and pollution-free. I sure would like to be using alcohol, better for the jets. Doesn't matter, most of the time I'm on freerail anyway. Probably 90 percent of my mileage is on solar station powered freerail . . . ."

"That's amazing," interrupts Bill.

"Look at our fuel consumption. Zero on the freerail. I get about 80 kilometers a liter on the accelrail. What did you get, Bill?"

"I didn't check it, but I know it was more than I got on the road."

"I would say about 100. Let's look it up!"

"I forgot the databoard keeps a log."

"Not only that, but sends its own owners a distance bill."

"That reminds me. How much will this ride cost?"

"Costs about a penny a kilometer. The freerail, like lunch, isn't. It pays for the solar power and to supplement the states who can't afford highway maintenance."

Coral breaks in. "The clutter in here sort of grows on me, Amos. I'm beginning to see the pattern. How long have you had it?"

"Got it in the summer of 84. It's an 82. Almost prototype. The guy I bought it from was a relative of the maker.

"That summer I got my first teaching job in Colorado. They had just finished the stretch from Salt Lake. My parents and everyone else still insisted it would never catch on — whatever that meant — so I got it. I felt like a pioneer, just a tie behind the laying crew. And what a trip that first one was! The speeds were between 100 and 120 then. They didn't think the vans could take the highway curves or some such nonsense. It was pretty much a new thing, still. All the people on the road were really with me, waving and cheering.

"It was like the CB craze all over again."

"Yeah, but this time with some reason. You know I was so happy, I just packed all my books — didn't have much else — and drove to Philly and started. The folks on the road shouted and waved; the CBs called me 'rail-splitter.' Once I started I didn't want to get off for anything. You know I just hadn't thought about it: on the road you stop, on the rail you just don't. There was five gallons of water, but no food. That was my parade: waving at people, joking with them on the waves and starving. I searched all around, hoping the nephew had left something; I practically licked the refrigerator. But no food! It got to be a matter of pride, not stopping. But I didn't get off the freerail; nonstop to Denver. I guess if I didn't have the water I would have had to!"

"That's a story!"

"And when I got to Denver, you know I wasn't hungry anymore. Just very tired. I had been going for thirty hours!"

Amos' mouth tasted like the bottom of Hetch Hetchy. In the bright morning flatness, he looked somber and unsettled and sleepy. Aura tried to claw her way back into sleep, ignoring his carping about the hot valley air and the alarm clock's ancestry. Amos touches the transition switch and the wheels begin slapping the first switchpoints. Aura gives up her digging.

Deceleration to 90, air pressure to maximum, tires inflating with a slight skid, the railvan makes a wobbling turn toward a slot in the right lane. "YOSEMITE PARK, VISITOR PARKING."

Amos glides down the off ramp. He turns left to 15 Street, cruising carefully with the second van in tow. The two-story garage on L Street proudly advertises its "complete open recreation deck," but Amos heads through the forest of willows, down two levels to the weekend section and finds a double stall. He turns off the turbine, listening to it whine down to a final squeak.

He opens the door, steps out on ribs of concrete and stone filled with squares of grass. Sunlight coming down through the many lightwells reminds Amos to search for his sunglasses.

"Are we there? How much time?"

"About twenty minutes. I think Bill and Coral are stirring, so hurry up."

Rays of sunlight bounce off the clear plastic sphere containing a bright butterfly captured intact on a small branch. The miniature diorama, with neatly lettered label underneath, is a piece of the swampy reality flashing by beyond the window. A sign low in the grass, "Snelling 2.0 km." Coral sits back in the high-backed corduroy booth and looks through the sphere watching the sunlight change as the train skims around a broad corner.

"You know, it's funny being in the train after last night. Being so enclosed there, so separate from the rest of the world, makes things very fundamental, strips the social layers away," Amos intones watching Coral's glazed eyes.

"Like space travelers coming face to face with survival by themselves?" Bill questions.

"Seems like we're going faster, but we're only doing about 60 or 70, isn't that right?" Aura says through her raspberries.

"We're so close to the trees and ground, it seems faster. Pass the cream, please." Amos drenches his raspberries. "Delicious."

"You've been up half the night. Anything would taste good," Aura takes the cream and pours it into her coffee.

"It was that bloody accident at the 880 junction. Some drunk drove right into the freerail lane.

"At least we don't have 50,000 deaths a year anymore. They seem to forget that every time they complain about . . . ."

"Are you calling 20,000 okay? Something we can live with?" Coral challenges both Amos and Aura.

"Becky behind the counter there told me these berries come from an inn up the canyon a ways. They grow on lattices suspended between walnut trees. That'll have to be seen."

"Bill, you're a fanatic. Any way to fill a space and you'll find ten ways to do it," Aura laughs. "Amos, what are you doing with those walnuts?"

"Well, if they grow together, why not eat them together."

"He has the eating habits of a bear!"

"Becky also told me, world travelers," Bill continues over a large glass of fresh orange and grapefruit juice, "that this train is going through to Hetch Hetchy after El Portal. How about a peek at what's been happening?"

They walk by the tradespeople on the platform and then past the open air market where flatcars and railtrucks are parked loaded with fresh produce.

The wide paths of the narrow flatland shelf turn into zig-zagging ramps, then stairways and passages through buildings, up and around corners. Speckled light through tree branches falls on their faces. Occasionally they look back at the Merced River between the trees. At the first street level, people ride by on horses and bikes, one electric truck purrs to a stop. Bird, water, people noises mingle with

odors. The town reveals itself like a perspective tilted at a steep angle. The shops tempt them, but the first they succumb to is the one with the model railway, the YR, in the window, as well as skeletons of squirrels, raccoons, coyotes and deer realistically displayed.

"Are these toys for children?"

The storekeeper smiles, fixing the hinge on her one bear skeleton's leg. "They're expensive, so difficult to find."

Bill looks at the fat tires of dirt bicycles handcrafted out of steel and wood and leather, while Coral reaches up to touch the sleighs hanging from the ceiling. Wood and plastic miniature windships — helium provided by Mrs Dougherty — are everywhere. One lifts off and floats around the shop — Mrs Dougherty giggles — wafting off the hanging toys and beribboned columns, taking a new tack at each obstacle before the helium expires and floats down to Amos' hand.

The odors from a bakery draw Aura first, then the others, out beyond a porch where kitchen tools sway from the awning. The bakery has a wide veranda shading the street and overlooking the lower town and station. They take off their knapsacks and sip teas and juice and pick at what they, in their exuberance, ordered.

Refreshed, they wander further up, around and through the switchback town. "It's really a completely linear town, even though the most curved, circuitous example anywhere."

"Amos, you're the only one who'd notice that," Coral laughs.

In front of the Miwuk Inn, the Hetch Hetchy train stops and all four look at one another. With instantaneous laughter they rush toward the train as it begins to move. Laughing and shoving they find they have a whole car to themselves.

resource
resourcefulness

IN LOS ANGELES

Co-Evolution Quarterly Precis
Spring 1987 issue

New urban and suburban expedients for handling water and energy and transportation based on survival and economic need started appearing in California in the 1980s. Some of these methods were adapted from work done in Yosemite Park, the Catalina Island Restoration, the Lake Tahoe Peripheral Railway and countless small urban experiments throughout the country. Since they sprang up, rather than were imposed, they are not unilateral nor do they conform to pattern. A mere list, however, can communicate some of the trends.

HOME CHANGES BY 1987 IN CALIFORNIA

Electric generation through in-home solarskin accounts for more than 91 percent of all home power use. Solarskinned houses use overload metering to prevent more than a preset consumption of power, reducing percentage of per capita income spent for home energy to under 2 to 3 percent.

The majority of light fixtures are the gas glow type which use less energy to manufacture, last up to twenty times longer and use approximately 40 percent less energy than filament bulbs.

Commercial gas and electric clothes washers are being shared by up to ten households. Solar drying is now common again.

Combination dish/clothes washers are used in 43 percent of homes.

Virtually all electric motors in home appliances, and televisions, video disks and stereos sold since 1982 are the high-efficiency/longlife type.

Uncommon power requirements are confined to low energy use times like late at night when other appliances and power drains are not used.

More than half the street lighting has been transferred to home-mounted and owner-maintained light. In communities where this is common, all exterior lighting is turned off on full moonlight nights.

Cooking by electric stoves amounts to less than 5 percent of use. Natural gas, LPG and/or methane are the common methods.

Use of wood as supplementary source of heat in times of extreme cold is up 500 percent. The concern that this would deplete forests caused a 5 to 10 percent increase in forested land.

General reduction in nonindigenous plants. In Los Angeles a shift has occurred away from lawns and similar high-water use vegetation towards species more acclimated to the area. For example — tremendous increases in citrus trees for ornamentation and food.

Substantial increase in home gardens for food production. Estimates as high as 45 percent of regional fruit and vegetables grown by homeowners and renters in San Francisco and Los Angeles regions.

Small-scale dairy farming within urban regions increased from approximately 10 percent to over 35 percent.

In Los Angeles area since 1980, number of homes constructed with or partially using adobe up 500 percent. There's been a similar increase in the use of adobe, stone and concrete block throughout Northern California.

Restoration of old homes up 340 percent since 1980 except for San Francisco which achieved this figure by the mid 1970s. Owner-built homes increased 900 percent and contractor or development home construction down to 11 percent (of 1975 levels) of total construction.

Home designs commonly use passive solar heating by placement of windows, relation to site, etcetera.

WATER

Use of imported water down 79 percent paralleling increased development of swimming pools, community reservoirs and ground water replenishment as collection for rainwater and storage for fire or drought. Most city reservoirs are filled with rainwater recycled via storm drains and sewage treatment plants.

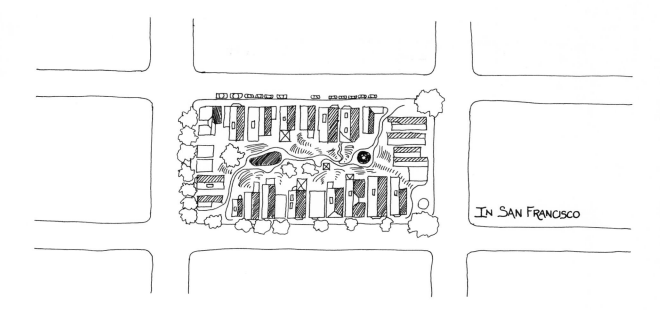

IN SAN FRANCISCO

Approximately 71 percent of toilets are waterless/digesting type. About 11 percent use septic tanks and/or leach lines, 2 percent simply use a hole and the remaining 16 percent flush into municipal recycling sewer systems.

Water pollution cleanup legislation and/or drought constraints required water recycling by large industrial users. Over 82 percent have completed the conversion by the installation of solar generators utilizing fuel-cell breakdown and recombining of oxygen and hydrogen for electrical storage.

Approximately 8 percent of industrial water users use small-scale reservoirs, desalinization or extant water systems.

Approximately 78 percent of large office buildings use recycled water from city water systems. The remaining 22 percent — mainly smaller buildings — utilize in-house water recycling, electric regeneration and heating by solar collection.

During the early 1980s 40 percent of parking lots and 25 percent of streets and other paved areas were returned to open land in order to increase the area capable of absorbing moisture.

Wildland within urban regions increased 21 percent. Many mini-parks and creekbeds that were flood control ditches are now opened to absorption of rainwater.

CENTRALIZED ELECTRIC GENERATION

Electricity generated by steam generating stations is down to 35 percent of 1975 figure. Now used as supplemental power for office buildings, foundries, and similar energy-intensive operations, and for small homes and businesses not yet converted to solar power. Part of this reduction is due to solar-skinned houses and small offices that pump back excess electricity into remaining utility lines.

Hydroelectric power averaged over ten years down to 15 percent of pre-1975 levels. Reason: low water levels in reservoirs, increased need of irrigation water and decreased consumer use.

Nuclear power plants shut down completely by 1985.

TRANSPORTATION

Automobile use by distance down by 35 percent since 1975. Approximate decrease in number of cars 21 percent. Gasoline consumption 65 percent of what it was in 1975.

Bicycles by quantity 800 percent increase since 1975. Estimated kilometer distance increased by 300 to 400 percent, while the use of horses for transportation has increased about half that percentage, particularly in beach and mountainous areas.

Foot/equestrian trails by kilometers built: up 2100 percent.

Bike trails apart from roadways up 1000 percent, mainly in suburban and rural areas.

Electric cars powered by house solarskins for urban use up from estimated 800 in 1975 to over 18,000.

Use of diesel buses up 1000 percent. Electric streetcars, rapid transit up 800 percent. Ferryboats up 400 percent.

Small-scale shopping and service areas have replaced shopping centers in many communities. Portions of these complexes have become community meeting and/or entertainment halls while their parking lots have often been converted to public gardens.

Use of intercity passenger trains up 800 percent.

Use of jet travel within and to/from California up 175 percent though fuel use remains about the 1975 level owing to increased efficiency of aircraft and their use.

216

PACKING with FATHER

June 24, 1988: El Portal to Mather

Father leans against the baggage car door, the open space between us. Both of us are leaning out, looking up at the passing branches, down at trees and rocks straight below us. At El Portal's cluster of roofs jutting out from the mountain-side hundreds of meters below. The four-car local bound for the Mather end of the track rumbles over the boards of a bridge spanning a mossy waterfall.

Father wipes his brow, leans into the wind as the train bends around a curve and looks down at the crowd visible along the river. "Good to get away from that mob, real good."

"Still think we should've stayed for the race."

"That many people? No way! Not in that heat. They're going to kayak all the way to the Pacific, portages and all, so what could we see there except the start? I'm looking forward to the cool of the forest. The Olympics'll still be going on all over the state. There's the races in San Francisco Bay in September. Now that's something to see! The new sailing ships competing against those old square riggers!"

"Yeah, but we're here and this race is the first of its kind. I think we're missing something. We could've ridden the event train following the course down the canyon!"

"Well, if it's any good we can read about it." Between two passing sugar pines, Father turns his nose down to the scattering of bright color barely visible against the Merced's white water.

"But we're here! Why get it secondhand? We could've seen it!"

He's turned away and isn't hearing me. And anyway what am I saying? We are on a train going the other way.

Just short of Mather the train slows, workers gather equipment from the baggage car and Father and I go off over the spongy soil where a track will soon be embedded. A glance back at the supplies being transferred from train to mules. The forest has the cool of thick pines all around us. We walk around mule apples on a trail clinging to the side of a ridge just north of the Tuolumne's Middle Fork. The trail is soon to be a railroad. I'll miss the trail.

"Pack okay?"

"Tight but comfortable. Haven't worn one of these since that trip up Rainier in 65. These new ones fit like a coat, a lot more comfortable on your body than the aluminum-framed things." He wiggles his shoulder blades to show me how tight it is. The only things that rattle are the extras — stove, knife and pot — he insisted we take.

"Hear what's loose?"

"Course I do. How do you know it's the *extra* stove that's rattling?" He doesn't mention the knife or pot. I know he's thinking, "You just wait, I'll bet we need an extra stove." We've played this game before. Some minor mishap and he'll proudly announce, "Aren't you glad I brought it along?" And I'll have to nod wondering if the whole thing didn't happen just because he brought the whatever in the first place. That's my father . . . and me.

Across the pond is a mill, even if it doesn't look mechanistic; rough pine boxy shapes are riddled with doors, skylights and open windows of all sizes. Seven lodgepole pines grow up through the roof. Swallows return to nests beneath the iris-filled windowboxes in the sunset light.

Catwalk galleries are suspended in the pine trusses over the grease-stained sawmill floor. Through the open doors, we see people slowly but deliberately scurry around, skirting whirring saws and skating slabs of fresh-cut clean-smelling pine.

"The mill burns scrap wood, generates its own power. It's self-sufficient."

"Huh? Sure is small. Doubt if they can make much money here," Father says handing me the plastic flask of brandy.

"Profit's only *one* of the reasons why it's here."

He watches me with a skeptical eye. "What's that mean?" He's partial to bare bones masculine technology.

"What's what mean? People here want to feel satisfied, enjoy what they do as well as make a profit."

"I'd never have thought of camping across a pond from a lumber mill. Guess they take care of it, it's spotless around here. Still can't see how they make any money."

"I don't know. May be a whole lot easier for them to deal with fluctuations in the lumber market. They've only got a small investment in machinery and they've planted gardens and orchards in and around the mill. Looks like they can keep goin' no matter what a 2x4 sells for."

"Silly when they can be making money!"

Sun's gone down behind the mill's roof, the steady hum slows as each machine shuts down the line. Father's cutting carrots and celery for soup, I'm slicing salami and cheese. We're both keeping an eye on the bats that've now taken over the swallows' rounds. Lights flicker on, casting reflections across the pond.

"Jeff, you know you're a dreamer. This kind of thing is impractical as hell. You know as well as I do that larger operations are more economical, despite all this trend to smaller companies."

"You can make figures say whatever you want them to. Besides, you talk as if money economics were the only concern. Seems to me that's only a small part of it."

"I grant you the return to small capitalism has worked in some places, but the economy is a big thing!"

"Look, right across the pond. That style of operation is working. It's one of many in the foothills, and they're a whole lot more locally owned all around the country. Some grew out of failing congloms, others just grew. You don't know the spirit here; people are really sick of the old rape-and-run big businesses."

"What about Weyerhauser's work with hybrids in Oregon? Doug firs developed to speed growth and facilitate clear-cutting. I think that's a pretty efficient way to manage a forest. And there are other lumber companies who've been pretty responsible about maintaining and stewarding their resources." Father sips the simmering soup, decides it's going to be good and pours more brandy into my cup, almost missing it in the sollight's dim glow.

"That was a valid approach, I guess. Their work was based on control of nature, but you know, a wild diverse forest is much more productive, and it doesn't require the management a domestic one does."

"I wouldn't toss it off so glibly. They're making money. I think there's some sound research going on there."

"Yeah, maybe so, but it bothers me that the whole thing rests on the premise that management is necessary. Forest took care of itself before we started meddling with it. Seems to me we'd be better fitting the tools to the wilderness than the wilderness to the tools. Look at what these people have done. They use a lightweight railway, draft horses in the woods, selective cutting and removal by helium balloon. You'd never know the logging went on so near the Park if it weren't for this mill."

"Still seems impractical to me. Ready for soup?" Father pours it slowly into my cup. I sprinkle a little salt in and sip the broth, biting a pine needle and a barely cooked carrot.

Mill's quiet, can't see the bats anymore, but the stars are incredible. I turned down the sollight. Father debated about having a fire, but I'm glad we decided against it. My parka's keeping me warm enough and the lack of extraneous light makes the stars bright and crisp.

It's very quiet. Occasionally I can detect the sound of water. Probably the Tuolumne or a waterfall back in the woods behind us. There's practically no noise nearby except the toads along the log pond's shore and the occasional squeak of a bat.

June 25, 1988: Cottonwood Creek

Glowing embers sting my eyes. I can hear the steps of animals in the woods. The fire barely illuminates the tree trunks around us. Looking into the blackness beyond the first ring of trees, I see creatures moving. Is it only the fire's after-image?

Father is sitting quietly on the foot of his mummybag, orange reflected on his glasses, his sunburned nose and gray sideburns. His face looks like a mask hanging in the darkness. His eyes are lost in the firelight. I don't know where he is.

We talked about the trail during another soup supper. We'd come up from Mather this morning, crossed into the Park and followed Cottonwood Creek till we got to a place that the map called Smith Meadow. The trail's incline and surface were gentle, easy walking for our first full day out.

"Jeff, you know what bothers me about our talk last night?"

". . ." I shrugged.

"This isn't a real world up here. It's a small community in the mountains built around a National Park. Here it's easy to decentralize and to — using your term — humanize. But these methods won't work in cities; they're too complicated and people don't care about community there. They feel imprisoned rather than at home, which is why such a large proportion of income is spent on driving. Less mobility seems synonymous today with a return to the nineteenth century. People will pay anything to remain mobile." Father looks back into the fire, resting his case.

"This isn't the real world? Seems to me it's more real than cities could ever be!"

"You know what I mean!" Father doesn't appreciate my remark. His face is tight, but I can't tell whether it's irritation with what he thinks are irresponsible opinions of mine or the tightening effect of the hot sun today.

"Well in the first place," I begin, "I think people drive around as much to find community as to escape it. America's this cat circling to get comfortable. It's no wonder people have to drive around the way everything's spread out to fit the automobile. There isn't much choice. And you're the one who's always telling me about the joys of walking around cities with less and less auto traffic, more streetcars and ferry systems. It parallels the revival of local communities, the celebration of small- instead of large-scale enterprise. It's happening in Seattle, Portland, Boston, Pittsburgh. Even Las Vegas built a streetcar system down the strip. Those systems were built by the communities they serve, and by doing that, the communities strengthened themselves. They wouldn't have been built if the people there hadn't wanted a higher quality of life, hadn't wanted to stay put and work for that quality."

"What you're saying happened in places that limited growth. The power was too expensive, or there was a lack of water or some resource limit. Those are isolated examples. Look what happened in parts of the Southwest when solar energy and water recycling in the early 80s started them growing again. People left the old to build new suburbs. The old routine of leaving mistakes for someone else to clean up while they move on."

The fire's almost out. Its crackling has given way to the breezy noise of pine trees in the wind. Needles are raining down, some landing in the coals and curling into orange flames that die as soon as they're born. I sense the presence of something large moving above my peripheral vision. A giant cloud covers the Milky Way, dividing it in half.

"Father, don't start that nonsense about people being greedy. We express every emotion, so we're greedy too. So what? I feel a basic intention to take care of *numero uno* and I'd bet even odds that everyone else feels the same no matter what they say to the contrary. It's fifty years of advertising and education preying on this ego reality that has institutionalized self-interest and turned it into greed."

"That's too simplistic. It's like the criticism in all the ineffectual liberal press. Goodness-of-mankind horseshit. If they could get the chance they would turn this Park into a housing tract."

"This may be obvious but that's why it's pointed out so much. When the government imposed horsepower limits on cars back in the late 70s, it implied a size limit as well. But there seems always to be those who want big cars no matter what the gas costs. The liberal press made noises about greedy people, about how much of the planet's resources were gobbled up by us, about the real shortage — prestige — not fuel. You remember that? Well, the cars got smaller, the one and a half ton limit was 83, and all that time they kept selling those guzzling V-6 dinosaurs."

"People're still buyin' 'em. They're the same people who have boats and second homes, who never use anything to its fullest, who just clutter the landscape with their toys. Now that's greed, Jeff."

"I've seen 'em, I've seen 'em all my life. But everybody knows what they're like. Sold on more technology to escape their ills. I think we have to look at places where people have taken control of their lives, not just their tools. Where self-interest is directed towards making life work. I flew down to Atlanta last month dreading the street violence that went on the last time I was there. But it was quiet and you could walk the streets. In fact the place was alive at night. The downtown community there had upgraded old office buildings that used to be half empty, made them into apartments and shops and offices mixed together, the whole neighborhood buying, refurbishing and renting them out. Now instead of vacant city streets at night, there's activity. They organized teams for crime prevention patrols. No cops or armed guards, just people taking turns making sure everything's calm in the streets, no harassment, just vigilance. Now the profit in all of it wasn't money but a fine place for people to live in and a real end to the violence. The profit was a renewed community."

"Those kinds of stories are getting to be clichés. They're the exceptions to the rule that the middle class moves out rather than deals with the problems."

"But doing that forces them to go after more monetary profit to pay someone else to do what they could easily, and more effectively, do themselves!"

Off with my clothes and into that sleeping bag. Father's in his already. Wind's coming up stronger and it feels like there might be some rain. Probably just a shower.

"Everybody can't do everything, take responsibility for everything!"

"Who says, Father? Just have to strike a new balance between professionals and everyone else. They still have cops for the violent crime in Atlanta. But keeping the peace in the streets is what the people who live there are doing."

"Well, I still don't see what's so different about what you're saying. And you have to admit it's only happening in some places."

June 26, 1988: Smith Peak and Cottonwood Creek trails junction

"Here, want a peach?"

"Thanks, these are awfully good. Too bad it's the last. Where'd you get them, Jeff?"

"At the El Portal station. They're grown down the canyon I think. She told me even the coyotes eat the ones on the low branches."

"Those beggars will eat anything. Why doesn't she fence in the trees?"

"Too much work? She probably doesn't care if some are eaten by the coyotes. They can't climb trees."

My butt's bruised from sitting on boulders the last few days. Feel like I've been speeding on the freerail for ten hours. We're sitting next to a beautiful little pond on a creek south of Hetch Hetchy. Trees bent over and almost cover the pool, so it's cool and shady. The water from a fall above us spreads out from a shallow pool over a brow of shiny granite. Then it collects in a trough and falls in a straight column breaking on the stub end of a log wedged into the rocks.

"Look at that bird. What the hell's he doing?"

"It's an ouzel."

"That's a Greek liqueur."

"That's ouzo. This little fellow builds a moss, mud and stick house beneath a waterfall. If we move over one rock, Dad, we'll probably see him fly in after he pops up out of the water."

"He wasn't drowning?"

"There, see it? The beehive-shaped thing, right behind the white water?" Father looks closely but doesn't see it till he follows the bird's flight, vanishing in his well camouflaged home.

"Amazing! I'd never heard of it before. Quite a piece of engineering."

"He's coming out! Quiet, don't move. Watch this!"

Light gray with a black streaked back and wings, about the size of a robin, rounder body, with a head that looks like a bump, brown beady eyes over an orange beak shaped like a tiny carrot: an ouzel.

"There he goes again, committing suicide!"

"Quiet!"

The bird stands in the shallows, then abruptly walks right under the clear foamy water. Father expects the plump body to bob up floating downstream. To the left, 30 degrees from where I assumed he'd be, the bird walks on the bottom of the knee-deep pool picking out worms and grubs on the sandy bottom, his body almost encased in a silvery gray bubble.

"He looks like a walking rock," Father says, bobbing his head like a duck. "Imagine us holding this protective skin of atmosphere around us."

"We do. Our shield from space. What's incredible is that it's only a thirty kilometer band of air. That's not very thick."

"I never thought of the atmosphere that way. Interesting. We walk on the bottom, too!"

"And it passes through us. Our skin is like a thick veil through which sweat exhausts and atmosphere enters. No stop and go, just elements flowing through us. We're composed of the sediment left behind."

"Like a mesh screen." Father uses his fingers to clarify the image.

"Yeah, exactly. I look on wilderness as a fine screen, a series of grids laid over one another. What we create is coarse by comparison. "

"What do you mean? You're getting at something. What?"

The ouzel has not reappeared. Evidently he's inhibited by our talking. We must be the first to interrupt him in a long time.

"Same stuff we've been talking about. We seem to be repeating this conversation in different forms. I feel an urge to resolve, somehow to complete it."

"Yeah, well, go on. Out with it."

"Well, it's like this project, the Yosemite Park thing. I never thought about it much until recently. I realized that our technology didn't fit. Standardization rarely has anything to do with place, the land we live on. The politics of Yosemite used to be too tight and correlated, didn't let real relationships through. What was wrong was trying to impose a technological grid on Yosemite. Too much time was spent manipulating the government rather than solving problems the machine was set up for. Now the people here are a tight interdependent network. They are part of the land now and the land is their means of expression. Paradoxically there's more freedom even though they're more entrenched on the land than before. They feel they can go anywhere and survive."

"You're being too general, Jeff. Talk to me concretely."

"Hmm, well, I guess it comes down to fundamental changes in our sources of energy. Two actually: the increasing efficiency of solar energy and the gradual decay of large congloms. Those two are like a dog chasing its tail. The big cumbersome corporations are sloppy, their products ill-conceived, poorly made, wasteful both in manufacture and use, too expensive, undependable and difficult to repair. The founding spirit left a long time ago, leaving rubber-stamp hierarchy climbers. While their centralized sources of power — steam generating stations, nuclear power plants, hydroelectric dams — are patently less dependable. Obviously the congloms couldn't grasp the value of solar, inherently a decentralized source of energy. And at first it did require careful conservation because then it was inefficient.

"You remember, Father, when Ford collapsed in 82? There must've been a dozen companies making cars within two years — coach builders. And then the freerail system required more sophisticated, quality cars no one could afford unless the cost could be spread out over years. So fewer cars are produced and what's built lasts longer. Small craftshops like that old used car dealer's in your neighborhood sprang up. Last time I looked in their showroom there must have been five railvans being built by people who had probably been the local hot-rodders five years ago. The point isn't that technology has changed, but the way it's changed — spreading power into the hands of more people — has caused us to see more intimate and fine-meshed relationships among ourselves. I mean . . . ."

"You've attracted an audience." Father points to a fox near a huge ponderosa pine watching us without moving a hair.

"Amazing. I didn't think it would come that close. Anyway do you see what I'm saying. Is it any clearer?"

"I suppose. I gather you feel this business with solar has really changed people fundamentally?"

"It's too early to tell, but I think we're seeing a seed with tremendous potential. We change the technology, that alters our behavior, and this causes more change in that technology. Smaller groups tend to make things with care because they share the responsibility with those they work with. Many people don't equate quality with size, but rather with the joy and intimacy of the building process. This may be a realization that close relationships foster creativity."

"Are you telling me that Einstein or Shakespeare didn't create by themselves?"

"One way or another they had a dialogue with the world that spawned their genius. It's not that they didn't do what they did alone, but that their location, who they interacted with, the intellectual and social climate they moved in was as fundamentally important to their production as their individual expression. Can you argue differently?"

"You mean then if we created the same situation, we'd have more Einsteins and Shakespeares?"

"No, obviously that's impossible. All I'm saying is that by emphasizing community — small towns and small communities among people in big cities — we deal more directly with our problems and institutions. Human habitats need simplification; the problems we face are enough without the further complications of alienation."

"And you think it's as simple as that?"

"Many of the towns in New England are very tight communities; some grew out of nineteenth century self-sufficient villages. You're always saying what a good way of life that was, yet you say it isn't workable today. But small community is the wellspring of civilization. It's the space we return to naturally if we allow ourselves the opportunity."

"No, it's not practical anymore. It won't work in the long run. We've got to go ahead, not turn back to the past. Let's get back to the trail."

"But it's . . . yeah, the trail."

The fox was gone and so was a headache I'd acquired on the walk up earlier. It was time to walk, not talk. The trail, a series of short switchbacks up a steep ridge, was behind us. From here it's an easy walk to the crest, Smith Peak; altitude 2300 meters. But we decided to head east to a place on the ridge where the whole Hetch Hetchy valley can be seen — rather, the reservoir that fills it.

June 27, 1988: Smith Peak Ridge

Damp, frost-edged pine needles all around me. Hot tea steaming in the first rays of morning light. A woodpecker's rapid tapping on a hollow tree reminds me of my alarm clock with its broken clapper.

"You awake?"

"Yeah, been watching the clouds clear out of the canyon down there. They've been turning into nothing for the past fifteen minutes."

Father rolls back, keeping his eye on the Tuolumne's Grand Canyon and then sits up. His sweat-stained undershirt is speckled with pine needles. In a second he's up and at 'em, pulling his new Levi's on with the speed of someone who doesn't want to feel the cold air in his crotch.

A very quick breakfast and we walk on talking about how much we'd seen the past few days, how elated we are at having not gone very far but taking the time to really look, to pause and study the forests and streams and creatures. I've learned again about all those tiny occurrences that make up the life of a wild planet. Again I've been struck with that peculiar feeling of my own strangeness. I can never tell whether it's just my city ways being interrupted or something more profound.

We've gotten in touch with one another's pace. Observations and comments come almost at the same instant, and it makes me think about fathers and sons.

Had I ever doubted the value of wild places it is this moment, intensified by the last few days, that opens my eyes. In the city we're coerced by social pressure to act in ways that are clearly understandable to both of us, ways that make it impossible to really communicate with one another. Confusion pure and complex prevents us from hearing one another. But out here the clarity of place, of wilderness frees us. Here we're two men living on planet Earth.

Since we started down into the Grand Canyon of the Tuolumne this afternoon, we've seen only three people. They all seem to have gone somewhere else. It's fine to walk along in seemingly virgin country!

A camp vacated by packers whose only trace are footprints uncollapsed by a night's moisture. We both nod almost at the same instant. Tuolumne's just beyond a row of pines; we'll hear it through the night and probably wake up in wet sleeping bags, but it'll be worth it.

"Jeff, I feel really in gear, finally. I've been thinking that your way is almost antithetical to mine. I mean you're not a bum or a nazi or anything weird, but I can't help but feel, well, like we're almost a different species."

"Whew! My back's tired. Those switchbacks! Climbing on the rocks really did it. Of course we're different. But for what it's worth, practically everything I expressed has grown out of what I learned from you. Remember when we went to Slick Rock in Colorado in the early 60s? Remember those high plateaus breaking off into a long large bowl? Bright red cliffs edging the winding brown river? Looked like something out of Doyle's *Lost World?* Or that valley north of Silverton where we climbed up to the sheepherders' old house and watched the bighorn? I'll never forget those places. They weren't pristine wilderness. They were ignored. Stark and desolate . . ."

"Before you go off on one of your tirades, let's get something straight. What in God's name do you mean by wilderness? I never thought of that valley as wilderness. It was wasteland as far as I was concerned."

"Aside from a few ranchers and the Indians the place hadn't been used by humans. It was the way it had come to be, without us. A place where you could tell the age of the planet. Richer — like all wilderness — in diversity than anything we could ever create.

The Tuolumne is roaring by in white rapids over boulders. The trees add their sound as the afternoon breeze comes up.

"I still don't see . . . ."

"I think out here we come closer to essence. I've said things out here that I would never say to you in the city."

"That's good to know. I guess I'm lucky to have a son who even cares to talk about these things . . . to me. But I'm still puzzled."

"I'm beginning to wonder whether the purpose of this trip unconsciously was to open up this dialogue with you!"

Father looks down as if hiding what he's ashamed of and continues to pull out the foodbags from his pack. Was this the right thing to do? Of course, dammit,

A rock on a boulder, balanced like a cue ball on a medicine ball. A squirrel sits on top chittering to a neighbor, his sound barely audible against the river noise filling the canyon, reverberating off the high walls as if trying to escape.

"Well . . . you've certainly tried to tell me something, but frankly I still don't get it. I've had the feeling all along that you've been saying something foreign."

"I'm not sure but I think I've been afraid to say we think differently. You think of what is wild in you — your intuition, your imagination — as something to be tamed or at least restrained. As if it interferes with the way you think your life should be. But it's precisely what I want to explore in me."

I've done it now. He's really quiet. I can't hear the river or anything else. Like being in a sense deprivation chamber.

Thank the universe for grizzly bears. He's walking along a ridge, a rock-cleft trail, paying no attention to us only to the hanging berries. In typical bear fashion, he's eating one and avoiding the harder-to-reach deeper ones. No wonder there's been so little fuss about their reintroduction!

"You think I'm afraid . . . of my feelings?"

"No, I don't know whether it's fear or what. But I get the impression that you feel people should be regulated, controlled — as if they can't be trusted. Guilty until proven innocent."

"Hmmm."

"I'm trying to say there are emotions in me — I guess I'm more aware of them being here — that I follow out: thought doesn't enter into it. And it's just this that you'd criticize."

"Because I'd say you weren't thinking things through enough?"

"But that's just what's not necessary. The emotion, the right feeling is so deep, you just go along with it."

"That's just confidence. Comes with age sometimes. I don't think things out as elaborately as I used to."

"But it's more than that. I trust what I feel like I trust that bear. If I'd thought about it, I'd be paralyzed with fear. Couple of years ago I would have been terrorized. Now I'm respectful, not fearful. Plants, animals and the whole Earth. The whole goddamn universe! You know what I mean? It's the same, right through me. How can I be afraid of something that's made of the same stuff as me?"

"I don't know, Jeff, I don't know. Look, it's getting dark. Barely see Piute Creek. Thanks for sharing this with me. Let's make dinner, I'm starving."

"Right."

As of May 15, 1987 Badger Pass Inn will be closed permanently.

On that date the inn will be taken down and the shuttle line into Badger and to the top of the slopes will be removed. The ski areas will be planted with seedlings to begin reforestation in that area of the Park. Cross-country skiing will continue in the Park.

Closing down the special skiing facility was brought about by recent years' insufficient snowfall to maintain the slopes on a profitable basis. The decision was made also in response to increasing criticism of Badger being "contrary to the spirit of wilderness restoration." The Three Company agreement, approved by a CCT vote, explained that "Yosemite Park doesn't have to try to cover all the bases, accommodate every aspect of human recreation to remain a National Park servicing millions of visitors each year. The primary focus of the Park's effort must be restoration of wilderness and making it available to visitors. Hindrances to that goal should be eliminated."

The conversion of Badger Pass, after decades of trying to mold it into a mini Squaw Valley, "will be speedy," the Overview Company member concluded. "Once a mistake is realized, there's no lingering over doubts. Just clear it up for the next try."

IV. 1100 m asl: 1142, 17 May 87

"Just heard a whistling of the wind. A slight and distant sound that caused me to turn and look up. It was a windship sailing northwest. Looked like it was just over Half Dome. As I gazed the sun glinted off her sails and for a second she was a sky jewel."

BIG TREES

In 1975 I visited the Mariposa Grove of Big Trees. I walked into the small dark forest of huge trees. I felt icy damp winter air held down by the overhead canopy. The tops of the tall trees were hidden by the lower level forest, white firs and other pines. Only at a few places through those dense frost-edged branches could I see the crown of bushy sequoias. And the massive trunks bare of branches for half their height were only dark shapes seen through a pine-needle screen.

In 1985 I returned to the Mariposa Grove of Big Trees. I strolled through the light spacious forest of trees larger than I remembered. This late winter it was cool, not cold or damp: sunlight reached the forest floor. Not only could I see the tops of many trees, but I could look among sequoias spaced far enough apart to see between them and beyond.

I could appreciate the Sequoia Giganteas' peculiar pleasing proportions. Against trunks whose diameters exceeded my height, I could look straight up to their suddenly tapering points. The once ubiquitous white firs were stumps or scattered piles of ash under crusty snow and new grass.

What had happened?

Yosemite Park had, a ranger enlightened me. The firs were removed by careful logging and the use of draft horses to minimize damage to the forest floor. The lumber was utilized for inn construction along the railline in the Park. After those species were completely removed, managed fires burned off the seedlings and the remaining slash.

That was last summer. The wild grasses, stunted and sparse in the shade of the fir forest floor, are regrouping. The remaining stumps are decomposing in soil.

That was initiated by man. Lightning fires are expected to burn the grass and strengthen the next growth. Wildfires for thousands of years had acted to prevent the firs--weedlike pests to the overstory monarchs--from taking over. For all that time, only the giant species, widely spaced, broke the carpet of grassy meadow forest floor. It was what Muir saw here and in the other groves long since cut. That was before we recognized the process of natural forest fire.

Already the growth of the sequoias has increased, a major event for trees over two thousand years old. The rings will record this sudden leap preceded by a short period of slowed growth. Sixty years of our fear measured in a few centimeters of rings. Will someone a thousand years from now, or even a hundred, remember why?

FLOOD PLANE

"C'mon! It's like all the rest of those magazine articles. Trying to isolate parts of the problem isn't getting at the root. That lies in the totality." Will releases his large frame to the seat of a bentwood lounger.

"But, Will, inherent in the problem *is* the solution." Gary pulls his other chair around to face Will's. "That's how we find it."

"Yeah, but it doesn't make any difference. That article talked about it. Played with the problem. But it's all the same hype, making people believe there's an answer in overviews like that. You get out there on that tractor every day and you'll know what a solution is," Will rubs his work-worn hands.

Southwest of La Grange on a grassy slope looking over the Tuolumne's delta, the house is still except for the buzz of crickets. Goldie comes across the porch shielding her eyes from the afternoon sun through the oak trees that rustle over Will's railing. She looks at her husband, then Gary McCready. "Do you wilderness lab people drink alcohol?"

"We're usually offered Wild Turkey. But here in the sultry delta I'll take a gin and tonic."

"And I suppose *you* want a mint julep?"

"Lemonade, please, but only with the good lemons."

"What else would I use? From my trees, organically grown and personally guarded from that crap you spray everything else with! That's the way to grow lemons!"

Will watches Goldie's satisfied return to the house.

"That article was informative and everything, Gary, but it won't have much effect on valley people. You didn't grow up around here. I did. Sold my dad's farm near Modesto because the soil was getting poorer. That agricultural conglom has put money into the old place, organic fertilizers to enrich the soil, tiles to drain off the alkalinity. Farmers like me can't afford that kind of operation. So I moved up here to work this farm. It's a lot smaller and hard as hell to make it pay with all the additives and sprays and now those sterility agents to kill the damn bugs."

"Your place doesn't look bad, for a chemical farm!"

"Okay, okay, I get enough of that from Goldie. I'm doing what I can. I mean look out there! The river's dead! The salmon swimming upstream die because the flow is so slow they can't figure out which direction is up! They die without spawning. The trout die. The water is so stagnant, it's hot. Dumb fishermen think they're getting something when they catch these puny hatchery fish. Why the poor flippers would die of laziness if they weren't caught first."

"Don't you think the wild breeds would strengthen and come back if the dams are removed?" Gary taps his hands on the chair's arms.

"You have an emotional investment in taking down the dams, Gary, I know that. And yet you don't even know if it's going to work! Too much has changed over too long a time. Loss of ground cover and wetland, the growing pollution and eutrophication, all of it. It's not just gonna go away with the dams!"

"'Course it's not just gonna go away. I think there's just barely enough left of the old patterns to restore . . . . But it'll take work . . . ."

"Don't you guys talk about anything else except the river and the soil?" Goldie slowly crosses the porch balancing the drinks, her own flatbread biscuits and a small block of jack cheese. The sun flashed behind a row of cottonwoods. "Look at that!" She points at a clump of vines around the dredge tailings near the river. "It's a pheasant, see it?"

"What a beautiful creature! See it, Will?"

"Oh yeah, I see it now. Goldie's my eyes. I can't see nothing beyond those trees. Blessed with nearsightedness like the rest of my family."

"Shortsightedness, I'd call it," Goldie smiles. "Left yourself wide open, Will, you always do." She sits down without taking her eyes off the pheasant. "How bright and colorful, yet hard to see. I never tire of watching birds, more so since they've become so scarce."

"If the river flooded again you'd see more birds than you ever dreamed of." Gary looks at the river musingly.

"Do you think it'd change the water table? Raise it?"

"It will probably take ten, maybe fifteen years for the water table around here to rise to the surface again. Maybe by 2010 artesian wells will be common again. But hopefully, what with flooding and streamside reservoirs there won't be that immediate need."

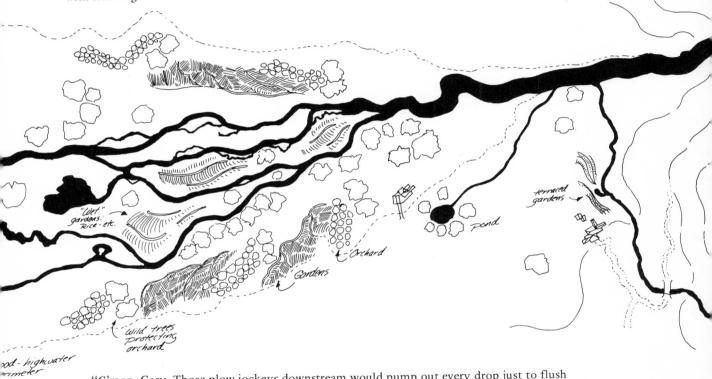

"C'mon, Gary. Those plow jockeys downstream would pump out every drop just to flush out the alkalinity. But why shouldn't they? They've got to feed the country, or at least a quarter of it. Besides can you really be serious about those people in Modesto doing without their dams? Or San Francisco without its aqueduct?"

"Won't take long before it won't make any difference what people in Modesto think about dams. You know perfectly well recycling is making the dams obsolete."

"You just want to make Gary convince you, don't you? Don't you, you old hayseed skeptic?" Goldie reaches over to Will's leg and pinches him.

"Maybe, woman. I'm just trying to drag the truth out of him."

"Water collection and recycling is so common already there's no real need for the dams anymore. You do it yourself with the roof and that pond down there. You don't need imported water anymore. Anyway there's been so little in the reservoirs, your irrigation ditch has been practically empty for the last three years." Gary points through the railing at yellow grass growing out of a concrete flume.

231

"I'm not convinced," Will squirms. "I'll bet you twenty bucks this recycling business is just a patch job, a band-aid that'll come off as soon as the droughts are forgotten. I'd use well water myself if that damn solarskin put out enough power to drive the deep pumps. How am I gonna grow stuff without water? Right now I've got a contract for river water. I use that windmill to pump it up here. But even so I've had to keep cutting back irrigation. Lost a couple of fields last year because the river was so low. I just don't see any other way but the dams and the aqueducts to keep up this valley's productivity." Will points his finger at Gary to make his point. "Taking the dams out is just going back in time, . . . making it primitive at the expense of producing food."

"Wild rivers, wilderness *and* small intensive farms can be economically more viable than continuing to try to control nature. I think we've begun to be aware recently of the awesome responsibility . . . ."

". . . and expense," adds Goldie.

"The staggering expense of maintaining flood control and the cost of irrigation projects! Once you control something, you're forever responsible for it."

"I hear you, but I still think you underestimate the situation. How you gonna turn back years of what's taken place in this valley and still produce enough food? I mean this place's developed into a giant food production system. You can't just stop it and go off in some new direction. If we leave it fallow for a hundred years it might work. But that's what it would take, not a minute less!"

"It doesn't just change like that," Gary snaps his fingers startling a small bug on his brow. "It takes small experiments like what we're planning for the Tuolumne. That'll tell us whether it's feasible. And if it works, then it'll spread on its own throughout the valley."

"Listen, Gary, I know Goldie's garden is very productive and doesn't use much water, and I know you've been involved in the gardens up in Yosemite. I'll grant you the big farms down here have learned a thing or two from the organic farms, but still to produce more than a small percentage . . ."

"That small percentage, Will, is up to about 20 percent nationwide, that's the prediction for this year, 1987. And the food can be produced cheaper. No overhead for large farm equipment," Goldie cuts in.

". . . well, whatever it's *predicted* to be, it still ain't much. To really produce volume you gotta have machines, and machines don't work on little gardens. To work them you gotta use your hands and that takes time. I mean where you gonna get the people to do all of that?"

"What about these people who've dropped out of the cities and moved up in the foothills? They work the gardens because it makes 'em feel good, stronger and less dependent . . . ."

"C'mon, those jokers are just hobbyists, not real farmers!"

"Will, if you'd open your eyes you'd see how widespread it's becoming, how it's become a trend, a movement. There're those farmworkers down near Fresno and Porterville that're working intensive farms cooperatively. They're managing okay. And their farms are human places instead of the farm factories that pollute this valley."

"Uhm."

"And there was that article you got such a kick out of the other day, the one about draft horses, in the *Bee*. People are returning to using horses and softer tech not because they're nostalgic, but because the ideas work. Draft horses turn out to be cheaper than small tractors *and* they provide you with a new model!"

"Be serious, Goldie! They can only do small gardens. Dammit, both of you don't seem to realize these trends you're pointing out are just minor frills. The major thrust is still mechanized large farms. That's where the money is, the productivity, the only way we can get more food that'll cost less. Once we get over these temporary crazy droughts."

232

"Now you're on my turf, Will. That reasoning isn't true anymore! If you measure the cost of water, energy, soil depletion, social disruption, the loss of the wild environment — the whole cost of the hidden factor of specialization — big, artificial agriculture isn't efficient. You've been toeing the agribusiness line too long. All they think is profit. And just look what the farm factory method has done to this valley. You've got to count that in your equation. It was once rich with black healthy soil, oak trees scattered across it, wildflowers everywhere; rivers full of fish bordered by jungles of marsh grass and trees. But they steadily harvested crops out of it and put nothing back: they plowed up grassland, let the soil dry out, killed wild plants with herbicides, farmed with heavy machinery that compacted the soil until it was hard and dry. Wind blew it away, sun baked out practically every drop of moisture. Soil's so hard now the alkali doesn't drain. It sits on the surface and burns roots and kills crops. The soil's so hard, the roots become more shallow every year and need more water because of evaporation. Mono-culture prevented natural insect control, so the farmers became as hooked on pesticides as on unnatural fertilizers. On top of all that, they produce crops low in nutrition for a low price, and to maintain that price they've got to accept government subsidies. This valley's a junkie dying of overdose. I mean the whole damn thing is sick. It hasn't anything to do with healthy life anymore."

"Yeah, we know, Gary. That's the problems I face every day of my life."

"Okay, so let's start talking about solutions. We've learned by studying Tuolumne Meadows, for example, how floodwater replenishes the soil while cleaning the shoreline and meadow of dead material at the same time. If we can try this in the Central Valley in a meaningful, useful way, we can begin turning around some of its problems."

"So we're going to see people killed, cars abandoned, cows washed away, houses wiped out, my farm flooded, just so that one day, maybe, the soil will be black again and the water table high?"

"Oh, Will, don't be ridiculous. You know that's not what Gary's saying!"

"We know where the floods will occur. The water would probably pass right down the hill, slowly washing over your lowest field."

"What about other people, lower land?"

"With just a little foresight, not a single person need be harmed nor any property damaged. You never hear about natural floods because we control rivers with security-blanket dams and build towns and cities in flood plains. The floods we see on television are devastating; the water has built up between the levees and overflows with sudden catastrophic results. What we're planning is analogous to the managed fires we use in Yosemite in order to get the forests ready for natural wildfire.

"We plan to subdue the flooding at first — after the dams are removed — with small diversion channels and reservoirs. The Tuolumne is a small river. It flows in a narrow flood plain with low hills defining it. It's a relatively small area, so it will be simple to restrain the tributary flow and minimize the suddenness of the flooding. Around here grassland watershed has a high runoff because the wild grass is gone. In just a few seasons wild grassland will return a greater absorption rate and we'll be able to let the natural flooding begin."

"Just like the wildfires in Yosemite," Goldie applauds. "Thing that really interests me is the restoration of elk and deer in the grassland like they're doing up at the 11 Bar 7 near Warnersville."

Will gets up to get a match for the candle. Bats dart through the garden below them. Goldie leans back and gazes up at the stars, her blond hair bunched up against the back of the chair and her smile as broad as her eyes are big. Will finds the candle and in the golden glow the circle tightens.

"Now I've decided what I want," Goldie announces. "I want another kid before I'm 35 and that's only three years away, so Will, we'd better get started, but not right now. What I want is a valley that's healthy, prospering for our kids, and theirs. I want to see happy faces when I go to town, people proud and strong, living without destroying the land or themselves."

Will watches Goldie with a quiet smile as she continues. "Will, you remember how hard it was to convince your folks to try anything but the accepted 4H practice? Squeezing crops in every corner of their land and driving the tractor half the night to make ends meet. They were too busy trying to make it to ever try anything new that just might be different, not pay off immediately. Your parents were the last of the pioneering breed who looked upon wilderness as something that had to be conquered and contained. But we don't have to restrict ourselves to that!"

"Goldie, I get the feeling you're trying to tell me something. That I'm as conservative as my parents?"

"I wouldn't say you're *as* conservative, but I wish you'd decide whether you're speaking for yourself, for what you know, or for those farmers out there. I mean I realize farm folk aren't your average liberals, but they're not as sluggish as you seem to think. Don't you think we could get a little air into your argument?"

Gary readjusts his butt, finishes his drink and plays with the ice as he leans closer to the candle. He pulls his dark hair back and scratches his beard. "The thing that concerns me the most isn't the land. It's the relationship of the land to weather, its effect on it. Those things I talked about before, farming techniques and dry soil? It's caused a permanent rise in air temperature over the valley. That, and the dust storms have encouraged the temperature to rise and sit over central California most of the year now. It acts as a barrier preventing storms and fogs from moving in off the ocean and delivering the moisture they used to. The storms are going around the valley now instead of flowing due east over the Sierra Nevada as they have for thousands of years. That's why the snowpack has been so low, why normal droughts are longer, more persistent, why the Central Valley is turning into a desert and why the water table is continuing to drop. This is a manmade change and even though we're dying of thirst, people can't see how we caused it even yet."

Gary glances down between the railing posts at the five meandering little jungles and the sixth filled with at least a dozen varieties of wild grass that Goldie's been experimenting with. He considers the rich variety of the natural plants and envisions a valley dotted with abundant, overflowing farms and gardens like theirs, with elk and deer herds grazing beyond.

"You know, I was just pondering Goldie's garden. It reminds me of something I tend to forget. That a whole system, once it begins to degrade into a less complex one, tends to accelerate in that direction. But what people forget is that it works both ways. When it starts to get healthy, that's the way it tends to continue. All we need to do is remove the blockages in the valley's natural flow, and let its primordial rhythm heal itself in time without benefit of our drugs!"

"It's so obvious, so simple. How can people continue to ignore it?" Goldie pouts. Will curls his lower lip between his thumb and forefinger and looks up into the just discernible Milky Way as he listens to Gary's challenging voice.

"Can you ignore it, Will? Can you ignore us? Can you say no to life in favor of . . . habit?"

Egypt is the gift of the Nile. --Herodotus, 5th century B.C.

MONO OFFS LA's FAUCET

(Bridgeport, California, March 21, 1988) The Supreme Court of California today upheld Mono County's injunction against the City and County of Los Angeles Department of Water and Power from "continuing to tap, divert or otherwise use water from Lee Vining Creek."

The unanimous decision handed down in the county seat by Chief Justice Sylvester Arnold restricted use of the city's aqueduct system from Mono County because of the "cumulative damage suffered by the lake and its environs by the water diverted to Los Angeles."

The Department of Water and Power has been drawing off Mono County water since early in the 1940s, but only by the middle 1960s did the level of water in the large lake start dropping about one meter a year, a rate considered alarming by Dr. Emmanuel Roth, co-director of the Wawona Wilderness Labs. "It seriously endangered Mono Lake's lifeforms and the area's ecology. If the injunction were not honored soon, the lake would die."

Chief Justice Arnold felt "that by this ruling, the natural watershed function of the lake would be restored so that the level of the inland lake would return to a level supporting birds and other wildlife." Dr. Roth predicted that this could happen within "three to five years. At least we can hope so."

The original action undertaken by citizens of Mono County and members of Yosemite Park was helped by the example of Owens Valley residents who are now witnessing the refilling of Owens Lake, dry since the 1940s.

This final appeal denial concludes the long legal battle waged since 1981 by Los Angeles to prevent the eastern Sierra Nevada county from cutting off this source of the city's water. *LA Times*

Since Lee Vining was settled over a hundred years ago, the majority of its structures have either faced highway 395--which bisects the town--or were hidden behind other buildings. Few had front views of Mono Lake. The building language of the place definitely had its back turned on the lake.

The coming of the Yosemite Railway in 1984, the continuing controversy over Mono Lake and the recent increase of visitors to the region have caused the four hundred residents of Lee Vining to take another look at the lake below the town's plateau.

Restaurants have been redesigned to accommodate windows with views, homes have been modified to open back storerooms and utility closets to the lake, while the first new tourist accommodation, the Paoha View Inn, actually advertising the lake view, was recently built on the site of an old gas station. Residents have definitely begun to look at their lake as an asset.

seer

Once I walked down a creek and saw a pool of soapsuds. By the way it looked, I could tell there were other humans using the water upstream and about how far they were. Well, the creek is continuous, water is happening together, so why couldn't I look ahead as knowledgeably as back?

Prophecy is sometimes nothing more than the ability to extrapolate--almost unconsciously--from what is seen. If you are clearly observing where you are, mightn't you be able to glimpse what lies ahead before you get to it?

I noticed all sorts of things floating down that creek and flying up along it. Many indicators but none of them gave me the slightest hint about what was ahead. Then, suddenly, I was aware of the wholeness, my standing there and being open to it all at once: the creek's relationship to the landform, where and what kinds of plants were growing; how the wind patterns influenced the spider about where to weave his web, the birds to build their nests. And the water's high mark and animal trails told me where the animals crossed in wintertime. I saw the creek in that one instant as a whole in itself, yet part of an ever-enlarging cycle. I saw the small repeated in the large, the large in the small and the end visible in the beginning.

By the frequency of webs and nest positions I could see that the wind accelerated here as it would after passing through a constriction. The high water marks concurred. I studied the vegetation to see what rock strata its growth patterns revealed. The position and composition of the soft crumbly stone suggested that the creek would shortly fall through a narrow gap. The creek was about to narrow.

I took a higher route with the assurance of knowing I was avoiding what would be difficult to traverse. And the river's two-meter fall was just about where I perceived it would be.

Excerpt from an address
by Winifred Larssen
at the Wholeness of Nature
Seminar, Wawona Wilderness Labs
October 3, 1988

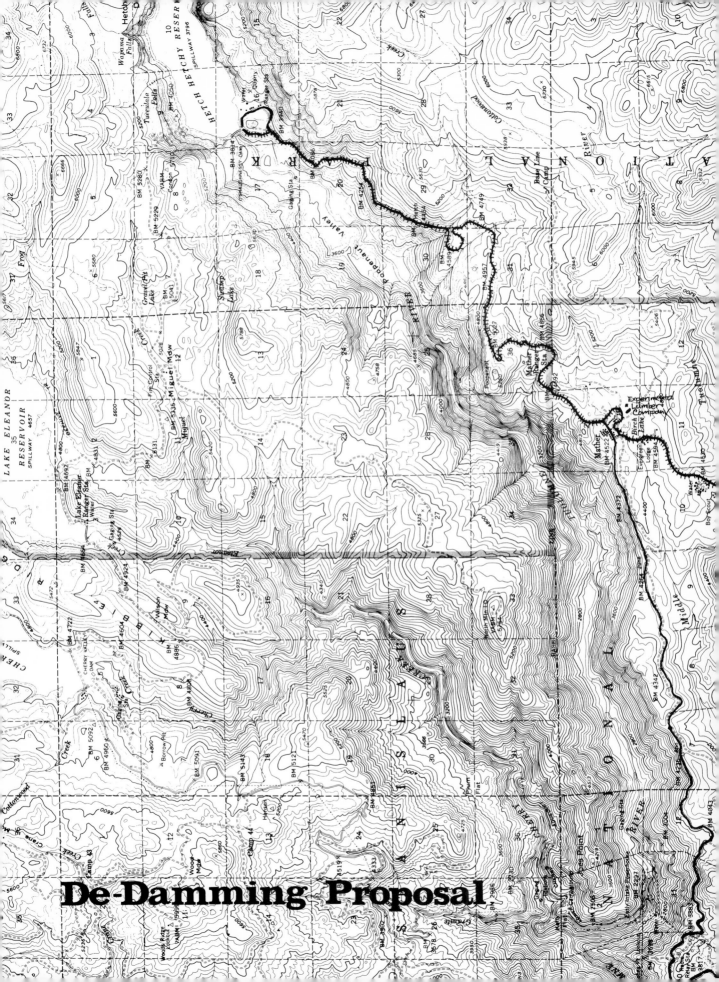

De-Damming Proposal

Our intention is to free the Tuolumne river of all man-made obstructions; insure that its flooding in coming winters is unimpeded and its ecosystem returns to a healthy, diverse wildlife; and introduce agricultural methods that are in tune with the river's natural tendencies and are integrated with its wildlife.

> Yosemite Overview Company
> Wawona Wilderness Labs
> National Park Service
> Tuolumne River Organic Growers

TUOLUMNE RIVER DAMS, IRRIGATION AND HYDROELECTRIC FACILITIES

Demolition

Extend Yosemite Railway from Mather to damsite replacing highway (ex-Hetch Hetchy RR grade) to facilitate movement of materials and workers.

Complete draining of Hetch Hetchy reservoir, Cherry Lake and Lake Eleanor reservoirs. Begin reseeding the lake bottom to prevent rapid erosion Spread indigenous grasses and clustered pines, with the emphasis on fast-growing species that will provide shade cover. If necessary construct temporary pump and sprinkler systems to encourage growth before winter.

Remove center section of O'Shaughnessy dam by rock-drilling and explosives. Remove center arch of Lake Eleanor dam by the same methods. Cherry dam is earth filled: remove approximately one third of the center, distributing removed debris upstream along creekbed. Plant seeding groups on all faces of the dam to begin the formation of topsoil.

Earthfill Don Pedro dam is in front of a smaller concrete structure. Complete Gilman Gulch drainage tunnel. Drain reservoir. By drilling and explosives, remove center of La Grange and old concrete Don Pedro dams. By crane excavation remove the center of the earthfill dam.

As the reservoir drains, begin reseeding, particularly the steeper slopes. Insure that the replanted species of indigenous shrubs and trees are varied and widespread. Plan water sprinkling by helicopter if necessary to encourage growth. Plant indigenous species of fast-growing weeds along all creekbeds and watercourses to minimize erosion.

Construct railway station on south side of O'Shaughnessy dam. Materials: concrete pieces recycled from dam, wood and local stone. Observatory with time-lapse camera equipment to be installed on the south rim of the damsite.

Remove high-tension towers and powerlines. Plant seedlings
along right-of-way. Dismantle steel aqueducts, penstocks
and other assemblies. Seal underground aqueducts, take
down portals and powerhouses, except Moccasin Powerhouse
which will become a museum.

Drain subsidiary reservoirs: Modesto, Turlock and Dawson
lakes. Little reseeding necessary since all three have
been below one quarter capacity for approximately eight
years.

Modify employee housing at Early Intake into river laboratory.
Construct second lab at Don Pedro damsite. Four more at La
Grange, Modesto, Waterford and Empire. Install sluice box
sediment collectors, holographic nutrient sampling viewers
with recorders and flow/velocity meters at ten kilometer
intervals.

DELTA REGION: LA GRANGE TO SAN JOAQUIN RIVER

Modifications

Define flood plain channels paralleling the present riverbed.
Flatten dredge tailings throughout delta to allow water to
disperse over a wide area. Open passages where trees and
old growth have obstructed flow. Insure that remaining vegetation will not cause serious blockages or damming. Use
dredge tailings to construct scattered islands or mounds to
guide flow into side passages.

Modify existing garden beds near La Grange to receive floodwaters. Relocate, or place on stilts, existing delta farmhouses.

Define borders of maximum and minimum flooding and insure
that there are no narrow high velocity conditions where un-
dermining or other deteriorations will threaten existing
manmade structures.

Construct observation towers for observing and photographing
flood patterns at seven kilometer intervals. Also install
flow gauges and seepage meters at five kilometer intervals
from La Grange to Waterford.

Relocate all highways, pathways and bridge structures to accommodate flood path. Construct high-water levees to protect buildings along edges of towns, particularly Modesto.

Design test garden and orchard plan. Three regions of study:
upper delta where higher velocity, richer water will disperse
rapidly. Determine form of gardens that can withstand that
rush; use weirs and other diversion techniques as supplementary devices to divert or strain flow.
Middle delta where water is likely to stagnate or slowly cir-
culate through vegetation: design gardens to capture water and
hold in slowly seeping pools.
In lower delta study insect and bird life relative to cleaning
effect of floodwaters, particularly near confluence with San
Joaquin river. Gardens in lower delta: emphasis on wet-zone
crops like rice.

MONITORING OF THE WHOLE PROJECT TO DETERMINE:

Relationship of the river's seasons and human nutrition needs.

Flow rate and watertable replenishment.

Relationship of snow level to watertable.

Rate and quality of silt flow.

Effect of downflow nutrients on: gardens, fish, birds, insects and mammals.

Effect of flooding on accumulation of delta organic material, fogging and atmospheric cooling.

How growing and garden patterns can accommodate floodwater.

What organic barriers can act as sieves to catch nutrients.

Effect of surrounding, overhanging leaf cover on delta storage ponds.

How evaporative loss from flood replenishes delta ponds.

Transpiration loss from gardens, delta trees and wildgrasses.

How long flooding takes to replenish soil in delta.

What methods are necessary and workable to accelerate replenishment of soil.

How long it takes to bring back the delta's wild game.

The best mixes and growing patterns for domestic grains, field crops and grasslands.

The best moisture-retaining mixtures of wild grasses and grain species.

The effect of wildfire on soil enrichment, grasslands, creekbeds and delta

Effect of wildfire on soil enrichment, grasslands, creekbeds and delta.

Relationship of farmers, their techniques and seasonal flooding.

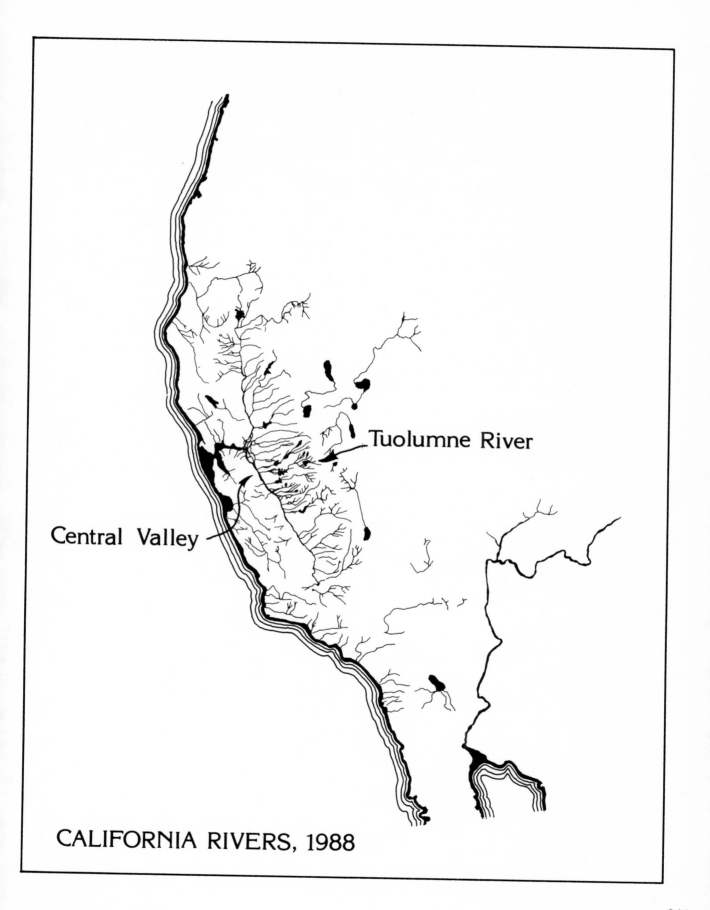

Tuolumne River

Central Valley

CALIFORNIA RIVERS, 1988

WW TO HH

3 Hetch Hetchy, California

On a dusty shelf cut out of a granite dome, the temporary rails are half-buried by gravel, sacks of cement and stacks of lumber. On the wall of a small plywood construction shack is a small sign where the history of the spot is memorialized: ". . . in order to complete the dam this shelf was cut as a railway yard for the Hetch Hetchy Railroad. Tracks were removed in the 30s and the route was converted to a highway . . ." Amos continues reading the sign as the others move on. He catches up with them next to a flatcar loaded with dynamite crates as Bill laughs at a sign that reads, "Visitors entering this area do so at their own risk."

"Amos, let's walk up to the canyon. That's the Grand Canyon of the Tuolumne, isn't it? I'm tired of all this construction confusion."

"Destruction, purposeful destruction," he answers.

"It's too hot," Coral says. "I want to get *in* that river, not look at it! C'mon, Bill."

"It's been quite a time since people swam in that river. A lot around here has changed!"

"I was thinking that, Bill. I was here four summers ago, 1984. Everything looked so new, like freshly turned earth. Uncomfortably clean, if you know what I mean."

"Didn't you like it?"

"No. I did, it's just that now things have sort of settled in, the buildings for example look more comfortable, weathered — less specifically planned. And the track: the Hetch Hetchy line looks like the whole system looked then. The ride through the Merced canyon? So much of the track is now overgrown and you can't see the old highway forms anymore. Trees have grown out over the track and the vegetation all around has come back — no more pollution, I guess."

"Did you see that wildfire burn in the logged area near, I think it was Mather Gate?" contributed Coral. "The new growth looked green and . . . ."

"Yeah, I saw a couple of areas like that. They sure grow fast after a wildfire — flowers, bushes, seedlings fairly burst, and the pines look greener."

"Well, what they're doing here. Won't that be like wildfire?"

"What do you mean, Aura?"

"More people will be drawn to this area so the concentration of visitors throughout the Park will lessen. That was the worst thing about the Park before the railroad. So many people in just a few spots. Larger numbers now of course, but they're spread out . . . ."

"Maybe our toleration of other people is getting better."

"Optimist!"

"At least people aren't afraid to come here in summer the way they used to be!"

"It's the train, it's having to come here by train . . . ." Aura sums it up.

"Not to mention by foot or horse."

"Something weekenders like us just don't do!"

"It's amazing that such a simple thing could have resulted in all this! And in only five years!"

"Even to removing the dam. It's getting late. Let's go down to the river, Coral. See you up here later, Amos. Not later than 1800?"

"In ten years I bet this'll all be forest," Bill shouts after Coral as they are forced to break into a run at the bottom of the increasingly steep trail. Bill chases Coral as they slide and skip, nearly tumbling into the rusty boiler of a steam donkey engine jettisoned during the dam's construction. Panting and sweating they stop at the Tuolumne, a meandering course through a waist-high maze of weeds that look evenly spread across the dusty silt plain.

"These trails are like deer paths!" Coral points.

"The deer sure'll have enough weeds to eat. They don't touch the fir seedlings."

"Gardeners to the Future Forests of Hetch Hetchy!"

"... all this you're seeing is the transition from one system to another. When old ways wear out, get new ones. In the 30s Sierra water was piped to San Francisco and damn near everywhere else. Nobody thought they were killing the land that feeds them in the process. The Central Valley seemed so rich, the mountain water so abundant. Who'd have ever considered that one day the dams would be thought of as a mistake? Really it wasn't a mistake, though; it was right for that time. People had to go through it, do it that way until it didn't work anymore."

"Ohhhh! Cold! I'm shivering!"

"I think it's deep enough here for a shallow dive," Bill takes off his pants.

"I can't do it that way. I'm a coward. I do it gradually, cent. by cent."

"Uh! That's the hard way!" SPLASH.

"You did it, you crazy . . . . How deep is it there?"

Only by the time the water reaches her waist does she give in to it, sliding into the current with a wide splash. A cloud of fine silt balloons up around her. "There's a lot of silt . . ."

"All the stuff the river'll be carrying downstream soon — Sierra black gold!"

"The treasure of the Sierra Nevada! Isn't slimy. I thought it would . . . it's like fine grit. It feels good between my toes."

Bill has found a flat rock in midstream. "Look, you can climb up here from this side!"

"Bill, look at that gravel pile there. I just noticed it. What is it?"

"I guess," Bill cups up cool water to spread on his hot perch, "that's river gravel dredged to make concrete. They probably never got around to this pile. On the train that de-damming brochure said five thousand boxcars of cement were brought up here by the old railroad, the HH Railroad . . . ."

Coral swims over to where Bill is lying stretched out in the sun. The urge is irresistible. Three minutes of a giggling, hysterical water fight. The war ends when Bill spouts a mouthful of water straight up.

"That's a water sign, not a treaty, you loser!"

"Not very many fish, but our fight sure scared all of them away."

"Yeah, look at all those bright green shoots and the matted grass there, lining those shallow pools."

Bill tests a warm puddle full of bleached pine needles. "Won't be long before there are more fish. It's amazing how fast it all takes hold. Twigs and seeds and stuff from upstream collect into a bed, then there's insects and fish . . ." he looks upriver. "You ever think how close this river is to the way our blood flows in us? Every time I swim in a river I think about that. I can almost feel my blood swimming within my skin when I'm swimming. A current within another current."

Coral swirls her hand in the river.

"I wonder," Bill continues. "From the train the river looked green and brown below the dam. I guess that will change when they blow the dam. But when the river's completely free, will the water be different? A different energy, perhaps?" he asks her.

"I can tell the difference between aerated tapwater and the kind that isn't. I suppose once it's really a river again — all the way up and down — it'll clean itself, be oxygenated, be an organism again."

"Not just aeration, it's the nutrients, the microorganisms — that stuff is food, liquid food."

They've reached a shelf that once was an access road. A corona of afternoon sunlight splays out above the dam, diffused through the drill dust. The dam's convex surface is stained with horizontal bands. From where they sit, the cut looks like a narrow slot forcing V-shaped sunlight into the valley.

"God, I'd like to be here when they bust the dam!"

"It won't be much of a charge! They're taking taking it down slowly; the last charge maybe will free only that muddy pool — what, five meters deep?" he estimates, pointing to the log boom and steel screen guarding the entrance to the diversion tunnel.

BOOM!

"What was that!"

"They detonated a charge. Look at that cloud! See, there, that crack?"

"Yeah."

"Now they can break out more concrete and haul it off somewhere."

"They look like they're having fun!"

"What do you mean? That's hard labor!"

"Maybe, but look at the way they're moving on that scaffold. Why I bet they'd rather be doing that than splashing in the river!"

"C'mon, Coral, you can't be serious. Who'd prefer sweating on that concrete to playing in the river?"

"Those men, that's who! They love it, look at them. Men hate to admit they love destroying as much as building — Maybe more!"

"C'mon."

"No. I think we all enjoy more things than we admit to," she cinches up the laces on her right boot.

"For instance?"

"Lemme see. Like when I had Alexis, I had no idea. I thought having a child was some simple even if painful process. It's not, it's violent. Joyful violence. There's no word for it — there should be. Those kinds of experience contain both pleasure and violence or destruction."

"What the hell's that got to do with blasting a dam?"

"Well, women who've had children actually felt the tension between joy and pain. Destroying things to make way for other things probably encourages a similar emotion. Maybe people would be better off if they could remember the pain and ecstasy of their own births."

"What difference would that make?"

"Remember how you said you felt when you watched Alexis being born? You said you'd never forget those eight hours! There were times when you felt you were experiencing what I was?"

"I remember."

"Well, I'm saying that you can't really feel that kind of painful joy. You may feel that you are sharing it, but you aren't really experiencing it."

"Chauvinist. I still don't see your point!"

"Well, maybe that's why those guys over there are having such a good time on that scaffolding. You don't see any women there!"

"Having babies makes women less violent than men!"

"You're being obtuse. It's just that there are different kinds of violence. Maybe women are able to differentiate better than men.

Look, things like earthquakes, hurricanes, floods, volcanoes are natural violences. We have become socially so afraid of them that we tend to lose sight of their function as part of a natural pattern. Because we've become capable of controlling some of them, we feel we must. But that's really a man's way, not necessarily a woman's. I think men feel they should control those things, a woman would simply get out of the way."

"And taking down the dam, is that a man's or a woman's way?"

Dark-brown, muskrat-like the little creature steps from rock to rock slowly following the course of a rivulet. The animal's dark body is silhouetted against the speckled gray granite. It disappears in a tangled thicket and then courageously hops to a bleached shelf: the beginning of the former reservoir. The drowned zone has not seen untold generations of its kind. Looking all around, walking from side to side, it scans the strange surface broken only by the weeds near the cascading creek. It takes another step down, then another and then its pace accelerates.

"Look! What's near that stream?"

"Looks like a beaver, a really small beaver, Coral."

"Shhhh."

Making its way down the beaver pauses near the huge boulders marking the creek's entrance into the river. At first it ventures little more than its length, searching among the weeds. The little mammal continues making larger forays into the thicker clumps of grass growing around the shallow pools. Stepping slowly, cautiously sniffing everything and then stepping back on the path to check again. It walks in farther, half swims, then immediately back on the shore. A few blades of grass waver, then fall. The beaver's eating.

Sunlight sparkles off the water and is broken by swirls as it moves out into the water. Small splashes as chunks of root and sand and rock are flicked by powerful forelegs. The mountain beaver disappears into his new home.

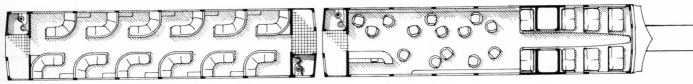

CINDER SNAPPERS
TOWER BUFFS
BOOMERS

Bonnie Alsup
Bill Anderson
Jim Bassett
Lucius Beebe
Pabby Betaincourt
Jean Cook
Addison DeWitt
Gloria Drayton
Becky Dwan
Kevin Dwan
Richard Fernau
Engel Ford
Nora Gallagher
Jeffrey Glazebrook
Joan Goodwin
Michael Goodwin
Bonnie Grossman
Seymour Grossman
Greg Guagnano
Karl Hess
Theresa Hess
Jeremy Hewes
Hank Johnston
Patricia Kepler
Cynthia Kerr
Ernest Kerr
Frank Kukula
Louise Lacey
Jeanne Lanstad
Leonard Leshandar
Howard Sheldon Levine
Peggy Levine
Lenny Lipton
Albert Morse
Jenifer Ann Padgett
Leslie Purcell
Ida Roaman
Morris Roaman
Martha Swan
Robert Swan
Lee Swenson
Charles Tucker
Ted Wurm
Byron Young

produced at the Swan-Levine House, Grass Valley, California